Emotion and High Politics

Frontispiece: Gladstone, age 23. Oil sketch by Hayter.
(Photo by Studio Morgan supplied by Oxford University Press)

Bismarck, age 11. Chalk drawing by Franz Krüger, 1826
(Courtesy of Archiv für Kunst and Geschichte, Berlin)

Salisbury, age 31. Drawing by George Richmond.
(Courtesy of the Marquess of Salisbury)

Emotion and High Politics

Personal Relations at the Summit in
Late Nineteenth-Century Britain and Germany

Judith M. Hughes

University of California Press

Berkeley / Los Angeles / London

An earlier version of the first part of chapter 3 appeared as "Toward the Psychological Drama of High Politics: The Case of Bismarck," *Central European History*, Volume X, Number 4 (December 1977), pp. 271–85. Used with permission.

University of California Press
Berkeley and Los Angeles, California

University of California Press, Ltd.
London, England

Printed in the United States of America

1   2   3   4   5   6   7   8   9

Library of Congress Cataloging in Publication Data

Hughes, Judith M.
   Emotion and high politics.

   Bibliography: p.
   Includes index.
   1. Great Britain—Foreign relations—Germany.
2. Germany—Foreign relations—Great Britain.
3. Great Britain—Foreign relations—19th century.
4. Statesmen—Great Britain—Psychology. 5. Statesmen—
Germany—Psychology.   6. Psychohistory.   I. Title.
DA47.2.H85   327.41043   82-4737
ISBN 0-520-04691-9   AACR2

For David

Contents

Preface   ix

1. **Past Misunderstanding and Present Insight**   1
   I. The Problem Posed: What I Am Doing and What I Am Not   1
   II. Psychoanalytic Portraits: What Is Feasible with Historical Data   6
   III. The Findings Foreseen: A Crisscross of Discourse   13

2. **Charismatic Authority and Cabinet Solidarity: Gladstone in the 1880s**   15
   I. A Political Genius under Restraint   16
   II. A Tribune Returns to Power   28
   III. The Psychodrama of Home Rule   38

3. **Charismatic Authority and Bureaucratic Administration: Bismarck in the 1880s**   45
   I. A Political Genius Making His Own Music   46
   II. A "Colossus" Holds onto Power   57
   III. The Opening Void   67

4. **Leadership from a Distance: Salisbury and His Colleagues, 1886–1892**   77
   I. Diffidence and Determination   78
   II. Emotional Surrogates   90

5. **Fabrication of a New "Authority Figure": Power in Berlin at the End of the Century**   113
   I. A Haunted Gray Eminence   114
   II. An "Orphaned" William   122
   III. Willy's Friend Phili   136
   IV. The Artifices of Bülow   144

6. **A Younger Generation Taking Over: The Heirs of Gladstone and Salisbury**   163
    I. The Ironies of the Great Mother: Queen Victoria and Her Male Maternal Surrogates   165
    II. Gladstone's Departure   175
    III. The Omnipresent Heir: Chamberlain   182
    IV. The Resourcefulness of Balfour   198
7. **Conclusion: Two Dissonant Tempers**   210
    I. The Scrupulous Temper   210
    II. The Fatalist Temper   215
Bibliographical Note   221
Index   223

Preface

The reader will not get very far into the first chapter before he discovers that this is not a traditional historical study. In that chapter I make clear the specific objective I am aiming at. What I want to do here is indicate more generally how, in setting out, I was led to depart from the well-trodden paths of my profession.

Most historians begin a project by locating a domain or finding a topic that interests them. They then look into the kinds of materials which fall within the domain or are relevant to the topic. When they have assured themselves that there is a plentiful supply of data, they proceed with the research—and, along the way, refine the topic. After a certain lapse of time during which data have been collected and pondered over, the investigator will start to arrange the material in some general pattern—or a larger interpretation may occur to him that will serve to order what he has uncovered. If all goes well, the weight of the data will lend credence to the interpretation he propounds. (It will not "prove" the interpretation.) If, however, the interpretation is found to be flawed—and historical interpretations of any scope are almost invariably flawed—the book can still be commended for the new information it provides. The interpretation may be regarded as controversial, but the historian can count on being praised for having made a scholarly contribution—for having added to the general fund of knowledge.

With this standard operating procedure well in mind, I set out on my venture. I was interested in late nineteenth-century European diplomacy, more particularly in overseas expansion and territorial acquisition. I spent the better part of a year reading British cabinet papers and German diplomatic documents in an effort to light upon a subject that had not yet been fully explored. I came away much better equipped to teach diplomatic history, but without a topic which could be handled in the usual fashion.

Instead of finding a topic, I was struck by a puzzle, more fully stated in the first chapter: the incomprehension between British and German leaders. I knew that to pursue this question would be to embark on a risky enterprise. In posing a problem and then seeking evidence which might lead to its solution—rather than letting a topic be shaped, in large measure, by the evidence itself—I would be forfeiting the security a topic-oriented historian derives from having a well-defined data base. I would not be able to promise to bring forth new facts. And indeed it was likely that there would be gaps in the evidence, making a resort to inferences and conjectures unavoidable. Despite these difficulties, I went ahead.

What I am now in a position to offer is an unusual perspective on British and German politics in the last decades of the nineteenth century. I am certain that the argument will be considered controversial; but I hope that the purpose of the study will be recognized and appreciated: to make the reader look at the past—if only briefly—in a new way.

■

For financial backing while this project was under way, I should like to thank Harvard University's Center for European Studies, the National Endowment for the Humanities, and the Academic Senate of the University of California, San Diego. For intellectual support, I should similarly like to thank my students at Harvard and the University of California, San Diego. The fortuitous circumstance of serving in the Social Studies Program at Harvard provided a stimulus I very much needed. I suppose most people feel after the completion of a doctoral thesis and its transformation into a book that they have lived too long in a state of claustrophobia. Thus teaching social theory was for me a welcome breath of fresh air—an education in its own right and a crucial supplement to the more arid training of graduate school. Since then, I have taken advantage of my students, in both graduate and undergraduate courses on a variety of subjects ranging from diplomacy to psychohistory, to test out my ideas in bits and pieces as they have occurred to me. An inability to convey them lucidly has frequently convinced me that I was off target and forced me to pursue a different line of attack.

More specifically I am grateful to Reva Greenburg, who went through a first draft of the manuscript, meticulously pointing out obscure passages and undeveloped arguments which might bewilder a future reader. More than that, over a period of many years she listened to and questioned me about the fragmentary speculations I served up between and after rallies on the tennis court. Peter J. Loewenberg gave generously of his time in reading a second version; his experience with clinical material and the insights springing from it that he offered have proved invaluable. During the final revisions, I have been most fortunate in being able to talk over troublesome issues with Melford E. Spiro. He has given me encouragement when my spirits have been at a particularly low ebb.

■

The reader will have no trouble in discovering that my enterprise reflects at every turn what may be called a domestic sensibility. When I finished my first book, I already acknowledged that my greatest debt was to my husband, Stuart. I thanked him for putting up with my demands for continual discussion of the work as it progressed and for the editorial assistance provided in the course of reading successive versions. These functions he has once again fulfilled with exemplary patience. But such intellectual support is only a part of what he has given me. Above all his unvarying kindness and affection have enabled me to be a mother to our son, David, and to derive from that experience a vision of my own.

Finally a word about David himself. Throughout this venture he has been both a companion and an inspiration. From an early age he became not only an object of observation, but a willing informant; he soon began to regard this book as his book. And in view of what he has had to endure from a mother's preoccupation, it is fitting that the final product should be dedicated to him.

Chapter 1

Past Misunderstanding and Present Insight

I. The Problem Posed: What I Am Doing and What I Am Not

Ever since the First World War, historians have been intrigued by the antagonism between Britain and Germany which preceded the outbreak of hostilities. Even when it became clear that this antagonism could not itself account for Europe's resort to war in 1914, Anglo-German relations retained their fascination. Why two countries, which in 1870 seemed to have much in common and little in dispute, should by the early twentieth century have come to regard themselves as potential foes ranked as a question worth asking in its own right. And numerous studies have addressed the question—so many, indeed, that another is scarcely needed.[1] Hence it is not this familiar problem that I want to pose. Rather what has struck me in studying the diplomacy of the prewar period, starting as early as the 1880s,[2] is the mutual, if not complete, incomprehension between British and German leaders—the fact that people separated by no insuperable

---

1. For the most recent and thorough book on the subject, see Paul M. Kennedy, *The Rise of Anglo-German Antagonism 1860–1914* (London: George Allen and Unwin, 1980).

2. See W. N. Medlicott, *Bismarck, Gladstone, and the Concert of Europe* (London: Athlone Press, 1956).

1

barrier of language or concepts still missed nearly totally each other's mental track.

This puzzle cannot be solved by attacking it head-on. Instead, to continue the military metaphor, the strategy of the indirect approach is called for. To gain insight into why the British and Germans spoke past each other, one must first understand how they spoke among themselves. Speech in this instance refers to privately constituted meanings which limit or facilitate personal interaction. How such meanings were shared among the British and among the Germans is crucial to the task I have set myself: the delineation of dissimilarities in personal relations at the summit in late nineteenth-century Britain and Germany.

■

Such a study of personal relations can be done only by focusing on selected individuals. Whatever number is chosen, that choice is open to criticism. No matter how small the cast of characters, some readers may argue that it should have been smaller still in order to provide a greater wealth of detail about the individuals in question. Other readers may claim that the number is too small to "prove" the existence of attitudes (or better, tempers) characteristic of British and German public life. In what appeared a potentially no-win situation, I allowed the choice to be made for me: with 1880 as the starting point prescribed by diplomatic history, I included those men who by virtue of their political roles in effect chose themselves.

This self-selected cast of characters falls into three categories. The first comprises the three statesmen whose long tenure as leaders made them architects of political cohesion: William Ewart Gladstone, Otto von Bismarck, and the Marquess of Salisbury. Their key collaborators constitute the second category. Three among these latter deserve extended treatment, and hence they too rank as protagonists of this study: the Marquess of Hartington, Friedrich von Holstein, and Arthur James Balfour. Holstein and Balfour also figure in the third group: the heirs of the statesmen who initially dominated the scene. Along with them, Emperor William II, Philipp zu Eulenburg, Bernhard von Bülow, and Joseph Chamberlain demand inclusion and complete the roster.

These categories in turn make more precise the task I am undertaking; they help refine the appropriate questions about personal relations at the summit. Initially, in the case of securely established authority figures, the crucial issue, then and now, is one of interaction between leaders and collaborators. The next series of questions follows logically. What happened to the men who had gathered around the leaders when those architects of cohesion left the stage? How was cohesion reknit after their power had waned? To answer these further questions entails—as the presence of "heirs" suggests— pursuing the study down to the turn of the century. By that time the transition to a new generation had, in both countries, been accomplished.

■

This study—resolutely and uncomprisingly individualistic—is based on the assumption that psychology cannot be derived from social institutions, that knowing an individual's social or professional position, for example, does not grant automatic access to his inmost being. Such an assumption may sound like a truism; nonetheless, it often appears to make historians uncomfortable. It implies that from readily available "hard" data one cannot reach demonstrable conclusions about the subjective states of historical actors. A pity: the task of reconstructing the past would be so much simpler if it were otherwise. More specifically, differences in economic development, politics, and family life cannot, even taken together, account for differences in how people spoke to one another.

Hence the immediate question confronting me is of a practical sort: How much discussion of institutional differences is necessary? How much knowledge of British and Prusso-German history can I take for granted? Let me start by ticking off three items which will, I assume, strike the reader as obvious. First, late nineteenth-century Britain had long been a well-established national state possessed of a large overseas empire, whereas the German Reich was of recent foundation and its place in both European and world politics remained uncertain. Second, in contrast to the early and relatively gradual industrialization of Britain, Germany's period of rapid economic change coincided with its unification. Third, the power of Britain's traditional state apparatus had been effectively curbed by the end of the seventeenth century; the power of the Prussian "military monarchy," on the other hand, had been extended by virtue of the dominant position it acquired in the newly unified nation.

The third item leads to a fourth that is equally obvious but nevertheless worth underlining: the institutional framework in which political activity was carried on. Power in Britain was located in the cabinet, which in turn depended upon a majority in the House of Commons—organized along party lines—for its continuance in office. The German Reichstag bore little resemblance to the House of Commons. The chancellor was not responsible to that elected body, but rather to the emperor, who at the same time was the king of

Prussia. On paper, then—the Germans, unlike the British, had a written constitution—power resided in the monarch and those he selected to advise him. In fact, it had no fixed location; it fluctuated in accordance with the ability of the chancellor to manipulate his sovereign, to mobilize his bureaucratic staff, and to keep a firm rein on the Prussian State Ministry, over which he usually presided. A British prime minister labored under the "liberal" constraints of cabinet government and party rule; a German chancellor found himself confined by "authoritarian" monarchical and bureaucratic structures. Which figure would prove able to exert more power was difficult to predict in advance.

These four items could, of course, be treated at much greater length. But I see no compelling need to go over familiar ground, to write a preliminary background chapter that would add little to what is already well known. A fifth item which may also be familiar does demand inclusion: the uncertainty associated with the transmission of power from one leader to another. One would anticipate that for the Germans, who lacked historical precedents, successions to chancellors (and to sovereigns) would prove troublesome indeed. A second look suggests that even for the British, who had ample experience to draw on, the transfer of power between and within parties was not without difficulties. Unlike the first four items, however, this matter cannot be relegated to the status of a preliminary consideration. Though the issue itself derived from the political realm, it was interpreted in a personal and emotional fashion by the protagonists of this study, and hence it should be analyzed along with the vicissitudes of these same individuals.

Thus far I have said nothing about family life. Again I am faced with a practical problem, but of a different sort. In this case there is no surfeit of familiar comparisons and contrasts; there is a dearth. Unlike the anthropological student of culture and personality, I cannot confidently expect to find two reliable and relatively complete sets of data. The first would comprise the objective facts of childrearing in a given culture (for the historian, read "class and country") at a given time. The second would include the objective facts of childrearing that obtained in the particular cases of the individuals to be studied. If the second set matched the first, then and only then might it be appropriate to use the first set of data as an independent variable which would help account for the dependent variable of individual personality.

The historian of nineteenth-century family life does not yet have adequate data of the first type; the sources available have not yet been systematically exploited and collated.[3] Two major categories stand out: prescriptive literature, broadly construed to include assumptions regarding parental responsibilities, and material about institutions intended to facilitate socialization. Each category poses difficulties. Prescriptive literature is always problematic when taken by itself: a careful social scientist would not, I think, want to explain the behavior and beliefs of an *individual* child born during the post–Second World War baby boom on the basis of Dr. Benjamin Spock's *Baby and Child Care*. Similarly, institutional settings are far from clear-cut. Even the common notion of "nannied" children turns out to be uncertain for the period I have chosen: the nanny as an institution was a midcentury development,[4] and my British protagonists were all born before 1850. No doubt this is an unsatisfactory state of affairs. But the effort required to put it right—to provide a reliable ethnographic account by utilizing data from a variety of sources—is beyond the scope of the present study.

Data of the second type, that is, information concerning the objective facts of childrearing in particular cases, though scanty, are available. And historians of the family depend heavily on this kind of information. By using it selectively and anecdotally, they flesh out a

3. The monumental work of Lawrence Stone is necessarily impressionistic and does not deal adequately with the nineteenth century: *The Family, Sex and Marriage in England 1500–1800* (New York: Harper and Row, 1977); for a perceptive critique, see the review by Philippe Ariès, *American Historical Review* 83 (December 1978): 1221–1224. A work comparable to Stone's in American history, which offers a sharply opposing view of the nineteenth century, is Carl N. Degler, *At Odds: Women and the Family in America from the Revolution to the Present* (New York: Oxford University Press, 1980); for a critique of this book along with Michel Foucault, *The History of Sexuality*, I: *An Introduction*, trans. Robert Hurley (New York: Pantheon, 1978), and Jacques Donzelot, *The Policing of Families*, trans. Robert Hurley (New York: Pantheon, 1979), see Christopher Lasch, "Life in the Therapeutic State," *New York Review of Books* 27 (June 12, 1980): 24–32. See also Randolph Trumbach, *The Rise of the Egalitarian Family: Aristocratic Kinship and Domestic Relations in Eighteenth-Century England* (New York: Academic Press, 1978), and Anthony S. Wohl, ed., *The Victorian Family: Structure and Stresses* (New York: St. Martin's Press, 1978). For the most complete bibliography of British materials, see S. Barbara Kanner, "The Women of England in a Century of Social Change, 1815–1914: A Select Bibliography," in Martha Vicinus, ed., *Suffer and Be Still: Women in the Victorian Age* (Bloomington: Indiana University Press, 1972), pp. 173–206, and Barbara Kanner, "The Women of England in a Century of Social Change, 1815–1914: A Select Bibliography, Part II," in Martha Vicinus, ed., *A Widening Sphere: Changing Roles of Victorian Women* (Bloomington: Indiana University Press, 1977), pp. 199–270. Comparable German studies are virtually lacking.

4. See Jonathan Gathorne-Hardy, *The Rise and Fall of the British Nanny* (London: Hodder and Stoughton, 1972).

general picture. But I am not writing family history; my purpose would not be advanced by trying to match data about the domestic environment and social milieu of individual protagonists with fragmentary, and possibly dubious, generalizations. These matters should instead be examined along the way. Where my work may be of value to historians of the family is in suggesting an orientation for future research. The psychoanalytic theory, which it is now time to introduce, may, at the very least, prompt a fresh series of questions.

II. Psychoanalytic Portraits: What Is Feasible with Historical Data

A comment about language is in order before proceeding further. In what follows I have strenuously tried to avoid technical terminology. The aesthetic appeal of literary English is overwhelming, and its use imperative if one hopes to reach a heterogeneous audience. Still more, the proliferation of technical terms often obscures agreement among analysts themselves. The elaboration of terminologies accentuates disputes over theory, some of which might well be settled if analysts took the trouble to translate each others' views into their own vocabularies, or, better yet, into the vernacular. Finally, the material itself virtually demands restraint; the abstract character of technical terminology would set up too great a distance between data and interpretation.

The Freudian and post-Freudian legacy is so complex that it is impossible for an historian concerned with psychoanalysis to avoid picking and choosing bits of theory to employ in his investigation. Selections, however, need to be made with an eye to consistency; that is, the items chosen should stand in a clear relation to the main Freudian corpus as well as being congruent with one another. For those conversant with psychoanalytic literature, I can state my own position simply: it derives from the British school of object-relations theory, more particularly from the writings of W. R. D. Fairbairn and D. W. Winnicott.[5] I cannot here give an account of their work,

5. W. Ronald D. Fairbairn, *Psychoanalytic Studies of the Personality* (London: Routledge and Kegan Paul, 1952); D. W. Winnicott, *The Maturational Process and the Facilitating Environment: Studies in the Theory of Emotional Development* (London: Hogarth Press, 1965), and *Through Pediatrics to Psycho-Analysis* (London: Hogarth Press, 1975). Behind the work of Fairbairn and Winnicott lies not only that of Freud, but also of Melanie Klein: Roger Money-Kyrle, ed., *The Writings of Melanie Klein*, 4 vols. (London: Hogarth Press, 1975). For a review of the work of the school as a whole, see Harry Guntrip, *Personality Structure and Human Interac-*

nor of the discrepancies between the two. What I should do, rather, is to indicate as clearly as possible how I have fitted together—in an effort to arrive at a coherent theoretical framework—the major themes they have explored.

Freud himself was at the origin of object-relations theory, though it had not yet acquired that name. His work in the early 1920s, his elaboration of the structural hypothesis of id, superego, and ego, and with it his renewed interest in the study of the ego, prepared the way for his deviant British followers. What remains recognizable in all their work, despite multiple reformulations, is Freud's conception of the superego's development. The notion of a child internalizing his parents at the point that he must renounce his attachment to them as *love* objects—the point Freud marked out as the resolution of the Oedipus complex—is the paradigm for the development of a world of *internal* objects. Relations to and among these objects constitute the central concern of the British school.

How to recognize such relations depends, of course, on knowing what one is looking for, that is, on pursuing the suggestions embodied in theories about emotional development. It is here that, in my view, the British school has made its most important contribution. Where Freud stressed the Oedipus complex, the triangle of father, mother, and child, as fundamental, the British analysts have focused their attention on the pre-Oedipal period, on the earliest tie between mother and child. Although Freud noted the importance of that tie, he never explored his own insight. For him the father loomed as the dominant figure, and psychohistorians, following his lead, have almost invariably concentrated on the father–son relationship. To shift the emphasis to the mother–child dyad, while it represents no more than a logical extension of Freud's pioneering work, nevertheless has entailed a far-reaching reassessment of childhood experience.

Inevitably the bond between mother and child will be disrupted. How the separation will come about in particular cases, one cannot know beforehand. Even afterward one can only piece together the

tion: The Developing Synthesis of Psychodynamic Theory (London: Hogarth Press, 1961). This approach is phenomenologically compatible with that of Heinz Kohut in his *The Analysis of the Self* (New York: International Universities Press, 1971), and his *The Restoration of the Self* (New York: International Universities Press, 1977); see also Kohut's "Thoughts on Narcissism and Narcissistic Rage," *The Psychoanalytic Study of the Child* 27 (1972): 360-400. For a summation of major parallel work in mother-child relations, see Margaret S. Mahler, Fred Pine, and Anni Bergman, *The Psychological Birth of the Human Infant: Symbiosis and Individuation* (New York: Basic Books, 1975).

drama in incomplete fashion. One can safely assume that the process begins when the infant starts to differentiate himself from his mother. But this mother is not a neutral figure, passively attending the child's growth; her own internal conflicts—as well as the material circumstances in which she must perform her tasks—shape her response to the infant's demands. In line with the British analysts, then, I attribute secondary importance to the father's interference (to which one should add that of siblings) in the widening gap between mother and child.

How does the child cope with this complex mother who has aroused in him not only love but angry feelings as well? It seems plausible to describe the child's response in terms of splitting and internalizing the mother figure. The mother is bound to frustrate the child, and the child internalizes this frustrating aspect in an effort to gain control over a person on whom he is utterly dependent; the tensions of the outer world are thereby reestablished in his inner domain. How can the relation between mother and child modify what is in danger of becoming a bleak inner prospect? The answer hinges on the mother's reliability: by serving as a steadying influence, she can sustain the child through bad experiences; over time he will become convinced that both he and his mother can master such experiences. If he has found this kind of safety, he has enjoyed an aspect of reality which he can take within him as something one may call a reassuring presence. Fortunate is the child who performs this crucial act; just as the one who does not succeed in accomplishing it remains eternally impoverished.

How can one of the "fortunate" safeguard a reassuring presence, how can he protect his mother against the anger he has already internalized? It is at this point—and not before—that the disposal of hate becomes an urgent and ongoing problem for the child. When he fails to shield his mother against his rage—and surely that must sometimes happen—she not only survives, but in the best of circumstances accepts his love as reparation. Her survival and acceptance, taken together, enable her child to imagine that he has made restitution for his anger. Still more, by offering such restitution, such amends, for the damage he feels he may have caused, he recreates and reinforces the memory of his mother's reassuring presence.

In the drama I have been tracing, the father has apparently disappeared. What has become of this formerly majestic figure? Though reduced to playing a secondary role, at some point he makes his entrance and establishes contact with his offspring. Now the child is confronted with two parents where earlier there had been only one.

His relationship with his father is fraught with vicissitudes similar to those he has already experienced with his mother, and, in turn, he employs once again the technique of splitting and internalizing he adopted for coping with her. His inner world has become complicated indeed.

To make this scene manageable, Fairbairn argues, the child, in effect, simplifies the parental objects and in so doing *"constitutes the Oedipus situation for himself."*[6]

> Psychologically speaking, the deeper significance of the situation would appear to reside in the fact that it represents a differentiation of the single object of the ambivalent (later oral) phase into two objects, one being an accepted object, identified with one of the parents, and the other being a rejected object, identified with the remaining parent. The guilt attached to the Oedipus situation, accordingly, is derived not so much from the fact that this situation is triangular as from the facts (1) that the incestuous wish represents a demand for parental love which does not seem freely bestowed, and (2) that there has arisen in the child a sense that his own love is rejected because it is bad.[7]

For Freud the Oedipus complex figured as an ultimate cause; for Fairbairn, "it is not a basic situation, but the derivative of a situation which has priority over it in the logical, but also in the temporal sense."[8] In short, the child's incestuous wishes, and his defenses against them, reflect the trials and tribulations of making emotional contact—initially with the mother; they reflect the hopes and disappointments he experiences in attempting to elicit love and thereby gain reassurance that his love is acceptable.

The child needs a responsive environment; so too does the mother. She looks for emotional sustenance from a variety of sources, including her own mother, and in her search her husband has an important part to play. He may have no opportunity to "mother" his child himself, yet in his relation to his wife he may provide encouragement and reliable assistance comparable to what she is giving their offspring. Indeed should he fail to do so, what would become of his position in the family? The question has rarely been asked. It cannot be answered here. What should be emphasized, however, in general terms, is that as a consequence of the mother's centrality in the emotional life of her children, she is also the central figure in the emotional life of the family. "Patriarchal" fathers no doubt have existed, men who

6. Fairbairn, *Psychoanalytic Studies of the Personality*, p. 124 (emphasis in the original).
7. Ibid., p. 37.
8. Ibid., p. 120.

have sought to lord it over wife and children. But such fathers, who in effect have rebelled against the status of mother's helpmate, have run the risk of becoming psychologically marginal within their own families, of being relegated to the sphere of public affairs.

Though one would hesitate to regard the emotional balance—or imbalance—achieved in childhood as fixed, one cannot help stressing the limited extent to which it is likely to change. For this to be the case, one is not obliged to argue (as does Melanie Klein) that developments within the first year of life are alone decisive. The central fact is that the early relationship with the mother is prolonged into the later stages of youth. The mother thus has the power to reinforce whatever came before, whether malignant or benign. New relationships might ideally hold out the possibility of starting afresh; in actuality, however, unresolved conflicts are all too often transferred onto subsequent attachments. To put it another way: what people seek are new objects to support the reassuring image of the mother, and this quest is constantly in danger of being undermined by the negative image which has also been installed in the unconscious.

■

A short digression on psychoanalytic explanations may help the reader assess the interpretations I shall be advancing. An initial point is that explanations, be they psychoanalytic, psychohistorical, or simply historical, are context-dependent. "The demand for explanations arises in . . . those situations, those contexts, in which there is perceived a puzzle, an incongruity, a lack of understanding about the way that certain facts or observations fit together." An explanation thus "logically requires that there be an incongruity, a conflict of fact or observation against which it is directed." It follows that different contexts may give rise to different explanations: what might be regarded as an appropriate explanation in one context might seem inappropriate in another.[9]

The second point concerns the criteria by which one evaluates a psychoanalytic explanation. The appropriateness already noted constitutes one criterion, but one insufficient by itself. Adequacy is another. Two standards of adequacy are widely recognized in both psychoanalytic and historical discourse: coherence—accommodating "the individual's behavior into a coherent whole"—and comprehensiveness—accounting for "every incongruent and puzzling circum-

9. Michael Sherwood, *The Logic of Explanation in Psychoanalysis* (New York: Academic Press, 1969), pp. 10, 12.

stance" (though not for every bit of behavior). A third standard of adequacy is less familiar to historians: consistency—making sure that "general statements about the individual . . . are consistent with each other."

> Taken together the three standards mentioned—self-consistency, coherence, and comprehensiveness—make up at least an important part of what we mean by judging an explanation of human behavior to be adequate. It must be remembered, however, that we are dealing with a spectrum of adequacy, a whole range along which we can place explanations. Moreover, just because we speak of partial and more or less complete explanations, we should not go on to the mistaken view that there is one absolutely complete explanation. To search for explanations that are more complete is quite feasible. But to demand a totally complete explanation is to demand the attainment of a logical standard for something which is essentially context-dependent. Such context-dependency makes total completeness logically impossible, for there is an infinite number of ways to approach any subject matter, and an infinite number of ways in which aspects of that subject matter may be incongruous.[10]

Adequacy is not, to be sure, the same as accuracy. In fact, context-dependence "allows for several explanations being equally adequate." As long as one sticks to the standards of "consistency, coherence, and comprehensiveness" it appears that several different explanations "might rank equally."[11] Something more than adequacy is thus expected; some sort of claim about truth is usually made. And in coming to the problem of accuracy—a third criterion of evaluation—one comes to the role of theory in filling out an explanation.

Truth claims are not themselves dependent upon the truth of the theory. The individual under scrutiny, not the theory, remains the final touchstone for determining the accuracy of an explanation. To the extent that assertions about the person in question are confirmed, "then the explanation can be regarded as at least partially true or accurate."[12] Theory does, however, play a supporting role. An explanation is considered more accurate if it accords with generally true statements about human behavior. Alternatively if an explanation contravenes such statements, the investigator is confronted with additional peculiarities that require explanation.

At this point the skeptic may well ask: Can I be certain that the psychoanalytic theory I am employing is valid? The answer, ob-

10. Ibid., pp. 247–249.
11. Ibid., p. 249.
12. Ibid., p. 251.

viously, is no. But I suspect that my predicament is similar to that of most historians who borrow—and historians are inveterate borrowers—from other disciplines. Few are able to demonstrate the validity of the theory which informs their explanations. They are not, after all, engaged in testing theory—nor am I. And if, perchance, mothers should prove psychologically insignificant for the emotional development of their children, the underpinnings of my study would collapse.

The skeptic might further wonder whether it is possible to draw psychoanalytic portraits of the dead at all. The charge is frequently made that since the data one can collect about historical figures are of neither the quality nor the quantity that an analyst gathers from a patient, psychohistory is doomed from the start. The problem of data is a real one—and psychohistorians are not the only researchers troubled thereby. Data *are* uneven, and hence explanations are uneven. Still more, though an historian make every effort to exploit what is available, his explanations are never immune to the ravages caused by the discovery of new data. The criteria already mentioned take these difficulties into account: they offer both ideal goals and realistic expectations.

■

In all cases, the likenesses of my protagonists have been fashioned according to the same principles. The first task has been to provide a context of explanation. How to do so was not, however, immediately apparent. Whatever starting point I might have chosen could have seemed arbitrary; after all, every "life story presents a variety of incongruities—events and attitudes demanding to be explained, to be brought within the framework of understandable human behavior."[13] I have tried to meet this difficulty by using, wherever possible, the same kind of material to establish context: a subjective statement—a written document—by the individual in question which represents his preferred emotional stance.

Although such material provides ample grounds for puzzlement, it is insufficient to resolve that perplexity. How, then, should conscious and relatively static self-images be handled? The emphasis should not fall on their factual content; an assessment of factual accuracy should not be the primary concern. Rather the emphasis should fall on what the particular figure wanted the world to believe, and, in

13. Ibid., p. 188.

turn, what he believed, about himself. There is little to be gained by subjecting such texts to rigorous literary analysis, by pursuing deep hidden meaning in patterns of rhetoric or imagery. At best one would arrive at debatable interpretations that would divert attention from the main purpose: to formulate questions about the individual's affective development from his childhood on.

The method of proceeding, then, is from a self-image constructed in maturity to the emotional experiences of childhood and then back to adult life. Superficially regarded, this method may appear circular. It is important to confront such a charge at the outset. Circularity is reprehensible only when the return journey marks no advance in understanding. One cannot be faulted for arriving once again at a starting point, or its vicinity, if the second time round that starting point has become more than a point, if it has become multidimensional. Such is quite evidently the case in the present investigation. What begins as a conscious and relatively static self-image ends as a dynamic tension between inner and outer worlds.

III. The Findings Foreseen: A Crisscross of Discourse

The tension between inner and outer worlds carries with it an implication that should be spelled out: there is no sharp separation between public and private life. If the emotional universe of childhood is transferred onto adult relationships, it follows that the realm of the family and the realm of public affairs cannot be viewed as neatly compartmentalized. In brief, the oppressiveness of the public sphere—not as abstraction but as personal experience—derives some of its power from reactivating internal persecutors already produced within the "security" of family life.

For the German protagonists of this study, both spheres were marked by an absence of trust, and, accordingly, interpersonal relations offered scant reassurance to the individuals involved. Fear, which acquired its force from a desolate inner landscape, was never far below the surface. It made men willing to accept a leader's authority; it also made their dependence on him irksome. From this dilemma, from the dilemma of a soul torn between dread and self-aggrandizement, there appeared no obvious means of escape.

For the British protagonists, trust in oneself—and in others—facilitated the passage to interpersonal relations based on mutuality and forbearance. Colleagues proved able to find reassurance in their association in large measure because they expected to find it. Among men so equipped, dependence and independence stood not as polar opposites but as necessary complements.

The problem requiring explanation has already been stated: the fact that the Germans and British missed nearly totally each other's mental track. The nub of the matter is that tempers so deeply rooted in childhood experience cannot easily be cast aside. They give rise to expectations about interpersonal behavior, expectations which are reinforced when "privately constituted meanings" overlap to a marked degree. And when they fail to overlap, what one hears is a crisscross of discourse.

Chapter 2

Charismatic Authority and Cabinet Solidarity

Gladstone in the 1880s

When William Ewart Gladstone formed his second ministry in 1880, his position as Liberal party leader and as British public figure was unrivaled and unprecedented. With his forays into mass politics during the preceding years, Gladstone had created about him an aura that was religious, if not magical. Both party and public seemed to hang on his person, to be malleable substances ready to assume their proper form according to his specifications.

Such power Max Weber called charisma, and for Weber, Gladstone was an exemplar of charismatic leadership. While that term and the qualities it connotes are elusive, its very ambiguity may help to focus a discussion of Gladstone and his colleagues. In the first instance, one must penetrate behind the quasi-mystical veil of charisma and explore the nature Gladstone's inner resources. Weber's readiness to locate such authority in the eyes of the beholder will not suffice. Yet his stress on the followers' acquiescence or recognition points to a second crucial concern: Of what stuff were Gladstone's co-workers made? What nourished their deference to him? And finally Weber himself posed a further riddle which he phrased in cumbersome terms as the routinization of charismatic authority. His own suggestions on this score were inconclusive. Nevertheless the question can be reworded more concretely and tangibly: How did Gladstone balance his own independence against the requirements of cabinet solidarity? In short, what qualities enabled Gladstone and his colleagues to conform to the conventions of parliamentary government?[1]

I. A Political Genius under Restraint

Before grappling with Gladstone a word of caution is in order. His outlook was defined by the religious framework of understanding and judging human behavior he had inherited. The psychoanalytic assumptions of this study obviously provide a very different perspective. Yet the two are not incompatible. To make their coexistence possible, one must avoid reducing Gladstone's religious sentiments to instinctual drives or suggesting that religious dogma simply veiled basic impulses. The effort required is one of translation, and Gladstone himself supplied the key in acknowledging that his religion was deeply anchored in affective ties. Hence the work of translation calls for delineating the personal relations which gave abstract religious categories their vitality.

One may start with Gladstone's apparent uncertainty about his own goodness. In an autobiographical fragment written in old age he remarked: "If I was not a bad boy, I think that I was a boy with a great absence of goodness." His summary comment on those early years echoed this doubt:

> I wish that in reviewing this period I could regard it as presenting . . . features of innocence and beauty . . . . The best I can say for it is that I do not think it was actually a vicious childhood. I do not think, trying to look at the past impartially, that I had a strong natural propensity then developed to what are termed the mortal sins. But truth obliges me to record this against myself. I have no recollection of being a loving or a winning child: or an earnest or diligent or knowledge-loving child.[2]

Yet Gladstone added a "palliating touch":

> I was a child of slow, in some points I think of singularly slow development: there was more in me perhaps than in the average boy, but it re-

1. For Weber's comments on Gladstone as a charismatic leader, see "Politics as a Vocation," in H. H. Gerth and C. Wright Mills, eds. and trans., *From Max Weber: Essays in Sociology* (New York: Oxford University Press, 1946), pp. 106, 113. For his discussion of charismatic authority, see ibid., pp. 245–252, and Talcott Parsons, ed., *Max Weber: The Theory of Social and Economic Organization*, trans. A. M. Henderson and Talcott Parsons (New York: Oxford University Press, 1947), pp. 358–392. For a discussion of the Gladstone cult, see D. A. Hamer, "Gladstone: The Making of a Political Myth," *Victorian Studies* 22 (Autumn 1978): 29–50.
2. W. E. Gladstone, "Infancy-Family-Childhood," July 8, 1892, in John Brooke and Mary Sorensen, eds., *The Prime Minister's Papers: W. E. Gladstone*, I: *Autobiographica* (London: H.M.S.O., 1971), pp. 20, 18.

quired greatly more time to set itself in order: and just so in adult, and in middle and later life, I acquired very tardily any knowledge of the world, and that simultaneous conspectus of the relations of persons and things which is necessary for the proper performance of duties in the world.[3]

In this regard one item in particular stands out: the slow—but eventually sure—development of Gladstone's conception of beauty.

I think that like other children, I had a faculty of imagination from the beginning, but it was one both weak and wild. I used to think or dream of myself as one furnished in certain odd ways for certain courses of life which I was then left to prosecute at my will. But there was a great want alike of definite purpose, and of dominant attraction, an emancipation from the rule of reason, without the distinct conception of the rule of beauty, or of any other allegiance. . . .

Notwithstanding all this it has undoubtedly happened that in the course of my life I have become and remained one of the most convinced and uncompromising asserters of the substantive character of beauty, in opposition to those who teach that it is conventional or that it takes rank below the dignity of an independent and changeless principle.[4]

It is Gladstone's juxtaposition of moral and aesthetic categories that is striking. Why should the "rule of beauty" have permitted what was in him to come to fruition? Why should an appreciation of beauty have enabled him to fill an "absence" or repair a "defect" in his "mental organisation"?[5] How does Gladstone's stress on beauty help one to understand both the self-confidence and the moral scruple which are so amply apparent? It is as if, given time, a vision of beauty can replace or restore what has been damaged—or to put it more concretely—what Gladstone may have believed he had damaged. When sustained by such a faith, moral scruple becomes tolerable; it does not undermine trust in oneself.

Gladstone's self-confidence and his scruples alike had their roots in his childhood. So too did his feeling for beauty—and the longing to make reparation it betokened.

■

What was most conspicuous in Gladstone's earliest years, from his birth in 1809 until his adolescence, was his close relationships with his mother and his older sister, Anne. The young daughter supplemented the mother's emotional nourishment without confusing or obscuring the primary maternal image. That image was of someone

3. Ibid., pp. 19–20.
4. Ibid., pp. 22–23.
5. Ibid., pp. 19, 22.

physically frail, yet firm in her Evangelical religious beliefs, of someone hypochondriacally concerned with bodily health, her own and
that of her children, yet intensely alive to their spiritual well-being.
A socially insecure and shy person, with a mind "full of taboos, inhibitions and piety,"[6] she nonetheless fostered in her fourth son and
fifth child the conviction "that there was ... something" in him
"worth the saving."[7]

In Gladstone's account of her death, he underlined the warmth of
her attachment to her children and hinted at the specialness of his
own position:

> And she said to me while I sat there, "My beloved William, my beloved
> son, are you there still? go to your bed." And again she said, "My pre-
> cious, why do not you go to rest?" Such were the epithets, which she was
> accustomed to bestow upon her children, while she esteemed herself vile.[8]

So long as his mother lived, Gladstone felt that he and she shared a
religious sensibility which required little "through the medium of
language" to sustain their bond.[9]

This sensibility received encouragement from Anne, a sister whose
portrait can be discerned only in the broadest outline. In the trying
circumstances of their mother's illnesses, she became the pillar of the
family, on whom parents and siblings alike relied, and an object of
adoration. Her self-confidence and poise under the weight of such
responsibilities are amply evident.[10] In Gladstone's diaries this sister,
who was both seven years his senior and his godmother, emerges as
his religious mentor, a role which made of her a mother surrogate.
From his sister (and his mother) William learned to cultivate a sense
of his own sinfulness—and he was to do so the rest of his life.

In line with Anne's prompting—and his obsessive concern with his
sinfulness—William began to keep private diaries, a practice he
maintained until his mid-eighties.[11] No intention of bequeathing to
posterity a document of literary or historical merit guided his pen.

6. S. G. Checkland, *The Gladstones: A Family Biography 1764–1851* (Cambridge:
Cambridge University Press, 1971), p. 88.

7. Gladstone, "Infancy-Family-Childhood," in *Autobiographica*, p. 19.

8. W. E. Gladstone, "Recollections of the last hours of my mother," September 23,
1835, in John Brooke and Mary Sorensen, eds., *The Prime Minister's Papers: W. E.
Gladstone*, II: *Autobiographical Memoranda 1832–1845* (London: H.M.S.O., 1972), p.
58.

9. W. E. Gladstone to John Gladstone, August 4, 1830, quoted in John Morley,
The Life of William Ewart Gladstone (London: Macmillan and Co., 1903), I: 640.

10. Checkland, *The Gladstones*, p. 89.

11. The following volumes of the diaries have been published to date: M. R. D.
Foot, ed., *The Gladstone Diaries*, I: *1825–1832*, II: *1833–1839* (Oxford: Clarendon
Press, 1968); M. R. D. Foot and H. C. G. Matthew, eds., *The Gladstone Diaries*, III:

"There is no striving for effect; there is earnest, continual striving after truth." Though many passages sound a jarring unctuous note, the "whole tone is that of a man making a powerful effort to be honest with himself,"[12] a man who is hypercritical rather than hypocritical. Above all, the diaries fulfilled the function Gladstone ascribed to confession: for in keeping his journal he came "face to face with his greater sins one by one. Many a flimsy extenuation" exploded "under the very act of bringing it into light, or by force of fair and legitimate questioning upon it."[13] But such self-scrutiny was not accompanied by fear and trembling. On the contrary, under Anne's tutelage religious doctrine had become suffused with hope: recognition of evil held out the prospect of forgiveness.[14] It was in encouraging William to look sin in the face that his sister's teaching had provided him the greatest comfort.

By the time William began, as an adolescent, to keep his diary, Anne was already ailing; she died in 1829, before her brother had turned twenty, and was promptly canonized by the mourning family she left behind. The atmosphere of suffering and death in which William had lived gave urgency to his mother and sister's religious injunction of self-restraint. It made him sensitive to the ways his own behavior might harm the persons who had first fostered his love. Though this love had been richly nourished, though he had known safety in emotional attachments, he had no doubt experienced frustration as well. But he kept in check whatever hostile sentiments had been aroused. Only then did he feel he could prevent what he unconsciously perceived as their devastating consequences: the destruction of the loved one itself. In short, William's scrupulousness offered him the means for preserving one and all. At the same time the hope of forgiveness it held out kept alive the possibility of making whole again what, in fantasy, he had broken up.

Hence the anxiety he expressed, shortly before his election to parliament, that he might be abandoning his family, whose fortunes at the time seemed less promising than his own:

Here is a noble trial: for me personally, to exercise a kindly and unselfish feeling, if amid the excitement and allurements now near me, I am en-

1840–1847, IV: *1848–1854* (Oxford: Clarendon Press, 1974); H. C. G. Matthew, ed., *The Gladstone Diaries*, V: *1855–1860*, VI: *1861–1868* (Oxford: Clarendon Press, 1978).

12. Editor's introduction to ibid., I: xx.

13. W. E. Gladstone, "On Confession-Reflexions," December 17, 1893, in *Autobiographica*, pp. 159–160; see also *The Gladstone Diaries*, III, December 25, 1840, p. 74.

14. See, for example, *The Gladstone Diaries*, I, December 29, 1829, p. 276; December 24, 1830, pp. 334–335; September 17, 1832, pp. 573–574.

abled duly to realise the bond of consanguinity, and *suffer with* those whom Providence has ordained to suffer.[15]

This concern for "the bond of consanguinity" had guided his relationship to his father. Though John Gladstone had been wondrously successful as a Liverpool merchant, his career had not brought with it the political and social situation which his son regarded as its "natural termination."[16] William understood full well that he himself was to do what his father had been obliged to leave undone. Originally he had preferred religion over politics. In a long letter to his father, written while he was still at Oxford, he had expressed a desire, which coincided with his mother's hopes, to enter the ministry.[17] Yet when the moment of choice came, he did not let his wish to serve God override his duties to his earthly father. In compliance with paternal direction, he planned to begin the study of the law—and was saved from a legal career only by the offer of a parliamentary seat in December 1832, at the age of twenty-three. In his first years in the House of Commons, where he made his mark as a defender of West Indian enterprise, the source of John Gladstone's fortune, he showed himself amply submissive to his father's guidance.[18]

When William Gladstone did loosen his ties to his family, the new attachments he formed continued and enlarged those he had already known. In 1835, the same year in which his mother died, he began his search for a wife. The earnestness with which he pursued his goal expressed a desperate attempt to recapture something of what he had lost with Anne and his mother's deaths and contributed to the failure of his first two courtships. In both cases he frightened the young women by the strenuousness of his religious belief and practice.[19] Finally, in Catherine Glynne, whom he married in 1839, he found an ideal mate, whose religious sensibility echoed his own. Politics, as well, drew them together. Catherine quickly became her husband's confidante; from the time of his marriage he told her all his political secrets, and, as he later commented, she "never once . . . *leaked.*"[20] If Gladstone's references to his wife in his diaries are brief, neither the

15. Ibid., I, November 7, 1832, pp. 584–585 (emphasis in the original).
16. Ibid., I, November 7, 1832, p. 585.
17. W. E. Gladstone to John Gladstone, August 4, 1830, quoted in Morley, *Gladstone*, I: 635–640.
18. On John Gladstone, his fortune and his politics, see Checkland, *The Gladstones.*
19. Philip Magnus, *Gladstone: A Biography* (London: John Murray, 1954), pp. 23–40.
20. Gladstone to Rosebery, August 25, 1895, Gladstone Papers, Add. MS. 44290 (emphasis in the original).

closeness of their tie nor her husband's high regard for her are in doubt. The recurrent motif that marks her appearance is summed up in the expression "hero-woman."[21]

Over the course of time Catherine's extended family became closer to Gladstone than his own. This shift reflected, in part, his rapid ascent beyond the social status of his parents. His early career reads like a textbook case in the smooth assimilation by the aristocratic political elite of a member of the commercial classes. Friendships formed at the prescribed educational institutions, Eton and Oxford, paved his way socially and politically. He owed his seat in Parliament to a friend's father, the Duke of Newcastle; but the impression he early made on that body testified to his own talents, and these were formidable indeed. To marry someone from the landed gentry, then, fitted the position he had already created for himself.

By the time Gladstone recited his marriage vows, the religious beacon which lighted his way had shifted from Evangelical to High Church. Writing years later on the Evangelical movement, he unintentionally suggested the personal reasons behind his change: excessive individualism he stigmatized as the "besetting weakness" of his childhood faith:

> Whether [*sic*] individualism is thus largely indulged, cohesion cannot well be durable; there must be expected . . . a remarkable want of permanence in personal and family tradition. . . .
> The Evangelical movement filled men so full with the wine of spiritual life, that larger and better vessels were required to hold it.[22]

Gladstone's statement contains a paradox. How could he reconcile his concern for permanence in family tradition and his break with his mother's Evangelical persuasion? For he had abandoned her distrust of church mediation—and just at the time when he disappointed her hopes by renouncing his inclination for a clerical career.[23] The answer lies in the nature of his staunch adherence to the Anglican es-

21. See, for example, *The Gladstone Diaries*, VI, January 6, 1862, p. 88. For Gladstone's most extended appreciation of Catherine and his own mental state at the time of his engagement, see ibid., II, February 6, 1839, pp. 576–577. For further glimpses of their marriage, see A. Tilney Bassett, ed., *Gladstone to his Wife* (London: Methuen and Co., 1936); Mary Drew, *Mrs. Gladstone* (New York and London: G. P. Putnam's Sons, 1920); Georgina Battiscombe, *Mrs. Gladstone: The Portrait of a Marriage* (London: Constable, 1956); Joyce Marlowe, *Mr. and Mrs. Gladstone: An Intimate Biography* (London: Weidenfeld and Nicolson, 1977).

22. W. E. Gladstone, "The Evangelical Movement: Its Parentage, Progress, and Issue" (1879), in W. E. Gladstone, *Gleanings of Past Years, 1860–1879* (London: John Murray, 1879), VII: 237, 232.

23. Morley, *Gladstone*, I: 87–88.

tablishment: in taking sustenance from those "larger and better vessels" he rediscovered a world which could hold and steady him as earlier his childhood home had done.

∎

That Gladstone underwent a prolonged psychic crisis in the late 1840s and early 1850s is now well known. His diaries provide a running account of years of turmoil. The symptoms by which this inner turmoil manifested itself, though titillating, are less significant than what brought on the crisis and how Gladstone eventually surmounted it. As his protective covering was stripped away, his earlier anxieties emerged, and also his techniques for dealing with them. The outcome was not so much a psychological rebirth as it was a consolidation of an emotional equilibrium temporarily, if severely, shaken.

A series of interlocking concerns runs through those crisis years: politics, religion, and sexuality. The political difficulties are the easiest to date and sort out. Gladstone's resignation from Sir Robert Peel's cabinet in 1845 certainly marked a major upset. It entailed a painful separation from the man he regarded as his political mentor. Fortunately it proved brief. The issue which led to his withdrawal was the government grant to Maynooth College, an establishment for training Roman Catholic priests in Ireland. Gladstone's own stance seemed quixotic: he left the cabinet, while voting for the grant in the House of Commons. His continued presence in the government, he felt, would have appeared as a self-interested abandonment of the position he had staked out in 1838—that the truth of the Anglican faith imposed upon the state an obligation of exclusive institutional support. At the same time his vote acknowledged that since the "vitality" of that obligation was no longer recognized by others, his position had ceased to be viable.[24] And in admitting that his view of the state as handmaiden to religion had become anachronistic, he found himself face to face with the fragmentariness of life.

Gladstone's sense that he had lost his bearings betokened a concern for the church which was more than institutional. It expressed the anguish of a man who experienced religion as a "personal and

---

24. For his lifelong concern with this subject, see D. C. Lathbury, ed., *Correspondence on Church and Religion of William Ewart Gladstone*, 2 vols. (London: John Murray, 1910). See also Deryck Schreuder, "Gladstone and the Conscience of the State," in Peter Marsh, ed., *The Conscience of the Victorian State* (Syracuse, N.Y.: Syracuse University Press, 1979), pp. 73–134, and Peter Stansky, *Gladstone: A Progress in Politics* (Boston: Little, Brown and Co., 1979).

living Church in the *body* of its Priests and members."[25] Throughout the 1840s a series of prominent Anglicans went over to Rome, and with their defection the state of the church became for Gladstone "a crushing care and affliction."[26] In 1851 his torment reached its peak. The two friends, James Hope and Henry Manning (the future cardinal), whom he called "the only supports" for his "intellect" were "wrenched away" from him, leaving him "lacerated . . . and barely conscious morally."[27]

> Such terrible blows not only overset and oppress but I fear also demoralise me: which tends to show that my trusts are Carnal or the withdrawal of them would not leave such a void.[28]

As that year drew to a close, Gladstone observed: "In truth the religious trials of the time have passed my capacity and grasp. I am bewildered, and reel under them."[29]

He was also buffeted by his own sexuality. Six years earlier he had drawn up a list of temptations and along with them a stringent set of rules designed to enforce a more perfect self-control. Thereafter he made a mark in his diary every time he violated one of these rules; he further noted the times, when to fortify his resistance or to punish an infraction, he resorted to the use of a scourge.[30] Though Gladstone was by no means alone among his contemporaries in self-flagellation, at the very least his obsessional practice represented a desperate effort to mitigate the anxiety that accompanied impermissible sexual wishes. He was caught in a vicious circle: the anxiety he labored under undoubtedly heightened his sexuality, while sexual desire exacerbated his anxiety.

Further woes followed. At the very time he was reeling under the blows inflicted on the church, he was mourning his second daughter, Jessy, who died suddenly in April 1850. Two months later Sir Robert Peel succumbed as the result of a riding accident; in December 1851 Gladstone's father breathed his last. Simultaneously financial troubles brought additional cares. Mismanagement had reduced

25. *The Gladstone Diaries*, IV, August 19, 1851, p. 353 (emphasis in the original, which was composed in Italian).
26. Ibid., IV, December 29, 1850, p. 296.
27. Ibid., IV, August 19, 1851, p. 353 (original in Italian). For Hope's view of the matter, see Robert Ornsby, *Memoirs of James Robert Hope-Scott*, 2 vols. (London: John Murray, 1884).
28. *The Gladstone Diaries*, IV, March 30, 1851, p. 319.
29. Ibid., IV, December 29, 1851, p. 382.
30. Ibid., III, October 26, 1845, pp. 492–493; IV, July 19, 1848, pp. 51–55, and April 22, 1849, pp. 116–117.

Catherine Gladstone's family to the brink of bankruptcy, and her husband undertook a worrisome and long-drawn-out salvage operation. These shocks coming all together proved harrowing indeed. Death and defection had brought about what Gladstone's scrupulousness had unconsciously been designed to ward off: the destruction of those he loved.

How can one make sense of the anguish he experienced? One must avoid the temptation to pounce on his anxiety as the product of a diseased imagination or as proof positive of mental instability. On the contrary one should stress the range of emotions to which Gladstone remained accessible. He did not in an effort to avoid anxiety cut off feelings, thereby administering an anesthetic to his emotional life. In this connection, one should recall that numbness, like repression, is unable to banish emotions; it simply removes them from any semblance of conscious control or modification. In short, psychic integration cannot be achieved without the risk-taking involved in remaining in touch with one's inner world.

How, one may further ask, did Gladstone reestablish something which might be called a "benign circle"?[31] How did he come to trust himself again, to tolerate the guilt for the damage he unconsciously felt he had wrought? The process was slow, and since the deepest of the anxieties he recognized were sexual, it is not surprising that that process involved women. To trust himself in relation to women emerged as crucial to his psychic integration.

Marriage had not spared Gladstone the problem of his own sexuality: Looking back "over more than twenty years since this plague began," he commented that the period of marriage was one "at which the evil was so to speak materially limited but it may also have been formally, essentially enhanced."[32] Unlike many of his contemporaries, who regarded sexual intercourse as sanctified by its reproductive purpose, Gladstone considered abstinence as morally preferable:

> Man as God made him is wonderfully made: I as I have made myself am strangely constituted. An ideal above the ordinary married state is commonly before me and ever returns upon me: while the very perils from which it commonly delivers still beset me as snares and pitfalls among which I walk.[33]

31. For this expression, see D. W. Winnicott, "The Depressive Position in Normal Emotional Development," in his *Through Pediatrics to Psycho-Analysis* (London: Hogarth Press, 1975), p. 270.
32. *The Gladstone Diaries*, IV, July 19, 1848, p. 53.
33. Ibid., IV, April 22, 1849, p. 117.

Behind this censorship of sexuality lay fear of its potential ruthless-
ness. If the violence latent in it—and in childhood the two are con-
fusedly experienced together—prompts the most determined efforts
at restraint, in Gladstone's case the danger had been borne in upon
him by the contrast between his father's robustness and his mother's
debilitation. After all, father and son had shared the same object of
sexual desire. Gladstone's own impulses had first been directed toward his mother—and his frail older sister, Anne; censorship of sexuality as incest thus reinforced censorship of sexuality as destruction.
And when Gladstone took Anne's place as religious mentor to his
younger sister, Helen, incestuous wishes no doubt penetrated their
spiritual relationship. In the diaries, Helen stands out as a central
figure during Gladstone's period of turmoil, refracting the anxieties
that threatened to overwhelm him.[34]
The youngest of the family and four years her brother's junior,
Helen, by the late 1830s, had become a severe trial to her relatives.
Years of ill health, both real and imaginary, had led to opium addic-
tion. Gladstone was horrified at the deterioration he observed. In
1840 he noted:

> There is an unsatisfied craving within her, a sentiment that her life is
> objectless, with some irregularity in the action of her powerful under-
> standing, and with unhappy disadvantages of habit. . . . Thank God that it
> is not mine to judge her in any respect: He has with a purer truth a larger
> love which will cover a thousand to us seeming anomalies. I write these
> lines with a heavy heart, as if they were a last tribute to one who is far
> less unworthy than I, with whom I have been most closely knit in bygone
> days: and whose affections are still real and powerful.[35]

Gladstone was far less sympathetic when two years later Helen
announced her conversion to the Roman Catholic church. Above all,
he vehemently denied any responsibility of his own for her submission to Rome. He rejected the notion that his High Church influence
had led her to abandon the faith he was so eager to defend. Moreover, he viewed this desertion as severing the spiritual bonds which
had linked them together; he bluntly told her "that doubtless it is
wise and just that all personal relations should be liable to convul-
sion, which are not founded in . . . the realised communion of the
Church."[36] Though reconciled to Helen in later years, after her

34. It was in late 1845, already harrowed by his resignation from Peel's cabinet
only a few months earlier and now commissioned to bring Helen home from Baden-
Baden, that Gladstone wrote down his list of sexual temptations and rules.
35. *The Gladstone Diaries*, III, June 13, 1840, p. 37.
36. Ibid., III, June 11, 1842, p. 206.

health had been restored by what she regarded as a miracle, he never acknowledged the faith which had produced the cure. When she died in 1880, he convinced himself that she was no longer a strict Catholic and proceeded to inter her according to the Anglican rite.[37]

His inability to master his complex feelings about Helen infused with urgency Gladstone's rescue work among the "fallen" women of London. Though this labor had begun at least a decade earlier and was to continue for the next forty years, it was during his time of troubles that it attained its maximum intensity. If Gladstone's strenuous involvement with prostitutes figured as a symptom of his mental distress, it also offered therapeutic gain. In this connection it is worth repeating (and at greater length) what he wrote in his diary when Hope and Manning were on the verge of submitting to Rome.

> Such terrible blows not only overset and oppress but I fear also demoralise me: which tends to show that my trusts are Carnal or the withdrawal of them would not leave such a void. *Was* it possibly from this that thinking P. L. [a prostitute] would look for me as turned out to be the fact, I had a second interview and conversation indoors here: and heard more history: yet I trusted without harm done.[38]

Clearly Gladstone's anguish was acute. Moreover with his two friends following the same course from High Church to Rome that Helen had taken, Gladstone's denial of any responsibility for his sister's conversion became hollow. So demoralized was he that he lost his self-control—the very reproach he had leveled at Helen—and succumbed to the impulse to converse once more with a "fallen" woman. Yet no "harm" had been done. Indeed what is most striking about the whole passage is the note of hope at its end. It is almost as if by taking responsibility for P. L., instead of Helen, and by helping her, Gladstone might find a way to ease his own anxiety.

Whether his efforts were in turn of benefit to P. L. and similar "unfortunate" creatures is less clear. He endeavored to dissuade them from continuing their wretched way of life, supplementing moral exhortation with material support. For many of the cases, his wife provided active assistance. In 1854 he drew up a summary of the results:

> This morning I lay awake till four with a sad and perplexing subject; it was reflecting on and counting up the numbers of those unhappy beings, now present to my memory with whom during now so many years I have

---

37. For details on Helen Gladstone, see Checkland, *The Gladstones.*
38. *The Gladstone Diaries,* IV, March 30, 1851, p. 319 (emphasis in the original).

conversed indoors and out. I reckoned from 80 to 90. Among these there is but one of whom I know that the miserable life has been abandoned *and* that I can fairly join that fact with influence of mine. Yet this were much more than enough for all the labour and the time, had it been purely spent on my part. But the case is far otherwise: and tho' probably in none of these instances have I not spoken good words, yet so bewildered have I been that they constitute the chief burden of my soul.[39]

In all likelihood the successful case Gladstone had in mind was that of Elizabeth Collins. He first encountered her shortly after Hope and Manning had left the Anglican fold, when he was so unstrung by their secession that he lacked the fortitude to administer his customary self-punishment.[40] "E. C." appears in the diaries as late as 1863,[41] but the bulk of the references to her fall between 1851 and 1854. Gladstone's early meetings with her produced strong emotion, though his sense of discipline revived sufficiently to enable him to scourge himself after "a strange and humbling scene."[42] (In this case, as in all others, he avoided the worst pitfall of "infidelity to the marriage-bed."[43]) The strength of his feeling is indicated by the use of Italian, a language he loved and frequently employed in discussing highly charged involvements with women. In a long passage he again linked his rescue work with the state of the church: he voiced his gratitude at being God's instrument in helping Collins and immediately thereafter expressed his grief at the Anglican church's loss of its leading lights.[44] The juxtaposition made manifest his own attempt to undertake the priestly function abandoned by his friends. And in turn his bewilderment suggested the psychic depths to which he was reaching.

More specifically, Gladstone consciously wished to give the prostitutes a refuge and haven—to shield them against outrageous fortune. At the same time, the intensity of his wish forced him to come to terms with what he regarded as failure—something he had not accomplished with Helen. After all, by his own account, his rescue work was not notably successful. In the case of the prostitutes, as opposed to Helen's, his "failure" aroused a sense of personal guilt; yet his efforts to provide a safe standing ground for the "fallen" al-

39. Ibid., IV, January 20, 1854, p. 586 (emphasis in the original).
40. See ibid., IV, June 11, 1851, p. 336, and May 11, 1851, p. 329.
41. Ibid., VI, July 30, 1863, p. 217.
42. Ibid., IV, July 13, 1851, p. 344.
43. Gladstone to his son Stephen, 1896, quoted by the editors in ibid., III: xlvi–xlvii.
44. Ibid., IV, August 19, 1851, pp. 352–353.

lowed him to tolerate that guilt. In going beyond mere scrupulous-ness—mere sexual restraint—to act out a role of succor or of nurture, he rediscovered a surer way of preserving one and all. A "benign circle" was once more in operation.

To be sure, a high-minded and sometimes single-minded deter-mination to assuage his sense of sinfulness always remained a marked feature of Gladstone's personality. But his work with the "fallen" permitted him to relax his demands on others. His capacity to think of himself as trustworthy, even though he might fail in his chosen mission, enabled him to forbear from judging harshly those who dif-fered with him. He did not require outward success to confirm his sense of personal worth, and by the same token he harbored no lin-gering rancor against those who refused to respond to his charismatic appeal.

II. A Tribune Returns to Power

To turn now to Gladstone as an architect of political cohesion: he found himself unable to enter upon his task without mental and moral reservations. The question in his mind was not whether politi-cal life offered a means to achieve dominance, but, on the contrary, whether it kept self-seeking sufficiently in check.[45] In 1868 at the beginning of his first ministry, he had used a powerful metaphor to convey the excessive demands of politics which left no "stock of moral energy unexhausted and available for other purposes."

> Swimming for his life, a man does not see much of the country through which the river winds, and I probably know little of these years through which I busily work and live, beyond this, how sin and frailty deface them, and how mercy crowns them.
>
> But other years as I hope are to come a few at least in which yet ampler mercy will permit to learn more of my own soul and to live for that kind of work which perhaps (I have never lost the belief) more specially be-longs to me.[46]

Sentiments of this sort had prompted Gladstone's retirement from the leadership of the Liberal party in 1875. As he later commented, he "deeply desired an interval between Parliament and the grave" for achieving serenity in religious reflection.[47] Similarly his wish for relief from "burdens under which he must fall and be crushed if he

45. See, for example, W. E. Gladstone [untitled], November 9, 1894, in *Auto-biographica*, pp. 138–139.

46. *The Gladstone Diaries*, VI, December 31, 1868, p. 655.

47. W. E. Gladstone, "1879–1894," in *Autobiographica*, p. 112. For Gladstone's

[looked] to the right or left" led him to misjudge the ease with which he could abandon both the discipline and the attachments of political life.[48] He seemed to forget the confession he had uttered at the height of his crisis in 1851. "My trusts are Carnal" he had exclaimed then, and so they remained. Only at great emotional risk could he break loose from the net that had enveloped him.

In joining, albeit belatedly, the popular agitation against Turkish atrocities and misrule in Bulgaria, Gladstone began the process of rescinding his ambiguous abdication. In part his slowness to act or to appreciate the outcry stemmed from his reluctance to admit that the news coming from the East touched a core of personal prehistory which lent it immediate significance.[49]

> When in 1876 the Eastern question was pressed forward by the distur-
> bances in the Turkish Empire, and especially by the cruel outrages in
> Bulgaria, I shrank naturally but perhaps unduly from recognising the
> claims they made upon me individually.... I had at length been com-
> pelled to perceive ... that as the only person in the House of Commons
> who had been responsible for the Crimean War and the levelling of the
> bulwark raised ... on behalf of the eastern Christians I could no longer
> remain indifferent.[50]

Gladstone's subsequent participation in the movement undoubtedly enabled him to regain what he had lost in his party's defeat of 1874, his rapport with the masses. At the same time he took care to safe-guard himself from the "insatiable demands" of political life;[51] he used his replenished sense of moral purpose to keep the world of party and parliament from impinging on him until he should feel ready to assume once more the burdens of leadership.

After the Liberal victory at the polls in 1880 and his own personal triumph in the Scottish constituency of Midlothian, he could delay no longer. His second ministry, formed in that year, has frequently been described in terms of his progressive loss of control and ultimate failure.[52] In contrast to the volume of constructive legislation his

---

critical comment on Peel's comparable behavior, see *The Gladstone Diaries*, III, July 10, 1846, p. 553, and July 13, 1846, pp. 559–560.

48. *The Gladstone Diaries*, VI, December 31, 1868, p. 655.

49. Compare R. T. Shannon, *Gladstone and the Bulgarian Agitation 1876* (London: Thomas Nelson and Son, 1963), p. 91.

50. Gladstone, "1879–1894," in *Autobiographica*, pp. 112–113.

51. *The Gladstone Diaries*, VI, December 31, 1868, p. 655.

52. For a detailed analysis of the government's weakness, see the editor's introduction in Agatha Ramma, ed., *The Political Correspondence of Mr. Gladstone and Lord Granville 1876–1886* (Oxford: Clarendon Press, 1962), I: xiii–xlviii; see also A. B. Cooke and J. R. Vincent, eds., *Lord Carlingford's Journal: Reflections of a Cabinet*

first cabinet had placed on the statute books, the record of his second has seemed thin and lacking a guiding purpose. In 1880 the Liberal party scarcely had a definite plan or shared political objectives, and the polemics of the electoral campaign proved inappropriate to. the new difficulties that soon emerged. Ireland quickly became the dominant issue, followed by the complexities of Egyptian affairs. Both divided a cabinet whose makeup itself reflected a spectrum of opinion rather than a common program. Earl Granville and the Marquess of Hartington, along with Earls Spencer, Northbrook, and Kimberley, could be counted on to espouse Whiggish sentiments, while Sir William Harcourt, John Bright, and Joseph Chamberlain manifested widely varying degrees of radicalism. The divisions among them on issues for which they found themselves unprepared have cast a shadow over the workings of the ministry and have obscured Gladstone's willingness to adapt his charismatic authority to a delicate cabinet structure—to let that authority function in a manner which could almost be called routine.

■

If Gladstone might temporarily postpone the baffling question of formulating coherent legislative proposals, he could not avoid the more pressing problem of molding his cabinet into a viable body. Despite the fact that he considered himself ultimately responsible for cabinet action—and hence his "obligation to act upon" his "own deliberate judgment" was not "in the slightest degree" diminished[53]— he sought to balance that obligation with tolerance of others, to preserve his personal integrity while demonstrating his appreciation for that of his colleagues.[54] To provide assurance that he accepted an individual as a person in his own right—and thereby encourage mutual forbearance—was the nub of the matter. Though Gladstone did not define his role in such explicit terms, his relations with certain of his intimates indicated his readiness to furnish what was needed from him.

In the published correspondence between Gladstone and Lord Granville one can discern the crucial role of personal sympathy.

Minister 1885 (Oxford: Clarendon Press, 1971), and D. A. Hamer, *Liberal Politics in the Age of Gladstone and Rosebery: A Study in Leadership and Policy* (Oxford: Clarendon Press, 1972), pp. 79–98.

53. *Gladstone and Granville Correspondence*, I, Gladstone to Granville, July 5, 1883, p. 385.

54. Membership in a cabinet, Gladstone believed—and so reminded erring colleagues—ought to act as a brake on deviance. He shared Granville's view that "no man has a right to play according to his own hand, without reference to the cards in his partner's." Ibid., II, Granville to Gladstone, December 4, 1883, p. 119.

Their paths had become permanently entwined when they served together under Lord Palmerston, though both men had earlier achieved political prominence and success. Throughout Gladstone's first ministry Granville was his closest associate, and after 1870, when Granville became foreign secretary, he and Gladstone jointly shaped their country's diplomatic policy. After Granville returned to that office in Gladstone's second government, the same kind of cooperation, initially at least, characterized their relationship. In conducting the negotiations with Turkey, which dominated the first few months, Granville constantly sought and received guidance from his chief. When Gladstone was briefly absent, Granville wrote that he missed "not having" him at his "elbow," and that his "only relief" was "being able to discuss every little detail" together.[55] During the following years Gladstone was so often preoccupied with domestic problems that their partnership in constructing foreign policy underwent many vicissitudes. While Granville, in his official work, might thus suffer from the prime minister's lack of attention, their long-standing intimacy allowed him no doubt of his own significance for Gladstone. More importantly, Granville never ceased to aid his friend in the task, which the latter often found trying, of giving personal recognition to the individual merit or self-esteem of other colleagues.

No one could have been a more appropriate helpmate than Granville. Born in 1815, educated at Eton and Christ Church, Granville was related to and thoroughly at home with the prominent aristocratic and landed families. To elaborate his ties with those families would delight a genealogist. In short, his was the social milieu of Hartington and the other Whig magnates. His was also the emotional milieu of a well-loved son, who had basked in the warmth of his parents' steadying support. When complimented on being unlike other Englishmen, on lacking their almost instinctive shyness, Granville demurred in such a way as to underline the ease and assurance of his manner. "He came of a shy family, he said, or at least of a family a great number of whom were very shy; but he had had one great advantage from his earliest youth, which might account for his having an undeserved reputation: he had nearly always been in an unquestioned position. This, he said, made all the difference. If you

55. Ibid., I, Granville to Gladstone, October 15, 1880, p. 202. For further comment on their relationship, as well as Gladstone's treatment of his secretaries, see Sir Edward W. Hamilton, *Mr. Gladstone: A Monograph* (London: John Murray, 1898); Sir Algernon West, *Recollections, 1832 to 1886* (New York and London: Harper and Brothers, 1900); Arthur Godley Kilbracken, *Reminiscences of Lord Kilbracken* (London: Macmillan and Co., 1931).

went to an official entertainment, or into a crowded room, or into a select circle . . . and you felt that nobody could doubt your right to be present, there was little excuse for shyness. This advantage he had almost invariably had."[56] Quite naturally, then, Granville became the social leader of the Liberal party. Entertaining a steady stream of guests, he played host to "all those . . . who counted for something."[57] His genial hospitality, devoid of any desire for self-advertisement, served the more general purpose of smoothing over personal jealousies and political rivalries.

The perplexing and often irritating behavior of Lord Rosebery and the way in which it was handled illustrate Granville and Gladstone's joint efforts to accommodate personal claims for recognition. Though Rosebery was merely a minor figure in Gladstone's second administration, the fact that he eventually became prime minister and, indeed, gained entrance into leading Liberal circles through his friendship with Gladstone makes their relations worth dwelling on. As a young Liberal Scottish peer Rosebery had early come to Granville's attention, but it was his management of the Midlothian campaign that brought him both intimacy with Gladstone and a certain political prominence. When the government was formed, Rosebery was offered the post of undersecretary in the India Office, a position that ordinarily would have been much appreciated by a man still in his early thirties. Rosebery, however, rejected the proposal, ostensibly to avoid the accusation of having curried favor with Gladstone in order to gain office. In writing to the prime minister's daughter Mary he enumerated other motives, placing first his "annoyance at not being asked to join the cabinet."[58] Rosebery clearly preferred to remain in the background rather than accept an offer that in either substance or manner he considered beneath his dignity.

The crux of the ensuing tension between Gladstone and Rosebery was simply this: Rosebery's notion of what was his due came into direct conflict with Gladstone's view of the proper political *cursus honorum*. The latter firmly believed that departmental service was a necessary prelude to cabinet office and only in rare cases should this

56. Lord Edmond Fitzmaurice, *The Life of Granville George Leveson Gower Second Earl Granville 1815–1891* (London: Longmans, Green, and Co., 1905), II: 131–132. For the atmosphere of his family, see his mother's correspondence: F. Leveson Gower, ed., *Letters of Harriet Countess Granville 1810–1845*, 2 vols. (London: Longmans, Green, and Co., 1894); see also the biography (including extensive correspondence) of his sister: Mme. Augustus Craven, *Lady Georgiana Fullerton, sa vie et ses oeuvres* (Paris: Perrin et Cie., 1888).

57. Fitzmaurice, *Life of Granville*, II: 126.

58. Rosebery to Mary Gladstone, April 27, 1880, quoted in Marquess of Crewe, *Lord Rosebery* (London: John Murray, 1931), I: 135; see also Rosebery to Gladstone,

stage be skipped. When in 1881 the Duke of Argyll resigned the Privy Seal and Rosebery displayed considerable pique at being neither offered the position nor even consulted about it, Gladstone found such presumption scarcely credible.[59] Granville, who fully understood that Rosebery was in earnest and like his chief was duly shocked, still advised Gladstone to try to "soothe" Rosebery by having "a little confidential talk with him, on the state of Affairs."[60] Though a few months later Rosebery did accept an undersecretaryship in the Home Office, by the end of the following year he was loudly expressing his dissatisfaction, which he focused on the existing arrangements for handling Scottish business. Gladstone was again surprised, commenting that it was "marvellous how a man of such character and such gifts" could "be so silly."[61] Once more Granville was "for dealing with him most tenderly," ready to admit his "claims to the next vacancy for a peer in the Cabinet," and willing to "give a sort of pledge" to him.[62] In mid-1883 Rosebery took the occasion of an indirect attack on him in the House of Commons to resign— though Gladstone and the cabinet had already agreed to introduce a local government bill for Scotland. Shortly thereafter the prime minister offered Rosebery the position that would be established in the event that the bill should pass. But Rosebery was "resolved not to take the post which the Cabinet decided to create really *for* him," because it would "not carry a seat in the Cabinet."[63] Such behavior was incomprehensible to Gladstone, who remarked that "to be on

April 25, 1880, Gladstone Papers, Add. MS. 44288. For the most recent biographical study, see Robert Rhodes James, *Rosebery: A Biography of Archibald Philip, Fifth Earl of Rosebery* (London: Weidenfeld and Nicolson, 1963).

59. Dudley W. R. Bahlman, ed., *The Diary of Sir Edward Walter Hamilton 1880–1885* (Oxford: Clarendon Press, 1972), I: April 22, 1881, p. 132.

60. *Gladstone and Granville Correspondence*, I, Granville to Gladstone, April 29, 1881, p. 272; see also Granville to Gladstone, April 16 [?], 1881, pp. 258–259; Gladstone to Granville, April 18, 1881, p. 260; Granville to Gladstone, April 18, 1881, p. 261; Gladstone to Granville, April 26, 1881, p. 266; Granville to Gladstone, April 27, 1881, p. 268.

61. Ibid., I, Gladstone to Granville, December 19, 1882, p. 471.

62. *Hamilton Diary*, I, December 26, 1882, p. 380; see also December 17, 1882, p. 377; December 22, 1882, p. 378; Mary Gladstone to Hamilton [December 1882], Hamilton Papers, Add. MS. 48611. That Gladstone sought to treat Rosebery gently is clear from the following letter he wrote to him: "I hope I have never written or spoken a word to imply that personal ambition was the spring of your present movement. I may have difficulties in putting a rational construction on the conduct of men from time to time: but I regard it as a base and commonly a misleading mode of escape to ascribe it to unworthy motives. In this case it would be monstrous." Gladstone to Rosebery, December 23, 1882, Gladstone Papers, Add. MS. 44288. For the calming effect of this letter on its recipient, see Spencer Lyttelton to Hamilton, December 27, 1882, Hamilton Papers, Add. MS. 48610.

63. *Hamilton Diary*, II, July 28, 1883, p. 465 (emphasis in the original); see also Rosebery to Gladstone, July 30, 1883, Gladstone Papers, Add. MS. 44288.

the rails ... and to be off the rails" were "two different things."[64] Obviously Rosebery was temporarily, at least, off the rails.

After Rosebery's return from a trip around the world, Gladstone resumed his efforts to bring him into the government. In late 1884 and early 1885 the prime minister conducted negotiations with the touchy Scottish peer about entering the cabinet as first commissioner of works. Rosebery, however, found fresh reasons for declining. Egyptian policy had replaced Scottish affairs as his source of discontent and become an insuperable obstacle to participation.[65] Then suddenly, in what would seem to have been an abrupt about-face, Rosebery volunteered to join up after catastrophic news of General Gordon's death in the Sudan reached London. "At a time of national disaster he thought that it became everyone to sink differences about details of policy and that, if the door was still open and if his services could be of real use, he was ready to place them absolutely at Mr. G[ladstone]'s disposal."[66] Following Granville's advice, the prime minister sweetened the original offer by adding the Privy Seal, and Rosebery, finally feeling that the nobility of his motives could no longer be in doubt, accepted.[67] Throughout these vicissitudes Gladstone, urged on by Granville, had done his utmost to satisfy Rosebery, even when the latter's conduct had passed his understanding.

■

While Gladstone had a reputation for exquisite courtesy, he was not credited with an equal degree of intuition: though he sought to give his colleagues personal reassurance, appreciation of firmly held convictions came more naturally to him. In the realm of principle he recognized the bedrock of an individual's psychological armoring. To his mind cabinet unity could be achieved only if such convictions had been given a proper hearing:

> In my opinion, differences of view stated, and if need be argued, and then advisedly surrendered with a view to a common conclusion are not "divisions in a Cabinet."
> By that phrase I understand unaccommodated differences on matters standing for immediate action.[68]

64. Quoted in *Hamilton Diary*, II, August 1, 1882, p. 467.
65. Rosebery to Gladstone, November 11, 1884, and Rosebery to Gladstone, February 1, 1885, Gladstone Papers, Add. MS. 44288.
66. *Hamilton Diary*, II, February 8, 1885, p. 791; see also Rosebery to Hamilton, February 5, 1885, Hamilton Papers, Add. MS. 48612 A, and Rosebery to Gladstone, February 8, 1885, Gladstone Papers, Add. MS. 44288.
67. *Gladstone and Granville Correspondence*, II, Granville to Gladstone, February 8, 1885, p. 335.
68. Ibid., II, Gladstone to Granville, March 24, 1884, p. 172.

To accommodate Hartington's views certainly ranked as one of Gladstone's most difficult tasks. Indeed Hartington's position was such that the survival of Gladstone's second ministry in large measure depended upon his willingness to stay at his post. Were he to withdraw, the government would lose the support of his Whig followers, and the party would be split. Were he to remain, the succession would surely be his. Since he had served as Liberal leader in the Commons during Gladstone's period of semiretirement, he was expected to take full charge when the elder stateman finally withdrew.[69] From the very start of the ministry, then, relations between the two men had been delicate, becoming even more strained through disputes over Irish policy. In those matters Hartington's personal stake could scarcely have been higher; his brother Lord Frederick Cavendish had been murdered in Phoenix Park (Dublin) in May 1882. Gladstone shared in his grief; Lord Frederick had been his nephew by marriage and someone very dear to him. As for Hartington, he took his sorrow unto himself, refusing to censure the chief who had sent his brother on his fatal mission. Though he yielded to no personal animus, in the face of this loss he clung more firmly than ever to the political convictions that offered him a standing ground.[70]

A statement from 1883 on franchise reform—characteristically flat in style—echoed what Hartington voiced on half a dozen occasions during his long association with Gladstone.

> There seems to be now no alternative for me between abandoning the position which I have publicly, perhaps prematurely, taken up, and sooner or later separating myself from the Government.
>
> I do not think it is possible for me to take the former course without so weakening my position in the country as to prevent my being of any further service to the Government. . . .
>
> I will not in this letter discuss the other alternative, although it seems to me to be the inevitable one. I would rather wait to hear your opinion on what I have already written, and I feel some hope that, unfortunate as are the differences which exist between colleagues and myself, and unfounded as you believe my objections to be, you will be inclined to agree with me that, after what has taken place, it would not be for the credit of the Government, or for my own, that I should now, even if it were possible, recede from the position which I have taken up.[71]

69. See, for example, ibid., I, Gladstone to Granville, November 15, 1881, p. 311.
70. For Gladstone's view of how Lord Frederick Cavendish's death affected Hartington, see *Hamilton Diary*, II, December 3, 1883, p. 518.
71. Hartington to Gladstone, December 2, 1883, quoted in Bernard Holland, *The Life of Spencer Compton Eighth Duke of Devonshire* (London: Longmans, Green, and Co., 1911), I: 396–397.

Clearly Hartington's stance of responsible politician acted in a crucial way to give him a sense of worthiness. Though this persona was
the one most readily available to someone of his Whig family background, his rigidity in maintaining the part suggested that it provided the carapace he found necessary for confronting the world. No
one could doubt his principles; some might feel he suffered from too
many scruples. Yet beneath his stiffness lay no fund of ruthless aggression—something ultimately more destructive of political cohesion than any amount of scruple.

About Hartington's early childhood his biographer tells us very
little. Two facts, however, stand out. His elder brother, the firstborn
and heir, died before he was three years old, when Hartington himself was scarcely more than an infant. In the five years following his
own birth in 1833, three other children were born, one daughter and
two sons, in that order. One can speculate that after the death of her
firstborn, Hartington's mother devoted particular attention to her
second son. In that event, her own death when he was close to seven
must have been all the more catastrophic for him.[72]

Hartington's loathing for English composition prevented him from
leaving his own account of his childhood. Yet it is evident that deep
feeling marked his relationship with his father, the Duke of Devonshire. Though the two of them always ranked as undemonstrative,
even among Cavendishes, who as a breed were known not to show
their emotions, the older man had tried to fill the void created by the
death of his wife. He kept his children by him when others of their
age and class were already away at school. Having been unhappy at
Eton himself, he had his sons taught at home. Hartington's first real
separation from his father did not come until he was sent to a tutor
to prepare for entering Cambridge. Even then his father continued to
guide him in well-trodden paths; he encouraged him to take his studies seriously, just as he was to support and counsel him in his public
endeavors. Hartington and his two brothers reciprocated this paternal devotion. As his sister-in-law Lady Frederick Cavendish noted:
"The three kept much with their father, and it was very comforting
to see them with him, and to know that they are *almost* like daughters to him."[73]

If his father, in encouraging him to assume his birthright of public
service, pointed out an acceptable way for Hartington to occupy himself, he was unable to stimulate his son to sustained activity. Har-

72. For biographical material, see ibid., I, chs. 1 and 2.
73. John Bailey, ed., *The Diary of Lady Frederick Cavendish* (London: John Murray, 1927), I, September 26, 1865, p. 286 (emphasis in the original).

tington never relished hard work, and the time-consuming labor of office required a constant struggle against his inclination toward a slower and easier pace, indeed toward lethargy. Doubtless there were times when he was disposed to answer in the affirmative the question asked by his cousin Lord Granville: "What are you going to do if you give up politics? Nothing but horseracing?"[74] As Granville pointed out to their chief, if Hartington "is not convinced as to his public duty, there is no other temptation for him. He dislikes office ... and, above all, he dreads the brilliant success which some time will fall to him."[75]

Hartington's reluctance reflected the limits he had early imposed on himself. The loss of his mother had not crippled his capacity for affection, as his lifelong attachment to the Duchess of Manchester attested.[76] Yet it had left him prone to fear that assertiveness might destroy those he loved. Under the cover of aristocratic obligation, he had learned to hide a hesitancy about pushing himself forward and a disinclination to transform political differences into matters of personal combat. This stance served his needs in so tidy a fashion that to outsiders he seemed a man "all of a piece."[77]

Gladstone in turn showed appreciation for firmly held convictions; he nonetheless tried to reduce the number of issues on which the accolade "matters of principle" might be bestowed. Thus he urged Hartington not to separate from his colleagues over Egyptian difficulties:

> If a rupture ... comes, ... it will come upon matters of principle, known and understood by the whole country, your duty will probably be clear and your position unembarassed: but I entreat you to use your utmost endeavor to avoid bringing about the rupture on one of the points of this Egyptian question, ... which does not turn upon clear principles of politics, and about which the country understands almost nothing.[78]

In a subsequent letter to Hartington, Gladstone made clear why Egyptian affairs did not fall under the rubric "principle":

74. Quoted in Holland, *Devonshire*, I: 398.

75. *Gladstone and Granville Correspondence*, II, December 19, 1883, p. 131; also quoted in Holland, *Devonshire*, I: 398.

76. For descriptions of Hartington and the Duchess of Manchester, see Reginald Viscount Esher, *Cloud-Capp'd Towers* (London: John Murray, 1927). For her political involvements earlier in her life, see A. L. Kennedy, ed., *'My Dear Duchess': Social and Political Letters to the Duchess of Manchester 1858–1869* (London: John Murray, 1956).

77. See, for example, Holland, *Devonshire*, I: 287–288.

78. Gladstone reported his conversation with Hartington to Granville: *Gladstone and Granville Correspondence*, II, Gladstone to Granville, January 22, 1885, pp. 326–327; see also *Hamilton Diary*, II, January 21, 1885, p. 778.

We certainly have worked hard. I believe that according to the measure of human infirmity, we have done fairly well: but the duties we have had to discharge have been duties, I mean in Egypt and the Sudan, which it was impossible to discharge with the ordinary measure of credit and satisfaction, which were beyond human strength.[79]

Principle, then, applied only to situations in which an individual was actually capable of shaping events. In such situations self-assertion offered a chance for reparation as well as for harm. In thus pointing out the path toward independence, Gladstone prefigured the course he would shortly take. By the same token he facilitated Hartington's separation from Gladstone himself—the rupture that in the long run could not be avoided.

III. The Psychodrama of Home Rule

Nothing in Gladstone's career raised such a storm as the commitment to Home Rule for Ireland which he unveiled at the outset of his third ministry in January 1886. His determination to settle a question that had plagued Britain throughout the nineteenth century—in effect, to undo the Act of Union of 1801—had fateful consequences for both his party and his reputation.[80] Though his chances for success were at best slim, he persevered in his quest long after it had come to try the patience of his most faithful lieutenants. Herein lies the problem for the present study. Was Gladstone's Irish policy compatible with his bearing as custodian of political cohesion? Did his championing of Home Rule undercut his efforts to keep his charismatic authority in check?

To solve this riddle one needs to take account of the psychological stress—the sense of loss as well as the longing to hold onto the past—attendant upon advancing age. The Irish issue reached far back into Gladstone's biography: it could serve to revivify earlier memories just at the point when that very weight of years made the formation of new attachments difficult. At the same time, it enabled Gladstone to be replenished by what in his past had retained the deepest meaning for him. In the stress of the mid-1880s, he succeeded in drawing on the emotional resources which the resolution of his crisis of almost four decades earlier had put permanently at his disposal.

79. Gladstone to Hartington, May 30, 1885, Gladstone Papers, Add. MS. 44148.
80. Besides the biographical studies of the participants already cited, the two most important (and widely divergent) treatments are J. L. Hammond, *Gladstone and the Irish Nation* (London: Longmans, Green, and Co, 1938), and A. B. Cooke and John Vincent, *The Governing Passion: Cabinet Government and Party Politics in Britain, 1885–1886* (Brighton: Harvester Press, 1974), Book I. For an intimate view, see Herbert Viscount Gladstone, *After Thirty Years* (London: Macmillan and Co., 1929).

Old age and death are rarely welcomed by those of sound mind and body. To this generalization Gladstone offered no exception. As early as 1859, when he had completed his fiftieth year, he noted in his diary: "There is in me a resistance to the passage of Time as if I could lay hands on it and stop it: as if youth were yet in me and life and youth were one."[81] On his next birthday he phrased this resistance in even stronger terms: "I feel within me the rebellious unspoken word, I will not be old."[82] In 1891 he had still not ceased his opposition. He reported to Lady Monkswell that "for the last thirty years" he had "felt . . . the desire and determination to fight with old age."[83] While Gladstone's revolt against religiously prescribed submission did not go uncensured, such self-censure merely heightened his appreciation for the attachments which held him fast:

> I am becoming alive to a new evil and danger in this that the ties that bind me to this world are growing more numerous and stronger. It appears to me that there are few persons who are so much as I am inclosed in . . . [an] invisible net. . . . I have never known what tedium was, have always found time full of calls and duties, life charged with every kind of interest. But now when I look calmly around me I see that these interests are for ever growing and grown too many and powerful and that were it to please God to Call me I might answer with reluctance. . . . Into politics I am drawn deeper every year: in the growing anxieties and struggles of the Church I have no less share than heretofore. . . . Seven children growing up around us and each the object of deeper thoughts and feelings and of higher hopes to Catherine and to me: what a network is here woven out of all the heart and all that the mind of man can supply.[84]

Almost from the outset of Gladstone's career, Ireland had been "charged with every kind of interest" for him. In 1845 he had penned what in retrospect sounded like a prophetic cry:

> Ireland, Ireland! that cloud in the west, that coming storm, the minister of God's retribution upon cruel and inveterate and but half-atoned injustice! Ireland forces upon us these great social and great religious questions— God grant that we may have the courage—to look them in the face and to work through them.[85]

What had prompted this outburst was Gladstone's anguish over the moral and institutional position of the state-supported Anglican

---

81. *The Gladstone Diaries*, V, December 29, 1859, p. 450.
82. Ibid., V, December 29, 1860, p. 541.
83. Quoted in E. C. F. Collier, ed., *A Victorian Diarist: Extracts from the Journals of Mary Lady Monkswell 1873–1895* (London: John Murray, 1944), p. 180.
84. *The Gladstone Diaries*, V, December 31, 1856, p. 183.
85. *Gladstone to his Wife*, William Gladstone to Catherine Gladstone, October 12, 1845, p. 64.

church amidst a hostile Catholic population. For a quarter-century religion remained for him the primary issue—down to its resolution by disestablishing the Anglican church in Ireland. But scarcely had Gladstone placed this momentous piece of legislation on the statute books when he turned his attention to the complex of issues involved in the Irish land question. Again he shepherded major bills through the House of Commons. This time, however, no resolution was achieved. Not long after Gladstone returned to office in 1880, the uneasy truce between tenant and landlord collapsed. For the next five years the cabinet resorted to land reform and coercion, either singly or in tandem, in what proved to be a vain effort to reestablish order on the troubled island.

Not least of the blows Ireland inflicted on Gladstone was the murder of Lord Frederick Cavendish in 1882. "The loss of F. Cavendish," Gladstone wrote his eldest son, would "ever be to us all as an unhealed wound." The young widow—Gladstone's niece—offered a model of how to endure that wound. "No Roman ... lady ever uttered a more heroic thing than was said by this English lady on first seeing Mr. Gladstone ... , 'You did right to send him to Ireland.'" "If his death were to work good to his fellow men," she added, she could accept parting with the husband who, as her diaries make clear, had been the object of her tenderest devotion.[86] "To work good" in Ireland rang out as a vague yet imperative injunction. If, as Gladstone had recognized in 1845, it would require an extensive concession, such a concession, he had stipulated twenty-three years later, should not be "the mere eccentricity, or even perversion, of an individual mind," but should connect itself "with silent changes ... in the very bed and basis of modern society."[87]

In the course of 1885 Gladstone became persuaded that Home Rule fulfilled these requirements. The political situation at Westminster unquestionably contributed to crystallizing into rational policy what had earlier been futuristic musings. In prompting Gladstone's conscious choice, the role of Charles Stewart Parnell, the leader of the Irish Home Rule party, should not be minimized. Throughout Gladstone's second ministry Parnell had been a power to be reckoned with, though that reckoning had been uncertain and contradictory. In the next parliament Parnell's position promised to be even more formidable. The Franchise Bill of 1884, with its wide extension of the suffrage in Ireland, meant that at last the "Irish nation" could speak out, and no one doubted that Parnell would

86. For these quotations, see Morley, *Gladstone*, III: 69–70.
87. *The Gladstone Diaries*, III, March 2, 1844, p. 355, and W. E. Gladstone, *A Chapter of Autobiography* (London: John Murray, 1868), p. 7.

emerge as its spokesman. While only the bare outlines of what Parnell might demand were clear, Gladstone was already beginning to turn over in his mind how to meet it.

Until the new electoral registers, to be drawn up in accordance with the Redistribution Bill of 1885, had been completed, Parnell's political strength could not be tested at the polls. Though Gladstone's ministry had fallen in June, Parliament continued to sit, and the Marquess of Salisbury, leader of the Conservative party, was heading an interim government. With both Liberals and Conservatives uncertain or divided over Irish policy, Gladstone watched hopefully for any sign that the Conservatives might move in the direction of Home Rule. Throughout the autumn of that year, his speculations on what the Conservative leadership might propose invariably ended on a wishful note. He fancied Salisbury repeating Sir Robert Peel's performance of 1846, with Home Rule substituting for repeal of the Corn Laws, while he, like Lord John Russell, would rally enough Liberals to insure that the dramatic concession received legislative approval.[88] In thus giving free rein to memories of four decades earlier, Gladstone seriously midjudged Salisbury's willingness to split his own party.

Even the election itself, which returned eighty-five Irish Nationalists, who together with two hundred and fifty Conservatives exactly equaled the Liberal total of three hundred and thirty-five, did not extinguish Gladstone's hopes. Nor did he fully appreciate the effect of what came to be known as the Hawarden kite—an interview his son gave the press in which he reported, in general terms, on his father's views. Only when the Conservative ministry met the new parliament and made clear that given the choice between Home Rule and coercion they were preparing to adopt the latter course did Gladstone abandon the notion of a bipartisan policy. In turning out Salisbury's government, Gladstone took upon himself the task of forming a ministry which would consider a measure, still unspecified, for Home Rule. In short, Gladstone appeared ready to do what Salisbury shrank from—to split his own party, or at least to accept numerous defections—in order to cut the Gordian knot that hobbled Westminster. He later expressed this determination in the strongest terms:

> Immediately on making up my mind about the ejection of the Government, I went to call upon Sir William Harcourt and informed him as to my intentions and the grounds of them. He said, "What, are you prepared

88. W. E. Gladstone, "Third Cabinet 1885–6," September 28, 1897, in *Autobiographica*, p. 109.

to go forward without either Hartington or Chamberlain?" I answered, "Yes." I believe it was in my mind to say, if I did not actually say it, that I was prepared to go forward without any body. That is to say without any known and positive assurance of support. This was one of the great Imperial occasions which call for such resolution.[89]

Whether or not the passage of years had led Gladstone to exaggerate the independence of his stance, at the time he was not engulfed in the self-absorption of a lonely crusader. His outward demeanor and personal deportment during the short life of the Home Rule ministry did not convey the impression of someone obsessed with a solitary mission.[90] To be sure, others joined him. But these colleagues, some new, like John Morley, and some old, like Lord Granville, were of lesser psychological significance than the reawakened spirit of Sir Robert Peel. Throughout Gladstone's negotiations to form his ministry, Peel's name hung in the air.[91] Gladstone's repeated references to his political mentor should not be dismissed simply as another instance of British veneration for historical precedent. When Salisbury had refused to act out Gladstone's fond hopes, that precedent had, after all, lost its political relevance. What still resonated in Gladstone's mind was the way Peel's direction had served to fix his political world in its course while he was struggling to surmount the collapse of his religiously based synthesis. With such comforting memories alive within him, Gladstone did not go forward unaccompanied.

Thus at the time when he was making a bold political move—whose boldness it is easy to exaggerate—he was also seeking to recreate in his inner world a sense of being protected. One might have assumed that this desire for protection would have induced a certain caution, or passivity, on Gladstone's part. But inaction provided no remedy for the current crisis; it offered no shield against the unremitting harassment of Irish problems. Home Rule did. At the very least, it permitted Gladstone to chart his course and to steady his position in the political world. At the same time, unlike the alternative policy of coercion, it fitted with the nurturing role that he had fashioned in his years of turmoil—and that had helped convince him of his own trustworthiness. Gladstone's commitment to Home Rule, then, expressed in highly condensed form both a public attitude of self-confidence and a private need for further reassurance.

89. Ibid., pp. 110–111.
90. Cooke and Vincent, *The Governing Passion*, p. 54.
91. See, for example, Lord Askwith, *Lord James of Hereford* (London: Ernest Benn, 1930), pp. 157, 163.

∎

When, in May and June of 1886, Gladstone at last unveiled his proposals and they were debated in the House of Commons, excitement in London reached its peak. According to John Morley, "Veteran observers declared that our generation had not seen anything like it. . . . Political differences were turned into social proscription. Whigs who could not accept the new policy were specially furious with Whigs who could. Great ladies purified their lists of the names of old intimates." But was Morley correct in concluding that such pruning of guest lists demonstrated "how thin after all is our social veneer, even when most highly polished"?[92]

The significance of good manners should not be minimized; courteous behavior is tantamount to kindness, and a lapse in manners is not unlike a slip of the tongue—the importance of which Freud was amply to demonstrate. The rupture of social contacts that Morley described suggests an effort to avoid angry confrontations rather than the breakdown of habitual constraints. Throughout the protracted discussion of Home Rule, no one relied more consistently on the technique of avoidance, first behind the scenes and then in public, than the person most directly affected by Gladstone's initiative, the Marquess of Hartington. Although in the past Hartington had had frequent differences with his chief, whether produced by deeply held principles or an excess of scruple, this time his scrupulousness served to make the parting as easy as possible.

During that trying period Hartington "showed truly ducal ability to play high and lose well;"[93] one never heard him "say an unkind or embittered word."[94] Indeed Hartington took pains to smoothe Gladstone's path, to make amends to the Liberal leader for his own inability to join the Home Rule ministry. Writing to his mistress, he sketched the scene in which he declined to enter Gladstone's government:

> He didn't argue much with me, and said that no man could decide for another how far he was bound . . . by . . . previous declarations; and we parted in a very friendly way. . . . I think now he has gone as far as he has, it is necessary that he should have a fair trial and should show his

92. Morley, *Gladstone*, III: 321–322.
93. Cooke and Vincent, *The Governing Passion*, p. 118.
94. Edward Hamilton's diary, May 9, 1886, quoted in ibid., p. 118 n. If one takes seriously G. W. E. Russell's contention that Hartington "had no manners," his courtesy toward Gladstone appears even more remarkable: *Portraits of the Seventies* (London: T. Fisher Urwin, 1916), p. 86.

hand. . . . If he is prevented from having a fair chance by premature opposition and obstruction then I don't believe that the country [Ireland] will be governable at all.[95]

The severance of political ties did not cut off the fund of mutuality which fostered ministerial cohesion. Trust in oneself and in others, independence for oneself and for others: these remained the sources from which British political life drew its sustenance.

95. Hartington to the Duchess of Manchester, January 30, 1886, quoted in Cooke and Vincent, *The Governing Passion*, p. 344.

Chapter 3

Charismatic Authority and Bureaucratic Administration

Bismarck in the 1880s

With Prince Otto von Bismarck's resignation as German chancellor in March 1890, an epoch seemed to come to a close. If at first glance his rule falls into two distinct phases—initially a period punctuated by the brief wars that served as milestones to the creation of a unified Germany, followed by years of outward tranquillity, now and then disturbed by complicated and potentially explosive conflicts in eastern Europe—this emphasis on the change in Bismarck's achievement merely underlines his own mastery. A brilliant diplomat, he had engineered the building of a new state with a mixture of foresight and improvisation, and then, with unceasing activity, fulfilled his self-appointed role as supreme manipulator among the great powers of Europe. For over a decade before his dismissal, he bestrode the continent "like a Colossus."

Though he appeared as such, and not only to German eyes, the image of a colossus was no more appropriate to the man Bismarck than to the man Caesar. Both had their strengths and their ambitions; yet both had weaknesses well known to their associates, which remained obscured or half-hidden until their downfall. While the analogy to the Shakespearean Caesar thus leads to an examination of Bismarck himself, it carries one beyond that single figure to those around him who first acknowledged his greatness, indeed magnified it, and then turned against what in part was their own illusion. In

short, one is led to ask not only what qualities in Bismarck and his
subordinates enabled him to maintain his dominant position, specifically in the 1880s, but also what eventually sapped an authority
which had seemed both indispensable and secure.

I. A Political Genius Making His Own Music

In Bismarck's *Reflections and Reminiscences* one has a document
which purports to be a factual and honest account of his statecraft.
Written during his forced retirement, it is so obviously self-serving
that historians must read it with more than their usual professional
skepticism.[1] If it should not be trusted as political narrative, can this
carefully constructed self-portrait serve as an introduction to prominent themes in the author's emotional life? The answer is yes. While
Bismarck was clearly intent upon creating a literary representation
of himself as the German national monument, the resulting image
was more than a fable designed to mold posterity's remembrance of
him. The portrait not only reflected what Bismarck wanted outsiders
to believe; it also revealed his convictions about himself. And in ex-
posing those cherished notions, he indicated the habitual ways of
staking out and defending his own standing ground which ordered
his relations with the world around him.

What is most striking about this work is the absence of references
to Bismarck's own growth and development. To be sure there are a
few comments relating to his youthful and unsatisfactory experience
in the Prussian bureaucracy. One gleans from these pages, which
serve mainly as background to Bismarck's emergence in the turmoil
of 1848, the impression that such a character, so independent and
farsighted, could not be harnessed to mere bureaucratic routine. And
when Bismarck, full grown, bursts onto the scene in 1848, his political self-confidence and determination immediately set him apart
from the frightened and vacillating figures of the Prussian court. Impervious to danger, relentless in his advice to quash the insurrection,
he remains stone deaf to appeals for appeasement and compromise.
That the king should refer to him as a man " 'only to be employed
when the bayonet governs unrestricted,' " Bismarck found both ap-

---

1. On the inception and composition of Bismarck's *Gedanken und Erinnerungen*,
see Ernst Schweninger, *Dem Andenken Bismarcks* (Leipzig: S. Hirzel, 1899), pt. 1.
See also the introduction to the critical edition: Gerhard Ritter and Rudolf Stadelmann, eds., *Otto von Bismarck: Die gesammelten Werke*, XV: *Erinnerung und
Gedanke* (Berlin: Deutsche Verlagsgesellschaft, 1932), pp. iv–xxviii.

propriate and flattering. In his view, to maneuver for short-term political gain ran counter to principle as well as reason.[2] Still more, such political tactics would have endangered his free-floating position above the infighting and intrigue of ordinary mortals.

While Bismarck notably neglected his early history, he struck the dominant chord with his depiction of himself as inhabiting a higher realm. Indeed to have described his political maturation, thereby inevitably suggesting that he was once something less than the heroic figure who appeared in 1848, would have detracted from his stature. Instead he accompanied his portrayal of a rocklike demeanor with expressions of unalterable, inborn faith in the German mission of Prussia; the staunch and bloody-minded statesman was thus outfitted with a suitably ambitious political vision. One may well question the perfection of this meshing. Yet in assigning himself the role of communing with the forces of history—of initiating and directing actions without which crucial opportunities might have been irreparably missed—Bismarck defined what he considered his proper sphere of being. Hence his lifelong passion for foreign affairs. The lonely and unceasing exertion that he believed the delicate nature of the task required offered an escape from personal relations too nearly approaching equality.[3]

More significantly, Bismarck seemed unable to imagine that emotional safety could be found in intimate alliances. In his *Reflections* figure after figure appear as consumed by base motives, inhabitants of a universe where political disagreement served merely as a screen for personal spite and vindictiveness. Scarcely anyone is spared in this sweeping indictment of both German politics and human nature. The focal point, the prime enemy, shifts frequently, from people at court, to government officials, military leaders, foreign diplomats, and conservative politicians. Indeed Bismarck depicts his opponents as so numerous that it is difficult to discriminate among them. Yet first place must be given to the Empress Augusta. Personal proximity to the king-emperor only partially accounts for the position assigned her; what Bismarck perceived as a consistently negative and au-

2. Otto von Bismarck, *Gedanken und Erinnerungen*, 2 vols. (Stuttgart: J. G. Cotta, 1898), translated under the supervision of A. J. Butler as *Bismarck, The Man and the Statesman: Being the Reflections and Reminiscences of Otto von Bismarck* (New York and London: Harper and Brothers, 1899), I: 55; see also chs. 1 and 2. The passages cited have been checked for accuracy against the critical edition. Since I have found retranslation unnecessary, references are to the English translation of the first edition.

3. Ibid., I: passim; note especially pp. 308, 313; ibid., II: 42, 58, 98.

thoritarian "petticoat influence" apparently unnerved him still more. While he managed to thwart this most dangerous opponent, as he did others whom he encountered in single combat, he always feared that common hostility to him would eventually cement his enemies into a solid bloc.[4]

Bismarck quite evidently intended to give an account of greatness triumphant, though constantly threatened. He not only exposed his beliefs about himself, but presented them as necessary armoring in a hostile environment—suggesting the symbiotic relationship between his rigid posture and his distrust of those around him. And just as a stance of overweening superiority had already become his habitual way of safeguarding his own psychological equilibrium before he entered the political arena, so too his fear of emotional involvement had its origin in his childhood. Bismarck's *Reflections* thus leads one to question what in his early affective life made the continual dominance of his aloof genius a prerequisite for his functioning in office.

The most prominent feature of Bismarck's first years was the unsatisfactory relations between mother and son. Wilhelmine von Bismarck, née Mencken, as the daughter of a high-ranking bourgeois civil servant, had grown up in a politically and intellectually vibrant atmosphere. At the age of sixteen she had married a petty aristocrat eighteen years her senior, whose caste position and rural existence turned her into an uprooted outsider. Then, in rapid succession, she gave birth to three sons; of these only Bernhard, the third, survived. Three more pregnancies followed, though less closely; Otto von Bismarck was born in 1815, his brother Franz, who died at the age of three, in 1819, and his sister, Malwine, in 1827. Wilhelmine's own sense of being restricted by her roles as woman and wife was palpable;[5] motherhood imposed at so early an age was bound to intensify her internal conflict. More specifically, through efforts to induce her sons to meet her high standards of performance, she strove to resolve

4. See, for example, ibid., I: 41, 136–139, 333; ibid., II: 143–144, 203, 312–313. For the views of the chancellor's enemies, see Julius Heyderhoff, ed., *Im Ring der Gegner Bismarcks: Denkschriften und politischer Briefwechsel Franz v. Roggenbachs mit Kaiserin Augusta und Albrecht v. Stosch 1865–1896* (Leipzig: Koehler and Amelang, 1943).

5. Erich Marcks, *Bismarck, Eine Biographie*, I: *Bismarcks Jugend, 1815–1848* (Stuttgart: J. G. Cotta, 1909), pp. 42–47. See also the famous description of Bismarck's mother by his cousin, Hedwig von Bismarck, *Erinnerungen aus dem Leben einer 95 jährigen*, 5th ed. (Halle: R. Mühlmann, 1910), pp. 28–31.

such conflict. Their achievements offered relief from the anxiety produced by her own warring emotions.

The demands she made on her elder son, who like his brother was to turn against her, emerge with full force from her letters to him. Shortly after Franz's death in 1822, she wrote Bernhard:

> You, dear Bernhard, are already reasonable enough to perceive that only through good behavior, through diligence, and through a zealous effort at constant self-improvement, can you give me joy and cheer me up after all the suffering I have endured.[6]

Nor was this motif of the elder brother as compensation sounded simply in his mother's moment of grief; it echoed throughout the correspondence. And along with it went a steady refrain of criticism and disapproval:

> I hope that it won't be a matter of indifference to you that you have incurred so many (but just) reproaches from a mother who loves you fervently and of all the people in the world most wishes that she need only praise you, and precisely because she loves you, cannot be indifferent to your faults. You have come to an age when you must try to deserve this love, which until now was simply given to you, and only in that way can you finally repay all the care and faith with which you have been fostered since your earliest childhood.[7]

The impression conveyed is that of a devoted mother who was determined at all costs not to spoil her son. But spoil him she did; he rebelled against her demands and disappointed her expectations. With her hopes dashed, her simultaneous possession and rejection of him fused into an intrusive examination of his feelings and failings:

> It is the old suffering with which I have already and so often reproached you in vain; but if I can no longer expect much success, it nonetheless remains my duty to tell you the truth, to hold before you the mirror in which you can both look at and judge your negligence, so that at least you don't entertain any doubt about your own worth and don't deceive yourself about it with flattering opinions. Your behavior toward me, the more or less hearty affection and intimacy on your part, have always been for me an infallible barometer of your moral worth. Your conscience does not permit you to approach me with these feelings if you feel unworthy of me;

6. Charlotte Sempell, "Briefe der Eltern Bismarcks an seinen Bruder Bernhard," *Historische Zeitschrift* 214 (June 1972), Wilhelmine von Bismarck to Bernhard, November 7, 1822, p. 564.

7. Ibid., Wilhelmine von Bismarck to Bernhard, without date [Spring 1825], pp. 566–567.

when I formerly missed these feelings in you, I consoled myself with the notion that your education was not yet completed and that its more advanced stage would turn such feelings back toward me again. ... I thought it the greatest good fortune I could achieve to have a grown-up son who, after having been educated under my eyes, would share my ideas, but who, as a man, would have been able to penetrate further into the realm of ideas than it was given to me as a woman. I looked forward to the exchange of ideas, to the mutual stimulation an intellectual life provides, and to the satisfaction of finding such delights in the intercourse with my son who was closest to me by nature, and who would become even closer through spiritual kinship. The time is here when such expectations should be fulfilled, but they have disappeared and—I must say— regretfully—forever.[8]

The letters of Wilhelmine von Bismarck to her younger son unfortunately have not survived. Bismarck's remarks alone remain as testimony to their relationship, more particularly in an oft-cited letter of 1847 to his fiancée, Johanna von Puttkamer—a letter composed the evening of his mother's birthday. Though she had already been dead for nine years, her birthday, as is often true of anniversaries, revived powerful emotions and painful memories:

My mother was a beautiful woman who loved external elegance, had a bright and lively intellect but little of what Berliners call *Gemüth*. She wished that I should learn much and amount to much, and often appeared cold and hard toward me. As a little child I hated her, later I deceived her successfully with falsehood.[9]

From this description it would seem that Wilhelmine treated the younger brother much the way she had treated the elder: at one and the same time attempting to appropriate him for the satisfaction of her inner needs and refusing to accept him as a person in his own right.

8. Ibid., Wilhelmine von Bismarck to Bernhard, without date [1830], pp. 577–578.
9. Wolfgang Windelband and Werner Frauendienst, eds., *Otto von Bismarck: Die gesammelten Werke*, XIV: *Briefe* (Berlin: Deutsche Verlagsgesellschaft, 1933), Bismarck to Johanna von Puttkamer, February 23, 1847, p. 67. For corrections and commentary on this edited text, see Charlotte Sempell, "Unbekannte Briefstellen Bismarcks," *Historische Zeitschrift* 207 (December 1968): 609–610. For citations of this letter, see Marcks, *Bismarcks Jugend*, p. 44; Otto Pflanze, "Toward a Psychoanalytic Interpretation of Bismarck," *American Historical Review* 77 (April 1972): 429; Charlotte Sempell, "Bismarck's Childhood: A Psychohistorical Study," *History of Childhood Quarterly* 2 (Summer 1974): 118. For evidence that Bismarck held to this view of his mother in his later life, see Rudolf Vierhaus, ed., *Das Tagebuch der Baronin Spitzemberg* (Göttingen: Vandenhoeck and Ruprecht, 1960), April 3, 1885, p. 218.

All his life Bismarck blamed his mother for exiling him to Plamann's Institute as a boarding pupil at the age of six:

> I was not properly educated. My mother was fond of society and did not trouble much about me. Afterwards I was sent to an educational establishment, where too severe a system prevailed, insufficient and poor food, plenty of hardening, thin jackets in winter, too much compulsion and routine, and unnatural training.[10]

Bismarck's judgment was harsh; his mother *had* troubled herself about her sons and in particular about their education. But the "compulsion"—whether deriving from school routine or from his mother's ambition—Bismarck experienced as an intrusion that spelled emotional neglect rather than concern.

The image of food, this time not as insufficient but as excessive, had also appeared in Bismarck's letter to Johanna. He recalled being fetched from school to celebrate his mother's birthday:

> There followed a gala dinner attended by many young officers who are now aging majors, and by much-decorated, gourmandizing old gentlemen, now eaten by worms. When I was sent from table as having had enough, my mother's personal maid received me in order to stuff me until I was sick with caviar and baisers she had put aside.[11]

The recollections Bismarck set down had an immediate sequel. With them still in his mind, he went to bed—and to a nightmare, which he communicated to his fiancée the following day: "I dreamt that you pushed me into the rolling sea from the plank I had grabbed when shipwrecked. It would not hold both of us, and you turned away, and I was poorer of a hope."[12] The memory and the dream taken together summarized Bismarck's feelings about his mother: tainted nourishment of the kind that made one ill was preferable to emotional shipwreck. At the very time he was evincing the bitterest antagonism toward her, he was longing for her love.

10. Moritz Busch, *Tagebuchblätter* (Leipzig: F. W. Grunow, 1899), II: 425. See also Bismarck, *Werke*, XIV, Bismarck to Johanna von Puttkamer, February 1, 1847, p. 51; Robert von Keudell, *Fürst und Fürstin Bismarck: Erinnerungen aus dem Jahren 1846 bis 1872* (Berlin and Stuttgart: W. Spemann, 1901), June 18, 1864, p. 160; Robert Freiherr Lucius von Ballhausen, *Bismarck-Erinnerungen des Staatsministers Freiherrn Lucius von Ballhausen* (Stuttgart and Berlin: J. G. Cotta, 1920), February 11, 1876, p. 85, and April 9, 1878, pp. 137–138.

11. Sempell, "Unbekannte Briefstellen Bismarcks," Bismarck to Johanna von Puttkamer, February 23, 1847, pp. 609–610.

12. Bismarck, *Werke*, XIV, Bismarck to Johanna von Puttkamer, February 25, 1847, p. 69.

Thus despite his mother's failure to convince him that he had been truly valued, her son could not simply renounce this primary bond: to have done so would have been the equivalent of psychic suicide. On the contrary, the erratic nurture he received intensified his emotional need, transforming it into an angry hunger to devour. It led not to an abandonment of his mother but to an extreme, if hostile, dependence on her internalized presence. Above all, Bismarck felt impelled to dominate what he could no longer escape and what now threatened him from within.

If the noxious sustenance of Bismarck's outer world heightened the importance of his inner world, that second domain proved far from comfortable. As he himself commented:

> Faust complains about having two souls in his breast, but I harbor a whole crowd of them and they quarrel. It is like being in a republic. . . . I tell most of what they say, but there are also whole provinces into which I will never let another person look.[13]

Bismarck's command within that inner realm remained precarious at best. It required more than deception and manipulation; it provoked an insatiable craving to conscript reinforcements, to incorporate others into his private world and private war. In short, Bismarck came to treat those around him (including his own father) as his mother had treated him.

What is most striking about his relationship with his father was its failure to deliver the boy from the oppressive maternal hold. In the same letter to his fiancée in which he wrote so bitterly of his mother, he gave a more nuanced account of his feelings toward his other parent, who had died two years before.

> I truly loved my father; when I was not with him I felt repentance about my behavior toward him, made resolutions which had little solidity; for how often did I return his truly boundless, disinterested, good-natured tenderness for me with coldness and moroseness, and many times, made a show of love out of my reluctance to violate what appeared to be good manners, when in reality I was hard and without love on account of his apparent weaknesses, which I had no right to judge, and which angered me only when they were coupled with a violation of good manners. Still I can't retract the statement that I loved him at the bottom of my soul.[14]

13. Willy Andreas, ed., *Otto von Bismarck: Die gesammelten Werke*, VII: *Gespräche* (Berlin: Deutsche Verlagsgesellschaft, 1924), Bismarck to Robert von Keudell, August 18, 1865, p. 101; also cited in Pflanze, "Toward a Psychoanalytic Interpretation of Bismarck," p. 432.

14. Sempell, "Unbekannte Briefstellen Bismarcks," Bismarck to Johanna von Puttkamer, February 23, 1847, p. 610.

Bismarck seemed confused. Did he love his father or did he not? At first glance his uncertainty suggests the ambivalence characteristic of the classic Oedipus complex. But Bismarck's father bore scant resemblance to Freud's majestic patriarch interposing himself between mother and son. The elder Bismarck was not an awesome figure. Dominated by his strong-minded and polished wife, this rustic and gauche man inspired contempt rather than fear. His very weakness may have prompted his son to seek a powerful substitute or have stimulated the boy to surpass him. Be that as it may, what remained crucial was Bismarck's relationship with his mother. His assertion of his own potency served in the first instance as a defense against maternal intrusiveness rather than as compensation for his father's lack of strength.

Still more, speculation about Oedipal conflict should not lead one to overlook the real pathos in Bismarck's confession: he could not express his love. Despite his father's "boundless, disinterested, good-natured tenderness," the son established no intimate relationship with the older man. Although the father invited love, the boy created a distance between the two. He locked his love within himself to guard against the emptiness that the act of giving would have entailed. Unable to bestow upon another human being what he regarded as a secret treasure, he continually mobilized his aggression to deal with the inhabitants of his external world. Unable to do more than hoard his love, he became a notoriously good hater instead.

■

The years from his late teens until his early thirties, roughly the decade and a half during which Bismarck studied in Göttingen and Berlin, served briefly in the Prussian bureaucracy, and then managed the family estates in Pomerania and Brandenburg, were ones of personal Sturm und Drang. Uncertain of his own direction, he rejected the careers generally regarded as suitable for someone of his station. In his famous letter to his cousin setting forth his reasons for leaving state service, he declared:

> The Prussian official resembles the individual in the orchestra; whether he plays the first violin or the triangle, without control or influence over the whole, he must play at sight his fragment as it is set him, whether he considers it good or bad. But I want to make music that I recognize as good, or none at all.[15]

15. Bismarck, *Werke*, XIV, Bismarck to his father, September 29, 1838, in which he enclosed his letter to his cousin, p. 15. For corrections and commentary on this second letter, which Bismarck later sent to his fiancée, see Sempell, "Unbekannte

Even the discordant tones of those years, however, were Bismarck's own creation. By adopting histrionic postures, playing a variety of roles, and, more tangibly, donning outlandish and eccentric costumes, he always managed to set himself apart from whatever circle temporarily surrounded him. Nor did his behavior change when, after his mother's death, he returned to a rural existence. Having hoped to find contentment in traditional landed pursuits, he soon discovered that he fitted into this life no better than into what had come before. While he shocked his neighbors—among whom he became known as *der tolle* Bismarck—by his rude and daredevil conduct, his restlessness and the despair it betokened reached their climax.[16]

The end of this period, the years 1846 and 1847, was marked by his friendship with Marie and Moritz von Blanckenburg and his subsequent engagement and marriage to Johanna von Puttkamer. What made it possible for Bismarck, who seemed destined for perpetual loneliness, to establish these intimate ties? What, one may also ask, was the nature of his religious conversion, which was encouraged by the Blanckenburgs and which provided a crucial point of contact with Johanna? The way he experienced communion with fellow-mortals as well as with an other-worldly being both echoed his earlier relationships and anticipated the pattern of his dealings with the political world, which, at the very same time, he definitively entered.

The specific event that precipitated Bismarck's conversion was the death of Marie von Blanckenburg in November 1846; as she lay dying, he uttered his first prayer. Until then her husband's patient attempts to bring Bismarck into their pietist fold had mostly been rebuffed. For nearly half a decade Moritz had sought to dispel his friend's gloom, to lead him—in part by the example of his own constancy—to a more trusting view of the people and the world around him. When Moritz married Marie von Thadden, he found in her someone willing to share his efforts. Thereafter Bismarck's visits to the Blanckenburgs became frequent; the "mad" Junker "soon felt at home in that circle" and was conscious of a "well-being ... previously unknown" to him—a family life in which he was "enveloped."[17] At the same time there was doubtless a romantic undercurrent in the relationship between Marie and Bismarck. Circum-

Briefstellen Bismarcks," Bismarck to Johanna von Puttkamer, February 13, 1847, pp. 610–611.

16. Marcks, *Bismarcks Jugend*, pp. 83–200. The new account by Lothar Gall, *Bismarck: Der weisse Revolutionär* (Berlin: Propyläen, 1980), adds little on this period.

17. Bismarck, *Werke*, XIV, Bismarck to Johanna's father, not dated [late December 1846], p. 47.

stances, of course, forbade the expression of such sentiments. When suddenly death was about to make irrevocable the separation between them, Bismarck granted what she and her husband had so patiently sought.[18] Since he was now forever barred from bestowing his affection, and hence no longer afraid to give some indication of his attachment, Bismarck finally accepted the spiritual nourishment Marie had offered. New life breathed within him, just at the point when his outer world suffered a grievous loss.

Less than two months after Marie was buried, Bismarck asked for the hand in marriage of her intimate friend Johanna von Puttkamer. The closeness in time of these two events would seem to suggest that Johanna had been chosen to fill the void caused by Marie's death. In fact, Marie had played the role of matchmaker, introducing Bismarck to Johanna, organizing an expedition which included her two friends through the Harz in the summer of 1846, an expedition that in retrospect figured as the seed time of their romance. What Bismarck evidently wanted from Johanna, who shared none of the high-spirited confidence of her deceased friend, was the assurance that he would be the whole world to her. He phrased this demand in a self-deprecating fashion, describing his morbid sensitivity about being momentarily put in the background by a preoccupation with "women friends, flowers, birds, books, dogs, etc."[19] The implication was clear: he needed to possess Johanna entirely. In so doing, he incorporated her love into his private world and exulted in a sense of triumph over her.

It is this note of triumph, indeed of exhilaration, in the months following Marie's death that is so striking. It sounded not only in relation to his fiancée, but in relation to the deity as well (and Bismarck had to give evidence of faith to win the consent of both Johanna's pietist parents and the girl herself). In the view of Erich Marcks, whose biography remains the most thorough and penetrating account of Bismarck's early manhood, he "needed the personal God and obtained fulfillment and peace only when he had him."[20] Yet this thirst for God had to be satisfied in a way "which did not bind Bismarck's personal powers, but instead strengthened them in their activity. He required high-handedness, or better still, auton-

18. Marcks, *Bismarcks Jugend*, pp. 272, 337–338.

19. Bismarck, *Werke*, XIV, Bismarck to Johanna von Puttkamer, March 16, 1847, p. 81. In another letter he sounded a note of self-deprecation to underline the male prowess he had displayed in previous sexual adventures: Sempell, "Unbekannte Briefstellen Bismarcks," Bismarck to Johanna von Puttkamer, February 13, 1847, pp. 611–612.

20. Marcks, *Bismarck Jugend*, p. 67. For the best account of Bismarck's relations with the Blankenburgs, his engagement and marriage, as well as his religious experi-

omy, vis à vis the world, and autonomy also in religious feeling and thought."[21] In short, Bismarck's religious sensibility derived its positive tone from a newly discovered "capacity to make requests" of the deity and from the sense of "confidence and energy" that this ability rekindled.[22]

Why such exuberance at a time when one might have expected despondency? To put matters simply: Bismarck did not mourn; he resorted to denial. Denial, perhaps, that Marie was dead, denial, most certainly, that feelings of his own endangered her—ambivalent feelings while she was still alive, angry feelings when she deserted him. Unable to make reparation, albeit unconsciously, for such emotions, unable to perform the imaginary act necessary for harboring a reassuring presence, Bismarck ran the risk of reactivating internal persecutors. Yet he did not succumb to depression. What emerged with full force in late 1846 was his capacity to choose the manic path instead, and in so doing to exert a more violent control over his inner world. And sustained by this mood, he was ready to extend his control to the outer world as well, to turn, at last, his mother's ambition to his own account.

Bismarck's triumphant exuberance and his corresponding sense of omnipotence come out in sharp relief in the famous dream he included in his *Reflections*. Writing to the Emperor William I in 1881, Bismarck reported a dream he had had eighteen years earlier, in his "hardest days . . . , when no human eye could see any possible issue."

> I dreamed (as I related the first thing next morning to my wife and other witnesses) that I was riding on a narrow Alpine path, precipice on the right, rocks on the left. The path grew narrower, so that the horse refused to proceed; and it was impossible to turn around or dismount, owing to lack of space. Then, with my whip in my left hand, I struck the smooth rock and called on God. The whip grew to endless length, the rocky wall dropped like a curtain and opened out a broader path, with a view over hills and forests, like a landscape in Bohemia; there were Prussian troops with banners, and even in my dream the thought came to me at once that I must report it to your Majesty. This dream was fulfilled, and I woke up rejoiced and strengthened.[23]

Hanns Sachs analyzed the dream in 1913, and Freud incorporated

---

ence, see ibid., pp. 200–451. For a contrasting view of Bismarck's religion, see Leonhard von Muralt, *Bismarcks Verantwortlichkeit* (Göttingen: Musterschmidt, 1955), pp. 94–140.

21. Marcks, *Bismarcks Jugend*, p. 340.

22. Bismarck, *Werke*, XIV, Bismarck to Johanna's father, not dated [late December 1846], p. 47.

23. Bismarck to William I, December 18, 1881, quoted in Bismarck, *Reflections and Reminiscences*, II: 212–213.

Sach's analysis in the 1919 edition of *The Interpretation of Dreams*.[24] Yet neither Sachs nor subsequent historians paid attention to the context in which the dream was retold.[25] Concerned with the childhood fantasies it might betray, they overlooked the audience to whom it was reported. Bismarck's account was prompted by William's confession of a disturbing dream of his own. The king-emperor, awakened by a nightmare, had spent the previous night in "a state of nervous agitation" about difficulties within his entourage.[26] In the first instance, then, Bismarck's narration of his dream was intended to reassure the anxious monarch.

How did he carry out his assignment? In simple terms, by self-aggrandizement. One may well doubt the significance of particular details; after all, Bismarck gave no indication of his associations with what he had dreamed almost two decades earlier. The central image, however—his self-comparison with the Moses of the Exodus—is stunning. It suggests that in his own fantasy Bismarck surpassed the ancient leader of the children of Israel. Moses had been punished for striking the rock; a similar action by Bismarck opened the way into the promised land. The message was clear: he was the semidivine figure who would deal with whatever crisis might arise. And William apparently understood it full well: in Bismarck's *Reflections* the monarch stands commended for having properly fulfilled his role as second fiddle in his chancellor's world-historical performance.[27]

By superimposing his grandiose visions on the public realm, Bismarck made politics intensely personal and himself indispensable. He was thus able to safeguard his position as the dominant figure because in his eyes there was no other. In so doing he unconsciously deprived his associates of their standing ground and by the same token assuaged his angry hunger to devour all about him.

II. A "Colossus" Holds onto Power

How did Bismarck fashion political cohesion? The portrait presented makes it clear that he was psychologically ill-equipped to dissipate the mistrust and suspicion which permeated German public life and which so clearly echoed his own sentiments. He himself derived little in the way of security from political ties: for the most part

24. Sigmund Freud, *The Interpretation of Dreams*, Standard Edition, trans. James Strachey (London: Hogarth Press, 1953), V: 378–381.

25. Pflanze interprets this dream as evidence of Bismarck's phallic-narcissistic character: "Toward a Psychoanalytic Interpretation of Bismarck," p. 427.

26. William I to Bismarck, December 18, 1881, quoted in Bismarck, *Reflections and Reminiscences*, II: 212.

27. See, for example, ibid., II: 320.

he shunned close associations. Yet his isolation did not blunt his appetite for power.

During the greater part of his career Bismarck had complained of bad health. His symptoms, of which he had a large variety, became most acute when he was under severe political pressure. On occasion he doubted whether his physical condition would permit him to continue in office. (He did surrender his post as Prussian minister president from 1872 to 1874.) While the threat of complete withdrawal was a useful political weapon, he, of course, had no intention of relinquishing power. Instead, each year he spent long periods away from Berlin on his estates, either at Varzin, which took twelve hours to reach, or at Friedrichsruh, which was closer and only four hours from the capital. Even after 1883, when his health improved—owing to the ministrations of Dr. Ernst Schweninger, who acted simultaneously as medical watchdog and emotional comforter—Bismarck continued to remain in the country for prolonged stays.[28] What is striking is the way his self-imposed seclusion suited his image of making his own music.

Baron Friedrich von Holstein, a counsellor and central figure at the Foreign Office, summed up the reality behind the image when he reported:

"In diplomatic affairs," the Chief said recently, "I fully recognize people's rights to contradict me and resist my plans. The bear has a right to defend itself against me. It is quite a different thing if the bear (i.e., a foreign power) bites or if my dog bites me."[29]

In short, Bismarck defined his task as one of insuring that the "dogs," that is, the highest Reich and Prussian officials, would be cautious about defending themselves—or perhaps even opening their mouths.

■

Certainly Bismarck's absences from Berlin made it easier for him to extend the kind of administrative practices which already existed in his private domain of foreign affairs. It is here that one finds the inspiration for the ideal type of German bureaucrat.[30] The chancellor's views were accepted as law by the inhabitants of the

28. On Bismarck's health problems and his relations to Dr. Ernst Schweninger, see Pflanze, "Toward a Psychoanalytic Interpretation of Bismarck," pp. 432–444.

29. Norman Rich and M. H. Fisher, eds., *The Holstein Papers*, II: *Diaries* (Cambridge: Cambridge University Press, 1957), April 14, 1884, p. 113; see also Lucius von Ballhausen, *Bismarck-Erinnerungen*, April 20, 1880, p. 184.

30. For an excellent description of how the Foreign Office operated, written by

Wilhelmstrasse, who busied themselves with collecting and preserving documents, with keeping the files in order. The officials' concentration on documents and files anticipated what Weber considered the defining attributes of bureaucracy, and their obedience foreshadowed his emphasis on a "firmly ordered system of super- and subordination" in which there was "supervision of the lower offices by the higher ones."[31] Regardless of who occupied the top position, he argued, "the principle of fixed . . . jurisdictional areas . . . generally ordered by rules" would continue to be followed. Clearly Weber had Bismarck's tenure in mind when he elaborated this type; Bismarck, he noted, had "during his long years in power . . . brought his ministerial colleagues into unconditional bureaucratic dependence."[32] In contrast to his strictures against a "leaderless democracy," Weber implied that the quality of leadership among bureaucrats was a lesser problem.[33] Here he missed the mark: he failed to recognize that in Bismarck's case "bureaucratic dependence" was scarcely bureaucratic at all; it was tantamount to subservience to the emotionally unreliable leader who exploited the system to enhance his own power.

Nonetheless in conformity with the model Weber was to devise, both Bismarck and his subordinates laid stress on the ability to perform bureaucratic duties with thoroughness, regularity, and dispatch. The existence of a shared standard exacerbated the sense that failure was the fault of the individual. Of course, Bismarck was always eager to heap blame on the unfortunate person whose actions did not coincide with his own wishes. The official's colleagues, as well, were ready to join in condemnation, phrasing it in terms of his inability to discharge his duties properly. Though the terms of disapproval remained fixed, estimates of performance oscillated rapidly; how to censure someone was clear, what was blameworthy was less so. In such a world, no one, aside from Bismarck himself, had a firm standing ground. And with little reason to expect support from his

---

one of Bismarck's subordinates, see Helmut Rogge, ed., *Im Dienste Bismarcks: Persönliche Erinnerungen von Arthur von Brauer* (Berlin: E. S. Mittler, 1936), pp. 93–103; see also Christoph von Tiedmann, *Aus sieben Jahrzehnten: Erinnerungen von Christoph von Tiedmann,* II: *Sechs Jahre Chef der Reichskanzlei unter dem Fürsten Bismarck* (Leipzig: S. Hirzel, 1909). For thorough studies of the higher levels of administration, see Rudolf Morsey, *Die oberste Reichsverwaltung unter Bismarck, 1867–1890* (Münster: Aschendorff, 1957), and Lamar Cecil, *The German Diplomatic Service, 1871–1914* (Princeton, N.J.: Princeton University Press, 1976).

31. H. H. Gerth and C. Wright Mills, eds. and trans., *From Max Weber: Essays in Sociology* (New York: Oxford University Press, 1946), pp. 197–198.

32. Ibid., pp. 196, 229.

33. For Weber's remark about "leaderless democracy," see "Politics as a Vocation," in ibid., p. 113.

co-workers, an individual might well doubt the merits of his own case. Thus the victim of Bismarck's hostility, criticized by his colleagues and himself finding their standards appropriate, was likely to temper his natural resentment with the suspicion that he had deserved his disgrace.

The way in which notions of bureaucratic conduct could be flexibly applied to reinforce Bismarck's determination to crush potential independence was nowhere clearer than in the case of Count Paul von Hatzfeldt. Hatzfeldt accepted the post of secretary of state for foreign affairs in 1881 with considerable reluctance; it meant giving up his easygoing life as ambassador in Constantinople, with a salary of 120,000 marks, in return for a 50,000 mark office job in Berlin.[34] From the outset Hatzfeldt's grand-seigneur manner set him apart from the other occupants of the Wilhelmstrasse. He never tried to emulate the regular habits of his associates; he refused to fill his day with detailed paperwork and instead allocated a certain period for tennis and a nap.[35] When he retired to bed because he was ill, Bismarck commented with astonishment as well as disapproval: " 'A molly-coddle, a pregnant woman, an egoist through and through. Wraps himself immediately in cotton wool. Doesn't even read his files when he's sick.' "[36] When Bismarck took to his bed, at least his files went with him!

Yet for the better part of four years, the bureaucratic rules were construed in Hatzfeldt's favor. During that time he was generally considered a success: his geniality made him a popular department head, and his talent earned him wide respect. Bismarck referred to him as "the best horse in his stable."[37] And Holstein, who was Hatzfeldt's long-time friend and had made every effort to persuade him to accept the appointment as secretary of state, considered him "the *only person,* after the Chief has gone, capable of surveying the diplomatic situation as a whole and of continuing calmly and skillfully the game of chessboard diplomacy. I know of no one who could even come near him."[38]

Only when Hatzfeldt became the object of Bismarck's suspicion, did this tolerance cease. The chancellor's hostility was initially

34. Norman Rich and M. H. Fisher, eds., *The Holstein Papers*, III: *Correspondence 1861–1896* (Cambridge: Cambridge University Press, 1961), Hatzfeldt to Holstein, September 15, 1881, p. 50; see also Holstein, *Diaries*, February 11, 1884, p. 78.

35. On Hatzfeldt's methods of work, see Brauer, *Im Dienste Bismarcks*, pp. 104–106.

36. Quoted in Holstein, *Diaries*, March 11, 1882, p. 13.

37. Quoted in Brauer, *Im Dienste Bismarcks*, p. 105.

38. Holstein, *Diaries*, February 22, 1884, p. 90 (emphasis in the original).

aroused by the good relations Hatzfeldt had established with the crown prince—which in the event of the prince's succession might turn Hatzfeldt into an independent agent.[39] Subsequently Bismarck determined that the surest means to maintain his own primacy would be to appoint his son Herbert as secretary of state. Hence by 1885 it was apparent that Hatzfeldt would have to go.[40] With his position rapidly deteriorating, behavior that had earlier been considered amusingly eccentric was regarded as the product of a flawed character. The major item of new evidence against him, which had always been in the background, was his inability to handle his ex-wife. Holstein remarked condescendingly that "no amount of support or pushing" was of "any use with him." One couldn't "make a back-bone out of a towel."[41] Quite obviously the slackness of both Hatzfeldt's personal and his professional life rendered him unsuitable for his office in Berlin. Such was the consensus that emerged, and which Hatzfeldt, who was transferred to the embassy in London, did not reject.[42] The smoothness of Hatzfeldt's departure almost makes one lose sight of the skill with which Bismarck had manipulated the bureaucratic system to remove someone he perceived as a potential rival.

Worse than that: he subverted the system itself. What emerges from the memoirs of Robert Freiherr Lucius von Ballhausen, who served as Prussian minister of agriculture from 1879 to 1890, is the steady erosion of the Prussian state ministry's standing and of the position of the men who composed it—with the result that Bismarck much preferred his chosen associates in that period to their predecessors.[43] Not only did the chancellor fail to treat the ministry as a group which might collectively offer advice and counsel, he scarcely kept it informed about the main outlines of his policy. One comes away from Lucius's detailed and almost daily account with a sense of astonishment at how little he knew. It was a rare occasion indeed

39. See, for example, ibid., February 11, 1884, pp. 77–78; April 16, 1884, p. 118; May 13, 1884, pp. 145–146.

40. See, for example, ibid., May 16, 1885, pp. 199–200; June 18, 1885, p. 209; June 30, 1885, p. 210.

41. Ibid., March 7, 1885, p. 173.

42. Nevertheless Hatzfeldt was chagrined by his displacement and resentful of how it had been managed. See ibid., October 27, 1885, p. 258; Holstein, *Correspondence 1861–1896*, Hatzfeldt to Holstein, October 25, 1885, pp. 156–157. For Hatzfeldt's reminiscences of his service under Bismarck, see his "Memoirenfragment," in Gerhard Ebed, ed., *Botschafter Paul Graf von Hatzfeldt Nachgelassene Papiere 1838–1901* (Boppard am Rhein: Harald Boldt Verlag, 1976) I: 1–96.

43. Lucius von Ballhausen, *Bismarck-Erinnerungen*, February 16, 1881, p. 196; May 5 and May 7, 1882, pp. 228–229; April 13, 1883, p. 262; January 10, 1884, p. 281. See also Holstein, *Diaries*, January 6, 1883, p. 26, and April 29, 1884, p. 130.

when Bismarck enlightened his ostensible colleagues either about relations with the Catholic church—a matter of immediate interest to them—or about developments in foreign affairs—to be sure, a subject of less direct concern. Since the chancellor frequently did not take the trouble to consult the appropriate department chiefs or inform them of his intentions, it became the minister's responsibility to divine his wishes. The possession of intuitive powers, rather than superior rationality, thus became the essential requirement for a successful German high official.

■

Why were the men around Bismarck willing to subordinate themselves to him? Clearly, the chancellor's inability to relate to people on a basis of mutuality meant that his associates were not required to bestow affection on him as a human being. They did not love him as a man; instead they venerated him as a national monument. Just as Bismarck's inner needs compelled him to maintain the image of his own superiority, so his associates felt it necessary to believe in its reality. One might speculate further that the chancellor's greatness served those under him as a pervasive eminence providing order and stability in a hostile world. Thus paradoxically he seems to have functioned as a defense against the slings and arrows which he himself so often launched.

The most notable and best documented example is that of Baron Friedrich von Holstein. Of the chancellor's younger subordinates, he had been the most intimate and long-standing associate. His ties to Bismarck dated from the early 1860s, when the future chancellor had served as minister to St. Petersburg and Holstein had been a very junior member of his staff. The young diplomat soon came to know the other members of the family, in particular the two boys, Herbert and Bill, who were at that time adolescents and toward whom he adopted a benevolent and avuncular attitude. In the mid-1870s, Holstein's role, albeit minor, in the trial of Bismarck's serious rival, Count Harry von Arnim, marked him as belonging to the chancellor's camp. It was only natural, then, that when Holstein arrived at the Wilhelmstrasse in 1876, he should have resumed frequent and easy contact with the family. He was a welcome dinner guest; the chancellor delighted in his company, enlivened and refreshed by the younger man's ability to carry on intelligent and amusing conversation.[44]

44. The most sensitive portrait of Holstein is the editor's introduction by Helmut Rogge to the collection of personal letters *Friedrich von Holstein Lebensbekenntnis in Briefen an eine Frau* (Berlin: Ullstein, 1932), pp. xiii–xxviii. On Holstein's early ca-

Holstein himself provided no summary account of his relationship with Bismarck—nor of his own life's work. On three occasions he set out to compose his memoirs, but he never completed the task. He simply put down as they came to him, so he reported, those impressions which had remained clear in his mind.[45] If the result lacked a single guiding theme, it mingled together a number of motifs; and in their association one can discern Holstein's psychic defenses at work.

Yet he did not make deciphering them easy. Indeed he comes across as a man with something to hide. Certainly he often voices the injunction to guard a secret, along with, or prompted by, the fear of being at the "mercy of anyone who shared the secret."[46] He emerges in his memoirs as morbidly sensitive about external appearances and intent on preserving the outward demeanor of a superior bureaucrat. By his criticism of colleagues in the foreign ministry, he furtively exhibited his sense of his own excellence. He alone, he implied, was capable of successfully balancing initiative with subordination, of combining intellectual independence with a talent for carrying out orders. With these gifts, it followed that he could be of special service to Bismarck. More than that, Holstein came to hint that he was indispensable to a chief determined to quash such overweening notions in others. It is at this point that one begins to suspect that Holstein's posture of "slave to the service" was mere dumb show.[47] Rather, one may conclude that as a great man's great man, he worked in the name of someone whom he unconsciously appropriated, thereby satisfying his own appetite for power.

The dominant figure in Holstein's early years—as in Bismarck's—had been his mother, with the father playing a more modest, if genial, role. Unlike Wilhelmine von Bismarck, however, Holstein's mother was not fond of society. On the contrary, she shunned it; only in her mid-forties did she enter upon matrimony, with motherhood following a year later. Hers had been a *mariage de raison*—con-

---

reer and relations with the Bismarcks, see Norman Rich, *Friedrich von Holstein: Politics and Diplomacy in the Era of Bismarck and William II* (Cambridge: Cambridge University Press, 1965), I: 3–96. See also George W. F. Hallgarten, "Fritz von Holsteins Geheimnis," *Historische Zeitschrift* 177 (1954): 75–83, and Norman Rich, "Eine Bemerkung über Friedrich von Holsteins Aufenthalt in Amerika," *Historische Zeitschrift* 186 (1958): 80–86. On the Arnim affair, see Norman Rich, "Holstein and the Arnim Affair," *Journal of Modern History* 28 (March 1956): 35–54; George O. Kent, *Arnim and Bismarck* (Oxford: Clarendon Press, 1968); Gerhard Kratzsch, *Harry von Arnim: Bismarck-Rivale und Frondeur: Die Arnim Prozesse, 1874–1875* (Göttingen, Frankfurt, Zürich: Musterschmidt, 1973).

45. Norman Rich and M. H. Fisher, eds., *The Holstein Papers*, I: *Memoirs* (Cambridge: Cambridge University Press, 1955), p. xxiv.

46. Ibid., p. 131.

47. Ibid., p. 45.

tracted to preserve an inheritance and continue a line—which apparently turned out to be one of compatibility as well. What this strongminded woman had done before she married is unclear. Thereafter she concentrated on her only child.

How her son responded can only be guessed at. He remained silent, strangely silent. His one comment that his childhood had been "too solitary to be happy" is both accurate and evasive.[48] Though Holstein lacked the companionship of children his own age, he did have that of his mother. Throughout many of his early years, in which he was educated privately, he and she were ailing together. If he was lonely in the presence of his mother, he was fearful too— fearful of (and fascinated by) the forces of disease. In Holstein's mind, physical defects or illness had devastating psychological consequences;[49] in later years he congratulated himself on eluding maladies that laid waste his less watchful associates.[50] In short, he seems seldom to have experienced a feeling of safety; rather he learned that catastrophe was always threatening.

Despite his geniality, Holstein's father offered scant reassurance. Not surprisingly, the elder Holstein was anxious about his son's health, or to be more precise, impatient with the boy's illness—as if illness were a fault of character. To harden their son's weak constitution had been the aim of both parents; their efforts, however, had proved unsatisfactory, and Holstein had been declared unfit for military service. To a father who had been a member of the officer corps, albeit an undistinguished one, this inability to perform military obligations was something to be ashamed of. He preferred advice to his son on how to counter the charge of having been a shirker,[51] an accusation which he himself may have been the first to imagine. Indeed the benevolence attributed to this former army officer, turned landed proprietor and later court chamberlain, does not altogether fit with the Polonius-like personality he revealed in his correspondence with his son.[52] The tone was hectoring rather than indulgent. The father's letters sounded a recurring motif, which was

48. Rogge, ed., *Friedrich von Holstein*, Holstein to Ida von Stülpnagel, October 22, 1908, p. 323.

49. See, for example, Holstein, *Memoirs*, pp. 57, 77. See also Norman Rich and M. H. Fisher, eds., *The Holstein Papers*, IV: *Correspondence 1897–1909* (Cambridge: Cambridge University Press, 1963), Holstein to Bülow, June 30, 1899, pp. 134–135.

50. See, for example, Rogge, ed., *Friedrich von Holstein*, Holstein to Ida von Stülpnagel, August 16, 1903, p. 225.

51. Holstein, *Correspondence 1861–1896*, August von Holstein to his son, January 30, 1861, p. 5.

52. For Holstein's appreciation of his father, see Rogge, ed., *Friedrich von Holstein*, Holstein to Minna von Holtzendorff, April 13, 1863, p. 32.

in harmony with his repeated admonitions to the young man to mind
his purse. In a world of jealousy and hostility, one could not be too
careful: "By a single ill-founded, ill-considered, or erroneous utterance one could forfeit one's standing . . . and once lost it would be
very difficult to regain."[53]

Above all, the elder Holstein spurred the young man to achievement:

> If . . . you have ambitious plans, and allow yourself to imagine big things,
> you must also have the strength of will to apply the means which lead to
> the goal. The truly ambitious man does this; he shuns no discomfort and
> trouble; and he usually succeeds, whereas the man who acts through van-
> ity takes it for granted that, due to his merits, his desires must be fulfilled
> without trouble; and he achieves nothing. . . . If therefore you wish to get
> something and do something exceptional, you must not shrink from any
> permissible means to achieve your end.[54]

Only by doing "something exceptional," it would seem, could Holstein buttress his standing. Only then could he impose his "individuality"—which both parents urged him not to suppress[55]—on a
dangerous world.

Holstein obviously took his father's injunctions to heart. Yet not
all of them. He did not heed his father's advice about social intercourse:

> Your position depends solely upon yourself. . . . It will not be at all diffi-
> cult with your personality to find acceptance. Dance and gossip with the
> best of them, and you will soon see that I am right. At social as dis-
> tinguished from purely diplomatic gatherings, talk in a lively and witty
> way and waste no time on intellectual profundities. Women love this and
> prefer indifferent witticisms and scandal to serious conversation. . . .
> Think all this over quietly and carefully and you will agree with me.[56]

In fact, with the personality he had, Holstein found society trying;
throughout his life he remained a reclusive bachelor, strictly limiting
his personal relations. In so doing, he demonstrated a logical consistency his father lacked: if the world was as treacherous as they both
imagined, was it not the better part of wisdom to reduce one's social
contacts? Of these two considerations, lack of trust, rather than
logic, no doubt proved decisive.

53. Holstein, *Correspondence 1861–1896*, August von Holstein to his son, February 27–March 2, 1861, p. 5.
    54. Ibid., August von Holstein to his son, April 13, 1861, p. 16.
    55. Ibid., August von Holstein to his son, April 9, 1861, p. 14.
    56. Ibid., August von Holstein to his son, April 9, 1861, pp. 13–14.

What, then, of Holstein's attachment to Bismarck? In 1883 he set down how he had come to know the future chancellor:

> As a child I had seen Bismarck once or twice at my parents' home. He was young and jovial then. Later I met him at Wiesbaden in 1859 when he was recuperating from a severe illness. In 1860 my father, who . . . realized I was not cut out for the law, asked me whether I would like to be a diplomat. I answered, "Yes, if Bismarck will take me on as an attaché." He was approached, gave his consent, and subsequently pushed through my appointment.[57]

In actuality it was Holstein himself who thought the law was not cut out for him; like Bismarck he was determined to play music he recognized as good or important, or none at all.[58] The future chancellor offered the kind of music the young man wanted: "I considered him a man of extraordinary abilities and with the blind faith of youth I felt sure he would make everything come right in the end."[59] And when Holstein arrived in St. Petersburg in early 1861, he stood in particular need of someone to "make everything come right": "As I walked back from the Legation to my pension along the quay, I was conscious perhaps for the only time in my life of a feeling of homelessness, or homesickness, as they say."[60] In this mournful state, Holstein yearned to possess Bismarck's strength as his own.

But Holstein's dependence on his chief did not transform the future chancellor into a trustworthy figure. If the young attaché had reason to agree with his father's judgment that Bismarck "went to quite exceptional lengths in championing and protecting, as well as commending, those among his subordinates who won his approval,"[61] he also came to appreciate that "the favor of tyrants" was "fickle."[62] Dependence and fear went hand in hand. These feelings persisted for a quarter century. By the mid-1880s, Holstein was increasingly taking pains to limit his social contact with the chancellor. He noted in his diary:

> With rough types like Herbert and his family there is only *one* way of avoiding the alternative between degradation and conflict, namely to

57. Holstein, *Memoirs*, p. 4.
58. Rich, *Holstein*, I: 10.
59. Holstein, *Memoirs*, p. 24.
60. Ibid., p. 4. For the atmosphere of the Prussian legation at the time, see Leopold von Schlözer, ed., *Petersburger Briefe von Kurd von Schlözer 1857–1862* (Stuttgart and Berlin: Deutsche Verlags-Anstalt, 1921).
61. Holstein, *Correspondence 1861–1896*, August von Holstein to his son, March 23, 1861, pp. 6–7.
62. Rogge, ed., *Friedrich von Holstein*, Holstein to Minna von Holtzendorff and Ida von Stülpnagel, January 11–13, 1871, p. 98.

withdraw of one's own accord. That is what I have done, and at first it gave me rather a jolt. But when I see how others are treated I am glad I made a clean break.[63]

Withdrawal was to prove no easy matter. For more than two decades Holstein had avoided conflict with his chief. Had he chosen degradation instead? Had he, in fact, debased his individuality? Far from it; he had fostered his own sense of self-importance by incorporating Bismarck in his private world.

III. The Opening Void

By the mid-1880s, the age and health of the Emperor William I had become the dominant fact of political life. Almost ninety years old, he could no longer be regarded as a permanent fixture of the German scene. If William's reign was nearing its end, might not Bismarck's also be drawing to a close? Constitutionally the chancellor was responsible to the monarch; his appointment or dismissal depended upon the will of the sovereign. Hence the approaching demise of the emperor necessarily called into question Bismarck's own standing. Yet the derivative quality of Bismarck's power— which even when he seemed the sole chief was never forgotten— does not account entirely for the uncertainty that now loomed over his position. Had the heir apparent, Crown Prince Frederick, shared his father's conservative views, both Bismarck and his subordinates would have felt far less threatened. Instead the crown prince and his English wife, Queen Victoria's eldest daughter, to whom Frederick had the reputation of being dangerously submissive, were known for their liberal outlook and were suspected of wishing to strengthen Germany's parliamentary institutions. On all sides it was taken for granted that once Frederick was on the throne, a collision between monarch and chancellor would ensue: men with such fundamentally divergent political beliefs could not be expected to remain harnessed together for long.

In the spring of 1887, less than ten months before the old emperor died, the crown prince became fatally ill. By the end of the year the diagnosis of throat cancer was firmly established and widely known. Thus even before Frederick reached the throne, which he occupied for barely three months in 1888, Bismarck and those serving under him were faced with the prospect of still another change of sov-

63. Holstein, *Diaries*, December 25, 1885, p. 272 (emphasis in the original).

ereign, that is, the accession of Frederick's son Prince William. In political outlook the second William was much closer to his grandfather than to his father. Indeed, in a family noted for its intergenerational strife, the hostility between the younger William and his father and more particularly between him and his mother ranked as unprecedented. Thrust into the limelight by his father's illness when not yet thirty, William made scarcely any effort to conceal his personal and political estrangement from his parents. Nor did he keep secret his desire to imprint his own mark upon his reign. Though he spent most of his time in the cloistered atmosphere of a Potsdam Guards regiment, he did not let his inexperience dampen his ardor to assert his manhood. He showed little inclination to play the role of schoolboy to a chancellor who had already passed his seventieth birthday. Where people had assumed that political differences between Bismarck and Frederick would lead to conflict, they now anticipated that age and youth would find accommodation difficult.

Thus throughout the second half of the 1880s, the elementary fact of the approaching succession of two different monarchs, both of whom were unsuited on either political or temperamental grounds to enduring or fostering the chancellor's mastery, flashed a signal to all that the tide was turning against Bismarck. How much time remained to him was unclear; most observers expected that Frederick and then William would find him indispensable for a number of years. The uncertainty, then, about the chancellor's position was likely to be protracted, and its duration alone sufficient to provoke anxious responses on the part of Bismarck and his subordinates. Still more, the stratagems Bismarck employed to safeguard his standing with the new sovereigns, devised without reference to the needs of those serving under him, so heightened his subordinates' uneasiness that some manifest resolution became the unspoken imperative.

■

In the disquieting circumstances of the aged emperor's impending death, did Bismarck alter what had become his normal mode of conduct? The answer is mixed. It is evident that he redoubled his efforts to demonstrate the necessity of his rule. His performance in 1887 was outstanding; with astonishing energy he played simultaneously two complicated games of chess. On the domestic front he maneuvered so adroitly in the Reichstag elections as finally to capture the long-sought prize of a conservative majority. In the diplomatic arena he devised a series of agreements in which Russia, Austria-Hungary, Italy, and Britain were induced to participate and which had his

own country as the fulcrum. His sheer brilliance in fabricating and
drawing together the threads of this complex network, and more particularly in keeping them from getting entangled with one another,
has awed subsequent historians. Whatever the ostensible purposes of
Bismarck's domestic and foreign activities, they served to buttress his
position with the most important, indeed crucial, member of his audience, Crown Prince Frederick. If Bismarck could not make certain
of Frederick's unconditional support by quiet efforts at moral sua-
sion—and mild-mannered behavior was alien to the chancellor's nature—he could hope to arrange the political situation in such a
fashion that only he would be in a position to assure the orderly conduct of business. Though the maneuvering of no other year was to be
comparable in dexterity to that of 1887, Bismarck did not give up his
attempt to constrain Frederick and subsequently the young William
to depend on him as his sole guide.

Yet in one vital respect the chancellor did change his tactics, or
rather made use of a new weapon in his arsenal. Where heretofore he
had absented himself from Berlin and remained content to rely primarily on the telegraph to convey his wishes, he now left behind him
his son Herbert as a tangible link to, and an active participant in, the
life of the court and of German officialdom. From early manhood
Herbert had been nurtured on affairs of state, and through frequent
employment as his father's private secretary and a variety of diplomatic missions, he had accumulated a wide experience. By mid-de-
cade Bismarck's intention to elevate his son to the position of secretary of state for foreign affairs, the place then held by Hatzfeldt, was
plain to see. Not until 1886 did the chancellor finally wrest consent
from the emperor to this unprecedented promotion of a man still in
his thirties. Once Herbert was installed in the Wilhelmstrasse,
Bismarck's tendency to avoid personal contact, be it with his sovereign or with those serving under him, became even more marked.[64]

That the instrument Bismarck had chosen to assist him in his
quest for aloof dominance and to buttress his position should have
turned out to be counterproductive was not without irony. The
emergence of Herbert as an irritating performer in the political
drama, as a palpable presence who spoke in a confusing mixture of

64. See Holstein, *Diaries*, June 28, 1885, p. 209, and June 30, 1885, p. 210; Brauer,
Im Dienste Bismarcks, p. 112; Heinrich Otto Meisner, ed., *Denkwürdigkeiten des
General-Feldmarschall Alfred Grafen von Waldersee* (Stuttgart and Berlin: Deutsche
Verlags-Anstalt, 1922), I, May 18, 1886, p. 292. For the fullest portrait, see the edi-
tor's introduction to Walter Bussmann, ed., *Staatssekretär Graf Herbert von Bismarck:
Aus seiner politischen Privatkorrespondenz* (Göttingen: Vandenhoeck and Ruprecht,
1964), pp. 8–67.

his father's voice and his own, skewed the perspective that the chancellor had so carefully delineated. Where Bismarck had anticipated that Herbert would maintain close connections with both the future monarchs and his father's subordinates, hostility toward the designated go-between corroded the image of the wise and purposeful, and above all indispensable chief.

Bismarck's reliance on his son, which went hand in hand with advancing years, requires a word of comment. In relieving the chancellor, as his brother Bill remarked, of the "unpleasant *faux frais*" of diplomatic and courtly exchanges,[65] Herbert obviously helped keep a hostile world from impinging on his father. So too did Dr. Schweninger, with whom Herbert stayed in close contact; both figured as emotional comforters to the aging chancellor. Herbert alone, however, could sustain the old man's belief that he might, indeed should, continue to dominate the public realm.

Bismarck found safety in relying on his son, for in no sense did he consider him an independent agent. That the chancellor was incapable of appreciating Herbert as a being separate from himself he had made amply apparent by his refusal, in 1881, to allow this adored offspring to marry the woman he loved. The elder Bismarck insisted that his son forswear his romantic attachment: Princess Elisabeth Carolath had the misfortune of being related to adherents of the Empress Augusta, whom he regarded as his archenemy. The conflict between father and son reached its dramatic climax when Bismarck threatened to commit suicide if Herbert carried out his marital plans. In short, the chancellor made no attempt to moderate his rage; instead he demanded that his son renounce his best hope of acquiring a psychological haven of his own. Such emotional blackmail could not be withstood; though Princess Carolath had divorced her husband with Herbert's encouragement, her beloved abandoned her.[66]

Herbert never expressed resentment at his father; his rage found other targets. On the contrary, he worried lest the violent upset he had precipitated might injure the chancellor's health. His father's potency, rather than his own, seemed his prime concern. Or were the

65. Holstein, *Correspondence 1861–1896*, Wilhelm von Bismarck to Holstein, October 20, 1887, p. 225.

66. The correspondence between Herbert Bismarck and Philipp Eulenburg provides a running account of Herbert's romantic problems: Johannes Haller, ed., *Aus 50 Jahren: Erinnerungen, Tagebücher und Briefe aus dem Nachlass des Fürsten Philipp zu Eulenburg-Hertefeld* (Berlin: Verlag von Gebrüder Paetel, 1925), pp. 81–107. For a perceptive account of the elder Bismarck's treatment of his son, see Fritz Stern, *Gold and Iron: Bismarck, Bleichröder, and the Building of the German Empire* (New York: Alfred A. Knopf, 1977), pp. 254–259; see also Louis L. Snyder, "Political Implications of Herbert von Bismarck's Marital Affairs, 1881, 1892," *Journal of Modern History* 36 (June 1964): 151–161.

two inextricably connected? Indeed the elder Bismarck, in opposing his son's marriage, offered him an opportunity to claim that potency for himself: "My father told me with sobs and tears . . . that he had had enough of life, that he still found consolation in all his battles only in his hopes for me, and if that now were also taken from him, he would be done for."[67] Although the sacrifice demanded of Herbert had been shattering, he had the satisfaction of knowing, as his brother wrote, that for their father "he would be *irreplaceable*."[68]

From this close relationship, Herbert sought to exclude his mother. Though his letters reflect a solicitude for both his parents, it is the solicitude of a licensed intruder. His mother should, he noted in a condescending tone, take better care of herself, even if that meant an absence from her husband's side:

> She has fabricated the illusion that she exists only to serve her husband and her children, she has artificially, so to speak, created for herself the role of chambermaid for us all, and she has the feeling that she is committing robbery if she ever thinks of herself. . . . I can call this nothing else than a fiction; Mama, without accounting for what she is doing, is not being honest with herself in this respect, and the painful result is that she is ruining her health.[69]

Yet at the same time as Herbert labeled his mother's self-sacrificing attitude a "fiction," he adopted that stance himself: he identified with what he simultaneously ridiculed.[70] Little wonder, then, that despite the cruel treatment he had received, he clung so tenaciously to his father's potency.

No one denied that Herbert was professionally well trained—though perhaps not quite ripe for the post his father had procured him. The younger Bismarck was generally credited with a flair for diplomacy—his mission to Britain at the height of the Anglo–German colonial conflict of the mid-1880s had earned him high marks—and with being both hard working and well-informed. Rather it was his personal behavior that made him repulsive. Even before Herbert replaced Hatzfeldt as state secretary, Holstein commented:

> Herbert's character is unevenly developed. He has alongside some outstanding qualities, others which hold down his *achievement* to the medi-

67. Eulenburg, *Erinnerungen*, Herbert Bismarck to Eulenburg, April 28, 1881, p. 92.

68. Holstein, *Correspondence 1861–1896*, Wilhelm von Bismarck to Holstein, October 20, 1887, p. 225 (emphasis in the original).

69. Bussmann, ed., *Herbert Bismarck: Privatkorrespondenz*, Herbert Bismarck to Rantzau, July 2, 1887, pp. 458–459.

70. See, for example, ibid., Herbert Bismarck to his father, October 26, 1886, p. 398.

ocre level, and will easily compass his downfall when his *position* has raised him above this level, whereas a mediocre but tactful person would muddle through. His defects are violence, arrogance and vanity. These first two qualities of his repel almost everybody, with the exception of the few who are clever enough to flatter him in the right way.[71]

Shortly thereafter, Holstein recounted an instance of such violent conduct. Herbert and his brother-in-law, Count Rantzau, had tested a new rifle by aiming the weapon at the windows of a mutual foreign office colleague, Arthur von Brauer. When another official observed that someone might have been injured in the course of this experiment, Herbert blithely replied:

> "Oh, no, because the first time I aimed at the upper panes and waited to see if any one came to the windows. When no one appeared I knew that the room was empty."
>
> Brauer remarked: "But, Count Bismarck, you might have hit a clerk bringing in files."
>
> "Yes," laughed Herbert, "and what silly faces the chaps would have made when the bullets went singing round their heads."
>
> The feelings of Brauer and Lindau (who works next-door to Brauer) can well be imagined. Furious, but they do not show it.
>
> Brauer said, half jesting, in his Baden dialect: "It reminds you of the darkest days of Nero."[72]

The unfortunate Brauer, in writing of Herbert, tried to be generous. He expressed sympathy for a son pushed forward by a father from whose shadow he could not escape and yet to whom he remained devotedly attached. He showed compassion for the inner torments that drove Herbert to seek comfort in drink. Though, according to Brauer, Herbert did not allow his drinking and his generally unhealthy mode of life to interfere with his duty—he engaged in this slow form of self-destruction only after the day's work had been finished—the excesses of the previous night betrayed themselves in his hung-over ill-humor of the following day. Despite the nuances Brauer added to his portrait, Herbert still appears as overbearing, if not downright odious, in his treatment of his co-workers.[73]

In the wake of the growing antagonism to his son, the chancellor himself was no longer spared. Holstein, for one, awoke from his spell, and during the last years of Bismarck's tenure in office, he became

71. Holstein, *Diaries*, May 16, 1885, p. 199 (emphasis in the original).

72. Ibid., December 25, 1885, p. 271.

73. Brauer, *Im Dienste Bismarcks*, pp. 140–142; see also Hugo Graf Lerchenfeld-Koefering, ed., *Erinnerungen und Denkwürdigkeiten von Hugo Graf Lerchenfeld-Koefering 1843 bis 1925* (Berlin: E. S. Mittler, 1935), pp. 270–273.

increasingly critical of his chief, both professionally and personally. What makes Holstein's complaints relevant here is their timing rather than their substance. (It is far from clear whether in the late 1880s Bismarck was actually following a course markedly different from the one he had entered upon after the Congress of Berlin in 1878 or after the signing of the Austro-German alliance in 1879.) Where earlier, Holstein had applauded his chief's initiatives, while scarcely troubling himself about their logic or necessity, where he had accepted as a matter of course that the chancellor never allowed *"his actions to be anticipated,"*[74] he now bemoaned Bismarck's "positive mania for secret treaties."[75] In Holstein's view,

> our policy with its crisscross of commitments . . . resembles the tangle of lines of a big railway station. The chief pointsman [i.e., switchman] thinks he can click everything into its proper place and hopes particularly that the greater the confusion the more indispensable he is.[76]

In short, Holstein had abandoned his faith that Bismarck was the man to "make everything come right." While he acknowledged the chancellor's "dialectical skill," he claimed, unaware of his own inconsistency, that his chief had lost "his breadth of vision and his energy" as well as "his nerve." He described Bismarck as "an unperceptive, unfeeling . . . old man," whose "memory" had "completely gone." Though "too lazy to study the files," the chancellor insisted "on making his marginal annotations as before, usually without consulting any one" and as a result, like an "hysterical old maid," he often contradicted himself.[77] Taken together, Holstein's laments about the excessive complexity of Bismarck's diplomatic arrangements and his supposedly failing powers suggest a preference for believing the worst rather than remaining in suspense any longer.[78]

How did Herbert figure in this unfolding psychic drama? To put matters simply: Bismarck's erratic behavior—his forceful intrusion

74. Holstein, *Diaries*, February 8, 1884, p. 76 (emphasis in the original).
75. Ibid., April 29, 1887, p. 339.
76. Ibid., January 11, 1887, p. 332, see also ibid., November 5, 1887, p. 355.
77. Ibid., October 3, 1886, pp. 306–307; April 29, 1887, pp. 339–340; October 22, 1888, p. 379.
78. For assessments of Holstein's views and activities, see Helmut Krausnick, *Holsteins Geheimpolitik in der Ära Bismarck 1886–1890* (Hamburg: Hanseatische Verlagsanstalt, 1942); Rich, *Friedrich von Holstein*, I: 204–221; Günter Richter, *Friedrich von Holstein: Ein Mitarbeiter Bismarcks* (Lübeck and Hamburg: Matthiesen, 1966), especially pp. 141–147. For echoes of Holstein's concerns, see Meisner, ed., *Waldersee Denkwürdigkeiten*, II, November 1, 1888, p. 13; December 2, 1888, p. 24; January 21, 1889, p. 32; January 28, 1889, p. 34; February 14, 1889, pp. 37–38; February 19, 1889, pp. 38–39; March 12, 1889, pp. 44–45.

into the lives of his subordinates, coupled with his emotional distance—was bearable for someone like Holstein so long as he could maintain his own fiction of being indispensable to his chief and thereby, in effect, appropriating him. With Herbert on the scene, this fiction became untenable. Bismarck's reliance on his son marked the younger man—and the younger man alone—as indispensable. It was as if an obnoxious sibling had disrupted what, in fantasy at least, had been a relationship *à deux*. And while the "sibling" might be loathsome in his own right, it was his tie with the parent which made him the object of burning jealousy. Only by denigrating the parent, would the "child" (in this case, Holstein) be able to avoid such pangs and the accompanying admission of defeat. Hence a father who depended on his son to guard him against the effects of changed circumstances and advancing years could no longer be considered a demigod. On the far shore of the widening gulf where Bismarck secluded himself from Berlin's political activities dwelt a mere mortal.

■

If Bismarck's subordinates experienced pain and panic in turning from the figure who not only had ordered the political world, but had given direction to their endeavors—who had for so long confirmed their sense of their own importance—Bismarck himself labored under a comparable difficulty: he too found it hard to imagine a Germany without his personal guiding force. He refused to admit the consequences of his success, to recognize that without him his achievements would still endure. How, then, would he bring his career to a close?

The story of Bismarck's last months in office is an oft-told tale which need not be recounted here. What is required for the purposes of this study is to set Bismarck's multiple efforts to hold onto power alongside Gladstone's exertions at almost exactly the same age. Their fates differed: while Gladstone remained on the political scene for nearly another full decade, Bismarck made a hasty exit. But emotional fortune, rather than political destiny, is the crucial concern. Neither man was spared the psychological stress which afflicts the elderly, regardless of station. Both Gladstone and Bismarck experienced a sense of loss, and both were forced to look backward, as well as forward, in coping with that loss. And herein one can discern fundamental differences between the two charismatic leaders.

Gladstone had a usable past at his disposal: he had known safety in close attachments and had come to trust his own capacity to keep those attachments safe. Revivifying and building on memories that soothed and reassured him, he was able to steady his inner world. He had no need to resort to anger to fix his political course.

In contrast, Bismarck found his psychic arsenal depleted: no reliable weapon lay at hand to combat fears of disintegration and decay. Once more, as he had done so decisively four decades earlier, he strove to reimpose control on his inner and outer worlds. And his failure to do so, his failure to reassert his manic omnipotence, left him enraged.

Bismarck anticipated that the proposals he devised in late 1889 and early 1890 would extend his lease on power, more particularly his domination over the young emperor. If Gladstone could be faulted for insufficient attention to certain of his colleagues before and during his Home Rule ministry, a similar charge cannot be leveled against Bismarck. Though he consulted no subordinates, he never lost sight of his prey. His determination to constrain William—and to humiliate him—gave coherence and purpose to what might otherwise have appeared a series of disjointed yet provocative acts: legislation which was bound to cause havoc in the Reichstag, mutterings about electoral reform and even about a coup d'état against the federal constitution itself.[79] By disorganizing political life, Bismarck apparently sought to demonstrate that he alone was capable of keeping chaos at bay. Still more, if this time he should fail to restore order, he would have the perverse satisfaction of watching the Reich founder. It was almost as if he preferred to see what had largely been his creation destroyed, rather than have it survive without him.

It was Bismarck, then, who inspired and set in motion the drama of his own downfall. While William had never been prepared to remain indefinitely eclipsed by his old chancellor, he had hoped that Bismarck would gradually relinquish his offices and gracefully retire from the political scene. This attitude was echoed by the chancellor's subordinates, who hesitated to take overt steps against their

79. For the details of these plans, see J. C. G. Röhl, "The Disintegration of the *Kartell* and the Politics of Bismarck's Fall from Power, 1887-90," *The Historical Journal* 9 (1966): 60-89, and "Staatsstreichplan oder Staatsstreichbereitschaft? Bismarcks Politik in der Entlassungskrise," *Historische Zeitschrift* 203 (December 1966): 610-624; E. Zechlin, *Staatsstreichpläne, Bismarcks und Wilhelm II, 1890-1894* (Stuttgart and Berlin: J. G. Cotta, 1929); W. Pöls, *Sozialistenfrage und Revolutionsfurcht in ihrem Zusammenhang mit den angeblichen Staatsstreichplänen Bismarcks* (Lübeck and Hamburg: Matthiesen, 1960); see also Michael Stürmer, "Staatsstreichgedanken im Bismarckreich," *Historische Zeitschrift* 209 (December 1969): 566-615.

chief. Thus although Bismarck had transformed himself into an agent of destruction, thereby upsetting the emotional equilibrium his dominance had formerly maintained, no Cassius emerged to galvanize his comrades to rid themselves of a man they now perceived as dangerous. Only after Bismarck had undermined what had been his own majority (and promised to become the emperor's) in the Reichstag elections held in late February, and was proceeding to provoke a conflict with its remnants, did William's advisers urge him to dismiss the chancellor.

Ironically Bismarck's reckless behavior cast William in the role of Brutus. Though the emperor felt personally thwarted by his chancellor—reason enough, one might surmise, for wanting to force him out—still William's determination to forestall governmental paralysis and political turmoil bears comparison with Brutus's reaction to the prospect of tyranny. In great haste the emperor decided to do the deed and assume the responsibility that constitutionally was his: to rid the state of the Caesar, more menacing than Shakespeare's character, who could not be endured. On March 15, 1890—the ides of March—William had a violent quarrel with Bismarck; the chancellor's actual resignation three days later was merely an anticlimax. But like Brutus, William was to learn that Caesar, though no longer a living presence, was mighty yet, that his spirit continued to walk abroad and would not be laid to rest.

Chapter 4

Leadership from a Distance

Salisbury and His Colleagues, 1886–1892

When the Marquess of Salisbury formed his first government in 1885, it was dubbed the "Ministry of Caretakers." Neither he nor his colleagues expected to remain in office more than a few months, and their expectations proved correct. When Salisbury resumed office the following year, after two general elections and the interlude of Gladstone's Home Rule ministry, his prospects were still in doubt. No one would have predicted that for thirteen of the next sixteen years he would continue as prime minister. Certainly this fact alone should assure Salisbury a place in history perhaps not equal but at least analogous to those of Gladstone and Bismarck. And though historians have not accorded Salisbury so exalted a rank, the delineation of British political relationships in the late nineteenth century requires that he be included along with his more celebrated contemporaries.

The ties between Gladstone and his colleagues and Bismarck and his subordinates have already been described. Though all was not smooth going with the British Liberal party chiefs, the contrast to their German counterparts is startling. The differences which emerged can be summed up schematically. Both leaders radiated the quality that had not yet been labeled charisma. But they were poles apart in how they interpreted what that authority entailed: Gladstone demonstrated respect for his co-workers as persons in their own right; Bismarck treated those around him as mere underlings. This differing behavior on the part of the leaders contributed to the character of the relations among their followers: mutual accommodation within the British cabinet and thinly veiled mistrust among German high officials. Gladstone's colleagues expected psychological support from one another; Bismarck's subordinates neither sought nor found emotional sustenance within their own ranks. And where co-workers could not depend on each other, their reliance on their leader, as if by default, became more pronounced. Of the two, then, Bismarck stood as psychologically the more significant figure for those around him.

In the case of Salisbury, as with Gladstone and Bismarck, one must start with the man himself, with a sketch of his personality. Here the focus should be on his difficulty in narrowing the emotional distance which separated him from his associates. And just as earlier the logical path went from the political chiefs to their co-workers, the next step must be to examine the way Salisbury's inability to be on intimate and easy terms with those working under him contributed to shaping relations among his collaborators. Despite such an ostensible handicap, Salisbury's Conservative cabinet functioned with greater harmony than Gladstone's second ministry. By what additional buttressing, one is thus led to ask, was Salisbury's personal leadership supplemented? Once this last question has been satisfactorily answered, common psychological features of Gladstone and Salisbury's governments should become clear.

I. Diffidence and Determination

What were the particular and characteristic set of emotional responses with which Salisbury confronted the world? Just as Gladstone's longing to make reparation and Bismarck's overweening sense of superiority gave direction to a discussion of their early attachments, similar guidance must be sought here. But where should one look? While there are firsthand accounts depicting Salisbury's behavior, of necessity these descriptions reflect an outsider's view. Salisbury left no autobiographical statement comparable to Bismarck's, where a conscious attempt to gain a special place in history might have shed light on his convictions about himself. Of his own literary productions, the most substantial were articles written primarily in the 1860s for the *Quarterly Review*. In these journalistic essays Salisbury intended to provide a concrete analysis of current political issues rather than a full and systematic elaboration of social and political theory. Nonetheless the articles go a considerable way toward defining his principles and beliefs, and hence offer precious evidence about his attitude toward the external world.[1]

One should not, of course, reduce political beliefs to mere manisfestations of psychic conflict. Yet at the same time one cannot make a sharp division between strictly rational and irrational mental phenomena. The line becomes blurred once one admits that certain beliefs are impervious to factual evidence and are held on grounds other than observation and logical inference. It certainly seems correct to stress the rootedness of a person's intellectual stance in his deepest psychological concerns. And Salisbury in charting the scope of political action, was unquestionably revealing his own emotional universe.

Salisbury's analysis of the situation confronting his generation of Conservative leaders was bleak indeed. In its bare outlines his description recalls Marx's writings, though from the other side of the political divide the class struggle was necessarily viewed not with relish but with alarm.[2] As Salisbury put it:

> The struggle between the English constitution on the one hand, and the democratic forces that are laboring to subvert it on the other, is now, in reality, when reduced to its simplest elements and stated in its most prosaic form, a struggle between those who have, to keep what they have got, and those who have not, to get it.[3]

In the 1860s it seemed clear to Salisbury that the opening battle in this impending conflict was to be fought over the question of franchise reform. Reform plainly meant that "the whole community" would "be governed by an ignorant multitude."[4] And once the political balance in the state had been irrevocably changed, it would be

---

1. For an excellent discussion of Salisbury's major political articles, see the editor's introduction in Paul Smith, ed., *Lord Salisbury on Politics: A Selection from his Articles in the Quarterly Review, 1860–1883* (Cambridge: Cambridge University Press, 1972), pp. 1–110. See also Michael Pinto-Duschinsky, *The Political Thought of Lord Salisbury, 1854–68* (London: Constable and Co., 1967), and Elie Kedourie, "Tory Ideologue: Salisbury as a Conservative Intellectual," *Encounter* 38, no. 6 (June 1972): 45–53. The author of the earlier articles, of course, was not yet the Marquess of Salisbury. Until the summer of 1865, when his elder brother died, he was called Lord Robert Cecil. From that date to the spring of 1868, as heir to the Marquisate, he bore the title of Lord Cranborne.

2. Salisbury himself did not refer to Marx. He knew of him, but was not conversant with his work. Salisbury did, however, cite Proudhon's *Qu'est-ce que la propriété?*: "The Budget and the Reform Bill" (*Quarterly Review*, no. 214, April 1860), in Paul Smith, ed., *Lord Salisbury on Politics*, p. 125.

3. "The Budget and the Reform Bill," in ibid., p. 125.

4. "The Budget and the Reform Bill," in ibid., p. 155.

but a short time before the system of taxation was altered to deprive the propertied of their wealth. Certainly Salisbury counted on the desperateness of the situation to rouse his readers to political action.

But in these unpropitious circumstances, what could be done? Salisbury's initial answer was simple: resistance. Given the nature of the political contest, he argued, the notion that peace and quiet could be bought with a moderate dose of reform was both illusory and pernicious.

> We might as well hope for the termination of the struggle for existence by which, some philosophers tell us, the existence or the modification of the various species of organized beings upon our planet is determined. The battle for political power is merely an effort, well or ill-judged, on the part of the classes who wage it to better or to secure their own position. Unless our social activity shall have become paralyzed, and the nation shall have lost its vitality, this battle must continue to rage.[5]

Above all, Conservatives must return to fundamental principles, must renew their faith in the existing social and political system. Here Salisbury struck his dominant chord; reverence for the status quo was the wellspring of political morality:

> Those who value the freedom and security we enjoy, now so hard to find elsewhere in a similar degree, are intelligibly jealous of experimental meddling with the body upon whose composition all the political blessings we possess depend. What the effect might be of the substitution of an absolutely new class of persons in the place of those who at present fill the House of Commons, it is, of course, impossible to predict with certainty. All we know is, that the attempt will be absolutely new. The forms may remain the same; the proceedings may be recorded in the same journals; the new assembly may meet within the old walls; but it will not be the old House of Commons. The existing body, with all its faults and merits, is dependent upon the social system out of which it is drawn.[6]

Thus did Salisbury unabashedly espouse the interests of his own class. He had no intention of renouncing his caste position. Quite the contrary, he expected others similarly placed to respond as he did.

Salisbury found it particularly paradoxical and inappropriate that the great Whig families should still look to Gladstone, now an advocate of electoral reform, for political leadership. As the "foremost

5. "The Change of Ministry" (*Quarterly Review*, no. 239, July 1866), in ibid., p. 242.

6. "The House of Commons" (*Quarterly Review*, no. 231, July 1864), in ibid., p. 175. For a similar discussion of the importance of manners and customs in regulating a polity, see *Lord Robert Cecil's Gold Field Diary*, with introduction and notes by Ernest Scott (Melbourne: Melbourne University Press, 1935).

representatives of English wealth, and the spokesmen of that peculiar form of culture which the social organisation of England" had produced, they had the "responsibility of guarding it from assault, and transmitting it to others . . . unimpaired."[7] Still more, as a swing group within the House of Commons—belonging to the Liberal party yet at loggerheads with its Radical wing—the Whigs could determine whether or not Gladstone would succeed. Their duty was plain: they must abandon their dangerous leader and close ranks with their erstwhile Conservative opponents. In short, Salisbury argued, it was "not the moment to quarrel about party badges, when the common enemy" was "at the gate."[8]

What had stood in the way of such a political realignment? The answer was clear: Derby and Disraeli's craving for office. In 1866 the Conservative leaders had formed a minority government after defections had brought about the fall of the Liberal ministry, and they had shown themselves determined to hold on at all costs. Instead of marshaling those eager to resist franchise reform as Salisbury had urged, they had quickly jettisoned their traditional principles. To win support from among the opposition, they had accepted far-reaching amendments to an initially moderate proposal and therewith taken their celebrated "leap in the dark." Such blatant treachery and crass ambition repelled Salisbury both in practice and in theory; he resigned from the cabinet and carefully dissociated himself from the government before attacking in print—albeit anonymously—his former chiefs.[9]

Nor was Salisbury's repugnance limited to unprincipled ambition. He felt the same disgust for political striving even when based on moral convictions. While he castigated Disraeli's unflinching resolve to put office above all else, he turned his choicest invective on what he regarded as Gladstone's particular combination of earnestness and self-seeking.

Many men allow their interests to overbear their convictions. A still greater number are biased by their interests in forming their convictions, and half-consciously drive their reason to conclusions to which it would not otherwise guide them. But such a description is not applicable to Mr.

7. "The Reform Bill" (*Quarterly Review*, no. 238, April 1886), in Paul Smith, ed., *Lord Salisbury on Politics*, p. 221.

8. "The Change of Ministry," in ibid., p. 251.

9. "The Conservative Surrender" (*Quarterly Review*, no. 246, October 1867), in ibid., pp. 272–279. On Salisbury's role in the Second Reform Bill crisis, see Maurice Cowling, *1867, Disraeli, Gladstone and Revolution: The Passing of the Second Reform Bill* (Cambridge: Cambridge University Press, 1967), and F. B. Smith, *The Making of the Reform Bill* (Cambridge: Cambridge University Press, 1966).

Gladstone. He is never, even half-consciously, insincere. But he is not, on that account, exempt from the action of the temptations which generate insincerity in other men, nor is his conduct free from the results which it produces upon the conduct of other men. His ambition has guided him in recent years as completely as it ever guided any statesman of the century; and yet there is not even a shade of untruth in the claim made for him by his friends, that he is guided wholly by his convictions. The process of self-deceit goes on in his mind without the faintest self-consciousness or self-suspicion. The result is that it goes on without check or stint.[10]

Was there no way for a politician to prove to himself as well as to others that he had not succumbed to crass ambition, let alone to the subtler forms of self-deception? For Salisbury there was only one answer—willingness to relinquish office:

> The idea that the convictions of politicians are never stable, that under adequate pressure every resistance will give way, every political profession will be obsequiously recast, is fatal to the existence of either confidence or respect. Neither trust nor fear will, in the long run, be inspired by a school of statesmen who, whatever else they sacrifice, never sacrifice themselves.[11]

But if self-denial was the mark of a statesman, then individual leadership must be deeply suspect. Thus Salisbury's fastidiousness—a clear indication of his own discomfort with direct forms of self-assertion—led him to renounce potential claims to personal dominance.

This attitude toward the permissible or possible range of individual action stood as the polar opposite to Bismarck's. Where the German chancellor extolled political genius—his own, to be sure—freed from constraint, the future British prime minister fettered it with moral scruples. In similar vein, while Bismarck saw the forces of history as familiars to be manipulated, Salisbury viewed them as overarching presences whose course might be delayed but not altered. Here one comes full circle, back to the nature of the political struggle. And at the same time one reaches the central paradox of Salisbury's position: once he had charted such a narrow field for personal action, his admonition to resistance lost its compelling power. All that remained was the hope that by a combination of forceful reasoning, common sense, and determination, he might induce Con-

10. "The Change of Ministry," in Paul Smith, ed., *Lord Salisbury on Politics*, p. 234. Despite political disagreements, Gladstone and Salisbury remained on friendly terms: H. C. G. Matthew, ed., *The Gladstone Diaries*, VI: *1861–1868* (Oxford: Clarendon Press, 1978), December 11, 1868, p. 647, and December 14, 1868, p. 648.

11. "Disintegration" (*Quarterly Review*, no. 312, October 1883), in Paul Smith, ed., *Lord Salisbury on Politics*, p. 234.

servatives to overcome their habitual lethargy. Though suffused with pessimism, his faith in his own rationality and that of others preserved him from despair. There was no other defense against the combined consequences of his personal diffidence and the course of history itself.

■

Salisbury's uneasiness about self-assertion, which he betrayed in his political writings, not unexpectedly had its roots in his childhood. It is equally clear that he must have mastered this anxiety to achieve the political prominence which was so long his. Since he eventually overcame the psychological handicaps of his youth, one might assume that those years could simply be ignored, that in this instance, at least, material about them is irrelevant. Yet it would be foolhardy to attempt a personality sketch without referring to his childhood. Not only did his early experiences leave indelible traces, but his defensive strategies, his ways of coping with long-standing emotional difficulties, cannot be understood apart from those very vulnerabilities. Without such a background, a variety of qualities might be attributed to Salisbury, but the figure would lack both core and connective tissue.

One should not be led astray by a titillating catalog of neurotic symptoms. Salisbury certainly had his share of them, which his daughter-biographer did not shrink from elaborating. A more recent commentator has noted:

> Such is the impression of mass and solidity, both physical and moral, presented by Salisbury in his later years that it is hard to realise how far, as a young man, he was a neurotic of the first water. In a weak and often ailing body, fretted by a powerful and remorselessly active intellect, his nervous system proved inordinately susceptible to strain. All his life, he would be liable to crises which he called "nerve storms," bringing depression, lassitude, and a hypersensitiveness of touch and hearing.[12]

But neurotic or eccentric traits do not disclose their meaning by themselves: they derive their significance from personal attachments. And it is on these latter that the emphasis must fall.

What of Salisbury's mother? In her published diaries she emerges as a woman with a flair for politics and with ample opportunity to satisfy that instinct. Unlike Wilhelmine von Bismarck, whose interests were more intellectual than political, the Marchionness of Salisbury did not feel thwarted or frustrated. Indeed hers was a

12. Editor's introduction in ibid., p. 10.

recognized position—a position reinforced, no doubt, by the general assumption that easy personal relations were crucial to political activity. What Bismarck angrily and fearfully referred to as "petticoat influence" was considered in Britain as legitimate—and frequently essential—emotional support. Such was the view of the Duke of Wellington, for whom Lady Salisbury figured as political confidante in the mid-1830s:

> He called me his friend twice over, with emphasis, as if he would have said "my first and best friend," and expressed a confidence in me which I feel with a gratitude and pleasure I cannot express. "With you," he said, "I think aloud."[13]

That Wellington should "think aloud" with a female is not to be wondered at: he regarded men as *generally* inferior in real and useful information to women."[14]

Interest in the public realm was not indulged at the expense of the private sphere; or rather, in acquiring status as the Duke's "friend," Lady Salisbury did not forfeit the esteem that accrued to her as wife and mother. Least of all from Wellington himself: his own "domestic" nature—his need for "some female society and some fireside" to which he could "always resort"[15]—prompted an appreciative participation in her family life. His fondness for children and his good-natured treatment of them evoked repeated praise from Lady Salisbury;[16] his behavior betokened his sympathy for the maternal role as well, and thereby eased her task.

How did Lady Salisbury carry out that assignment? More specifically, what was her relationship with Robert, the future prime minister? When he, her third son, was born in February 1830, two months before term, the second was already dead. His elder brother was eight years old and had been "afflicted from birth with a form of nervous debility which, before he grew up, resulted in a complete

13. Carola Oman, *The Gascoyne Heiress: The Life and Diaries of Frances Mary Gascoyne Cecil 1802-39* (London: Hodder and Stoughton, 1968), November 26, 1834, p. 145. Gladstone also had a fond remembrance of Lady Salisbury: see his letter to her son, February 18, 1898, quoted in Lady Gwendolen Cecil, *Life of Robert, Marquis of Salisbury* (London: Hodder and Stoughton, 1921-1932), I: 8.

14. Oman, *The Gascoyne Heiress*, December 22, 1833, p. 100 (emphasis in the original).

15. Ibid., August 2, 1834, p. 133.

16. See, for example, ibid., March 8, 1835, p. 156; September 9, 1835, p. 177; December 24, 1835, p. 191. Wellington continued to manifest sympathy for and interest in the mother's role with the marquess's second wife: see Lady Burghclere, *A Great Man's Friendship: Letters of the Duke of Wellington to Mary, Marchioness of Salisbury 1850-1852* (London: John Murray, 1927).

loss of sight, and which was manifested further in a general feebleness of constitution which went on increasing until he died, prac-
tically of old age, before he was fifty."[17] Indeed the state of the boy's
health appears as a constant source of anxiety in his mother's diary.
If "the others" were all she "could wish,"[18] her experience with her
first two sons nonetheless induced a certain guardedness toward the
third.

This impression is confirmed by Robert's daughter-biographer. Although she had little to say about her grandmother, her comments
and their paucity are both significant. One can infer from their scant-
iness that her father spoke little about his mother; she had died when
he was nine years old, and he was obviously loath to uncover a
wound which had never completely healed. His older sisters, who
had had a chance to know their mother longer and better, did not
live to an advanced enough age to pass on an oral tradition to an
inquisitive granddaughter. Her remark, then, that "intimate records" showed Lady Salisbury "possessed of deep religious faith,
strong feelings and warm enthusiasms; but their outward expression
must have been severely restrained"[19]—this remark should be read as
an indication that Robert had not grasped his mother's fund of feeling.

Still more, it suggests his unwillingness to intrude upon her private world: the nurture he had received had not led him to covet her
emotional resources; he had in fact acquired a modest portion of his
own. Rather what he had needed was assurance that she would remain intact. The "feebleness of animal energies" which plagued him
throughout his boyhood,[20] though he suffered from no specific
organic ailment, served as an outward and visible sign of his anxious
state. And between the ages of four and nine, the sensitive child sustained a series of shocks that confirmed the grimmest of forebodings.

The sequence of events proceeded as follows. When Robert was
four years old, his mother gave birth to another child, her fourth son.
Such a pregnancy and birth is a common enough, though trying, occurrence in childhood. What happened the following year, on the
other hand, was gruesome in the extreme. One of the wings of Hatfield, the family's ancestral residence, was destroyed by fire, and

17. Cecil, *Marquis of Salisbury*, I: 8. There has been no recent study of Salisbury
that supersedes his daughter's biography. The treatments by A. L. Kennedy, *Salisbury,
1830–1903: Portrait of a Statesman* (London: John Murray, 1953) and Robert Taylor,
Lord Salisbury (London: Allen Lane, 1975) are disappointingly thin.
18. Oman, *The Gascoyne Heiress*, August 30, 1834, p. 134.
19. Cecil, *Marquis of Salisbury*, I: 7.
20. Ibid., I: 11.

Robert's paternal grandmother was burned alive inside.[21] Then at the age of six Robert was sent to board at a local preparatory school, which he likened to "existence among devils," ever afterward maintaining that children were unready to be separated from home at so early an age. The final and most appalling loss in this succession of blows was the death of Robert's mother before the boy was ten years old.[22]

Little wonder he was frightened and dejected. Anxiety and depression went hand in hand: fearful of abandonment, he stood by helplessly as that very fear became a living nightmare. No action of his own could stay the sentence which had been pronounced against him. And failure on so grand a scale brought disillusionment: he could never imagine that what he did would be of much consequence. The best he could manage was to hold on to whatever earlier memories of comfort remained with him.

Instead of obtaining consolation from his father, Robert found his surviving parent unresponsive. "Never," Robert's daughter later commented, "were two men of the same blood more hopelessly antagonistic in all their tastes and interests."[23] Whereas the Duke of Devonshire kept his son the Marquess of Hartington close by him in an effort to heal the wound caused by the death of the boy's mother, Lord Robert Cecil's father made no similar attempt. On the contrary he pushed his child into the rough and tumble of public school life at Eton. Since Robert was then merely a younger son who, despite the family's position, would have to make his own way, his father may have reasoned that the boy should not be coddled. He urged his son to intellectual and physical exertion which together might make a man of him. At first Robert advanced rapidly in his schoolwork, only to find himself in class with boys two or three years older than himself. The merciless bullying he then endured at the unreformed school so undermined his health and his studies that at last when he was fifteen his father removed him from that noxious environment.[24]

Following his departure from Eton, Robert led a carefully circumscribed life; two tranquil years were spent at home before he went to Christ Church, Oxford, where he left few traces, but apparently was not molested and may even have met a few congenial associates. It was not till he had taken his degree and was attempting to read for

21. For an account of the tragedy, see Oman, *The Gascoyne Heiress*, November 27, 1835, pp. 184–186.
22. Cecil, *Marquis of Salisbury*, I: 2, 9.
23. Ibid., I: 49–50.
24. Ibid., I: 10–18.

the bar that his physical and emotional health gave way. "His nervous system had completely broken down, and there were besides threatenings of organic mischief."[25] Only with some difficulty was his father convinced of the seriousness of his son's condition and persuaded of the advisability of a long sea voyage, which included extended stays in South Africa, Australia, and New Zealand. Fourteen months later, as the time for his return approached, Robert took up again the unnerving subject of his future career. When Bismarck had found himself in a comparable quandary, he had disdainfully rejected the usual occupations as not offering him immediate dominance. Although Robert Cecil similarly considered "all modes of life ... equally uninviting," unlike Bismarck, he was convinced of his own "inaptitude for gaining personal influence."[26] His lack of hopefulness and self-deprecation had left him world-weary at the age of twenty-two.

How did he find his way out of this miasma of discouragement? There was no clear turning point, no dramatic encounter or conversion, that transformed his sense of self and endowed him with a confidence hitherto unknown. Rather through religious and marital experiences he gradually took heart. That religion should figure prominently in the biography of Robert Cecil, as well as of Gladstone and Bismarck, is not surprising: it was the lingua franca of mid-nineteenth-century emotional and moral expression. But its very prevalence may obscure the nuances of meaning and feeling among individual believers. Gladstone's religiosity suffused his being, acting as an integrating force which cemented private relationships, shaped his political style, and justified his purpose. For Bismarck the deity was also experienced as intensely personal, not, however, as a commanding presence whose work must be done, but as one that enhanced his own powers to undertake and complete the tasks he assigned himself. Yet for both Gladstone and Bismarck their religious sensibility foreshortened the distance between their inner and outer worlds, helping them make manifest, without embarrassment or self-consciousness, their long-standing convictions about themselves.

Robert Cecil's religious feeling was of another sort, private, yet at the same time impersonal. For him religion was the realm of "unsolved mystery." With an uncharacteristic rejection of intellectual scrutiny, which itself betrayed his emotional involvement in religious

25. Ibid., I: 25.
26. Lord Robert Cecil to the Marquess of Salisbury, September 2, 1852, quoted in ibid., I: 36–37.

certainty, he refused "to tolerate any ... attempt to subject God's action to the analysis of human reason."[27] "The dilemma which he postulated between the power and love of God on the one hand and the tragedy of the world's evil on the other was to him absolute, admitting of no issue but a confession of incomprehension."[28] Nor did he find assurance of redemption in religious faith; though the sinner might repent, Robert believed he could never know whether or not he had been restored to grace.

What, then, gave his religion its dynamic force? According to his daughter, "the doctrine of the Incarnation and the Gospel story read in the light of its revelation ... stood at the centre of his creed."[29] "He worshipped Christ,—not the Christ-type or the Christ-ideal or the 'Divine revealed in the human.' The vision ... was to the end apprehended with all the direct simplicity of childhood."[30] The reference to "simplicity" and "childhood" suggests that Robert had retained from his earliest years a reservoir of trust which even his heartrending losses had not entirely depleted.

In his late teens Robert's religious concerns had formed a bond between him and his elder married sister Lady Blanche Balfour.[31] In his mid-twenties they strengthened his attachment to Georgina Alderson, whom he had the good fortune to marry in 1857.[32] His intention to make Miss Alderson his wife had met with paternal opposition on the grounds that marrying someone financially ill-provided would insure a penurious future. Robert, however, had not been dissuaded: he had made it abundantly clear, in writing to his father, that he would brook no interference in his marital choice: "I am exceedingly sorry that my adherence to this marriage should cause you annoyance: but my conviction that I am right is too strong for me to give it up: and it is *my* happiness, not yours, that is at stake."[33] In this matter, at least, determination overcame diffidence.

27. Ibid., I: 113. See also Paul Smith, ed., *Lord Salisbury on Politics*, pp. 15–17.
28. Cecil, *Marquis of Salisbury*, I: 117–118.
29. Ibid., I: 119.
30. Ibid., I: 114.
31. Ibid., I: 17–18.
32. For Gladstone's appreciation of Miss Alderson, see H. C. G. Matthew, ed., *The Gladstone Diaries*, V: *1855–1860* (Oxford: Clarendon Press, 1978), May 14, 1856, p. 133.
33. Lord Robert Cecil to the Marquess of Salisbury, November 27, 1856, quoted in Cecil, *Marquis of Salisbury*, I: 59 (emphasis in the original). The vicissitudes of the relations between father and son are suggested by Lord Rosebery's diary entry for September 3, 1865: "Mrs. Disraeli said that she had been present at the reconciliation between Lord Robert Cecil and Lord Salisbury which took place within the last year." Quoted in Marquess of Crewe, *Lord Rosebery* (London: John Murray, 1931), I: 31.

Georgina offered him emotional support which he had not known before, devotion which assured him of his worthiness and alleviated his continual despondency. His domestic happiness, however, remained circumscribed: marriage did not enlarge his sympathies; human drama failed to stir his curiosity. Just as he relied on his wife's charm and vivacity to maintain their social relations, so too he depended on her insight and compassion in forming judgments of those they encountered together.[34] Yet at least through religion and marriage he had now taken possession of a standing-ground that could be called his own.

■

When Robert Cecil had canvassed the possible careers open to him, his first choice, which he had deemed impractical, had been to enter the House of Commons. In 1853, however, his cousin, the Marquess of Exeter, offered to use the preponderant family influence to secure his uncontested election at Stamford. Robert Cecil was to represent that borough until his elevation to the House of Lords at his father's death, his elder brother having predeceased the second Marquess of Salisbury. During this period, his criticisms of the Conservative party leadership, and in particular his breach with Disraeli, incensed his father. And indeed the older man had reason to be distressed by the passionate temper his son displayed.

It was as an outcast that Robert Cecil liked to picture himself. "In after years he used to declare that, in the House, he had been an Ishmaelite,—his hand against every man and every man's hand against him."[35] His daughter may be correct in suggesting that he exaggerated; but invective and sarcasm—and a frequently violent tone—in fact marked his style of disputation. Still more, the figure of Ishmael, cast out by his father Abraham, conveyed Robert's own sense of personal menace. This vulnerability helps explain his deep involvement in the American Civil War. In his enthusiasm for the Confederate side—for those driven to rebellion to protect liberties which he considered rightfully theirs—he refused to abandon hope.

---

34. Cecil, *Marquis of Salisbury*, I: 52–69. For lively descriptions of Lord and Lady Salisbury and family life at Hatfield, see Viscountess Milner, *My Picture Gallery, 1886–1901* (London: John Murray, 1951), pp. 79–85, and Viscount Cecil of Chelwood, *All the Way* (London: Hodder and Stoughton, 1949), ch. 1. See also Kenneth Rose, *The Later Cecils* (London: Weidenfeld and Nicolson, 1975). For insightful comments on the relationship between Lord and Lady Salisbury, see Lady Frances Balfour, *Ne Obliviscaris* (London: Hodder and Stoughton, 1930), I: 340–341.

35. Cecil, *Marquis of Salisbury*, I: 123, 38–52, 70–98.

And as an insurrection he deemed legitimate was being crushed, he himself verged on collapse:

> There were moments when the nervous strain upon him became so great as to seriously alarm his wife for his health, if not for his reason. He took to walking in his sleep, and she used to recall her alarm when, on waking one night, she saw him standing at the wide open window of a second-floor bedroom, fast asleep, but in a state of strong excitement and preparing to resist forcibly some dreamt-of-intrusion of enemies—presumably Federal soldiers or revolutionary mob leaders. She recorded that never in her knowledge of him did he suffer from such extremes of depression and nervous misery as at that time.[36]

Recovery came rapidly: the apprehensiveness diminished, though it never disappeared, and the violence subsided. Unlike Bismarck, in whom aggression and an overweening sense of superiority went hand in hand, Robert Cecil could not vent such feelings with impunity. Anger provoked "nerve storms" which depleted rather than nourished him. To put matters simply: at one and the same time Bismarck's angry hunger derived from and served to defend against his deepest psychic hurt. In contrast, Robert Cecil's fury reopened old wounds: to a child's mind the losses he had sustained bore witness to the destruction he had wrought—in short, anger itself was frightening. This contrast, rather than differences (or similarities) of neurotic traits, is crucial in delineating Bismarck and Salisbury's relations with their co-workers.

Paradoxically enough, the very guardedness of Robert Cecil's contact with the outside world facilitated his recovery. If self-control proved an inadequate barrier against temper, avoidance reduced the demand for that kind of control. Space served as a buffer to keep the external world from impinging painfully on his inner world. Where Bismarck required distance to make music of his own, the third Marquess of Salisbury was to find that it enabled him to play in harmony with others.

II. Emotional Surrogates

How did Salisbury shape political cohesion? It was clear from the start that if he were ever to become a commanding figure, the struggle would have to be transformed into his own type of battle. He could deploy his troops only in set positions: for the most part, movement was beyond his strategic capacity. On the level of tactics, he

36. Ibid., I: 170.

was similarly ill-equipped to give day-by-day reassurance. Both Gladstone and Bismarck, with mixed results, relied on others to buttress
or sustain the political relationships they had created. Salisbury did
so too; but more consistently than they, he sought surrogates to compensate for his deficiencies and inhibitions.

These surrogates had to bear the brunt of attacks upon the cabinet
and its policies, to act as lightning rods for the opposition's hostility,
and at the same time to spearhead assaults launched by their own
forces. Canalizing aggression through delimiting its object became
the nub of the matter. Employing it appropriately rather than letting
it feed on itself reduced to a minimum the damage which aggression
entailed. By the same token, success in this regard provided personal
reassurance all around.

■

Resignation from office, accompanied by hard-hitting attacks on
one's former chiefs, is not the usual path to party leadership. And
when, on the death of his father in April 1868, Robert Cecil had
inherited the title of Marquess of Salisbury and entered the House of
Lords, the road to preeminence through influence and mastery in the
Commons was forever blocked. Yet in retrospect it is the advantages
of this elevation that stand out. Though Salisbury expressed sorrow
at leaving the House of Commons, his daughter doubted whether
someone of his febrile temperament would ever have been able to
dominate that body.[37] Furthermore, he was spared the necessity of
fighting a contested election; the borough from which he had been
returned unopposed since 1853 was disenfranchised in 1868 in accordance with the Reform Bill of the preceding year. Finally, with Salisbury and Disraeli in different houses, friction between the two might
be reduced—and a reconciliation was essential to Salisbury's political career.

The reconciliation, however, had not progressed very far by 1874,
when Disraeli was again called upon to form a government; only
with the greatest difficulty did a variety of intermediaries and then
the prime minister-designate himself convince Salisbury that his virtue would be safe in such a government.[38] Eventually he agreed to
accept the India Office. But he increasingly became involved in foreign policy, first, on special assignment in Constantinople and later
as foreign secretary. Here Salisbury found not only his proper field of

37. Ibid., I: 297.
38. Ibid., II: 40-51.

action, where his talent for hardheaded analysis and his preference for stability were at a premium, but a meeting ground that brought him and his chief into close and harmonious contact which lasted until they left office together in 1880.[39]

Disraeli had gone to the House of Lords in 1876 with the title of Earl of Beaconsfield, designating Sir Stafford Northcote as leader in the House of Commons. When Beaconsfield died in 1881, it was natural for Salisbury to take charge of the Conservatives in the upper house; but with Northcote still in command in the lower chamber, the naming of a single party leader remained in suspense. Not until June 1885, when the queen asked Salisbury to form a ministry, was that issue definitively settled. Even then Salisbury had reason to be uncertain of his position. In large measure he had won the leadership by default, Northcote's inadequacies and infirmities having made him generally unacceptable. In addition, he assumed office on an interim basis: Gladstone's government had been defeated, but because the new electoral registers mandated by the Redistribution Bill of 1885 were still incomplete, Parliament could not be dissolved. The ambiguities of this situation were compounded by confusion over Irish policy, both within the cabinet and in the wider political world. When the election in December produced a new House of Commons in which Liberal strength was equal to that of the Conservatives and Irish Nationalists combined, Salisbury felt a sense of relief. In writing to a colleague he commented: "I am feverishly anxious to be out. Internally as well as externally our position as a Government is intolerable."[40]

With the formation of Gladstone's Home Rule ministry in late January 1886, the Irish miasma began to lift. When the Liberal chief

39. For a firstrate discussion of Salisbury's conduct of foreign policy in the late 1870s, see ibid., II: 76–383.

40. Lord Salisbury to the Earl of Carnarvon, January 3, 1886, quoted in ibid., III: 283–284. For a provocative account of Salisbury's first government, see A. B. Cooke and John Vincent, *The Governing Passion: Cabinet Government and Party Politics in Britain, 1885–1886* (Brighton: Harvester Press, 1974), pp. 61–83. See also the perceptive and wide-ranging study by Peter Marsh, *The Discipline of Popular Government: Lord Salisbury's Domestic Statecraft, 1881–1902* (Hassocks, Sussex: Harvester Press, 1978). For information and detail on the government's Irish policy, see Arthur Hardinge, *The Life of Henry Howard Molyneux Herbert, Fourth Earl of Carnarvon 1831–1890* (London: Oxford University Press, 1925), III: 160–216, and A. B. Cooke and J. R. Vincent, eds., "Ireland and party politics, 1885-7: an unpublished Conservative memoir," *Irish Historical Studies* 16, no. 62 (September 1968): 154–172, 16, no. 63 (March 1969): 321–338, 16, no. 64 (September 1969): 446–471. See also the masterly account by L. P. Curtis, Jr., *Coercion and Conciliation in Ireland, 1880–1892: A Study in Conservative Unionism* (Princeton, N.J.: Princeton University Press, 1963), pp. 15–95.

had finally made his intentions sufficiently precise to convince the Marquess of Hartington, leader of the Whigs, not to join the government—and in the next two months had proved sufficiently stubborn to induce Joseph Chamberlain, leader of the Radicals, to hand in his resignation—Salisbury found himself in a situation strikingly similar to what he had devoutly wished for in 1866: Gladstone's readiness to contemplate, and even to undertake, the overhaul of existing political institutions had finally driven the Whigs to abandon him. Though Hartington and Chamberlain had led their followers into the opposition lobby, thereby defeating Gladstone's Home Rule bill and bringing down his government, Salisbury could not count on this Liberal fissure becoming a permanent feature of the political landscape. And after the election of July 1886, the Liberal Unionists, as those who opposed Home Rule were called, held the balance. As the prospective prime minister, Salisbury now had a rallying cry, but he had not yet consolidated his forces.

Certainly Gladstone's espousal of the Irish cause had acted as a stimulant to Salisbury himself. In withstanding so drastic an innovation, he was able to set his own course on a conveniently fixed point. With the substitution of Home Rule for electoral Reform, but with the same arch villain, he could revert to his stance of the mid-1860s. Still more, he now felt free to make claims on the loyalty and support of those he began to gather around him, claims he had been loath to press during his first ministry. Only a great cause, he had argued in 1867, could reconcile independent and high-minded men to accept "so largely the responsibility for other men's acts and thoughts." Though he himself remained steadfast, eschewing the devious example of Derby and Disraeli, he could not be sure whether his own determination would continue to strike a responsive chord. Provisionally, at least, he could rely on Hartington; but Chamberlain was an unknown quantity. His Radical past and his penchant for novel combinations disquieted Salisbury and suggested that the conservative prime minister-designate could not count on opposition alone to cement the disparate anti-Home Rule groups.[41] To consolidate that majority the rallying cry must take on a dynamic tone and not merely sound the note of stubborn resistance.

41. "The Conservative Surrender" in Paul Smith, ed., *Lord Salisbury on Politics*, p. 271. For indications of Salisbury's concern about Chamberlain, see Memorandum by Queen Victoria, May 19, 1886, in George Earle Buckle, ed., *The Letters of Queen Victoria*, 3rd Series (London: John Murray, 1930–1932), I: 132; Salisbury to Queen Victoria, British Cabinet Papers, Cab. 41/20/23, August 5, 1886. For Chamberlain's

When Salisbury formed his second ministry in July 1886, he selected Lord Randolph Churchill to be both chancellor of the exchequer and leader in the House of Commons—in effect, to serve as his surrogate. Though most observers regarded as risky the appointment of the young and explosive Churchill to so prominent a place, few were surprised. Within the space of six years, Churchill had acquired an unprecedented position in the Commons. As chief spokesman of the so-called Fourth party, Churchill had launched repeated attacks on Gladstone and his government. He had probed the prime minister's weak spots, political and personal, and demonstrated an unrivaled ability to nettle the older man and so lead him into an undignified display of temper. At the same time Churchill's debating triumphs added ammunition to the campaign he was conducting against the Conservative leader in the House of Commons, Sir Stafford Northcote. On this second front Churchill's victory was complete: he made Northcote's retirement from leadership in the Commons a condition for entering Salisbury's interim ministry in 1885, and Salisbury reluctantly gave way. Northcote went to the House of Lords, and Sir Michael Hicks Beach took the posts of leader in the House of Commons and chancellor of the exchequer. When in the following year, Salisbury decided that Hicks Beach would be more useful as Irish secretary, the choice of Churchill to fill the positions Beach had occupied seemed to impose itself. As Hartington remarked: "R. Churchill is certainly a dangerous experiment; but as he would in any case have been the real Leader, or have influenced the Leader, it may be better that he should have the responsibility as well as the power."[42]

---

own views, see the letter from him to Hartington, August 1, 1886, quoted in Joseph Chamberlain, *A Political Memoir 1880–1892*, edited from the original manuscript by C. H. D. Howard (London: Batchwork Press, 1953), pp. 229–230; see also J. L. Garvin, *The Life of Joseph Chamberlain*, II: *Disruption and Combat, 1885–1895* (London: Macmillan and Co., 1933), pp. 263–269, and Peter Davis, "The Liberal Unionist Party and the Irish Policy of Lord Salisbury's Government, 1886–1892," *The Historical Journal* 18 (March 1975), 85–104.

42. Hartington to Goschen, August 1, 1886, quoted in Arthur D. Elliot, *The Life of George Joachim Goschen, First Viscount Goschen 1831–1907* (London: Longmans, Green, and Co., 1911), II: 101. For an appreciation of Churchill's behavior by a close associate of Gladstone, see Dudley W. R. Bahlman, ed., *The Diary of Sir Edward Walter Hamilton 1880–1885* (Oxford: Clarendon Press, 1972), I, November 2, 1881, p. 181. Churchill's biography by his son, although eminently readable, is peppered with errors: Winston S. Churchill, *Lord Randolph Churchill*, new edition (London: Odhams Press, 1951); see also Lord Rosebery, *Lord Randolph Churchill* (London: Arthur L. Humphreys, 1906), and Robert Rhodes James, *Lord Randolph Churchill* (London: Weidenfeld and Nicolson, 1959). R. F. Foster's *Lord Randolph Churchill: A*

Though Churchill might make Hartington uneasy, he had the esteem and confidence of Joseph Chamberlain. And it was precisely his relationship to Chamberlain that made him both attractive and dangerous to the Conservatives. He alone could act as a link between his party colleagues and the erstwhile Radical leader. Yet their common impatience with conventional party politics carried the threat of joint action between them toward a new alignment. Thus, while Churchill's personal force seemed to answer the requirements of the situation, it needed to be controlled and directed. If not, he would have to be disarmed.

And what of Salisbury? What were his hopes and expectations for this young lord who could neither be excluded nor ignored? By 1886 Salisbury had had enough experience of Churchill's waywardness and spoiled behavior to be apprehensive. Writing to a friend during the Sudan crisis in 1884, he had compared Churchill to the Madhi: "The Madhi pretends to be half mad, and is very sane in reality; Randolph occupies exactly the converse position."[43] During the Caretaker ministry, Churchill had shown himself sensitive and petulant, prone to take offense at the least slight, and ready to threaten resignation in order to have his own way. True to his reluctance to enter into personal contact with his colleagues, Salisbury had resorted to a steady correspondence with Churchill and by a combination of wit and tact had tried to soothe the young man's constantly frayed nerves. Even this private diplomacy had not entirely succeeded in keeping Churchill on the rails; at the time the ministry finally fell, he was once again on the verge of resigning. Certainly

---

Political Life (Oxford: Clarendon Press, 1981) appeared too late to be used for this study. For further assessments of Churchill's rise to prominence and selection as leader of the House of Commons and chancellor of the exchequer, see Cecil, *Marquis of Salisbury*, III: 138–139, 309–316; Andrew Lang, *Life, Letters, and Diaries of Sir Stafford Northcote, First Earl of Iddesleigh* (Edinburgh and London: William Blackwood and Sons, 1890), II: 185–215; Lady Victoria Hicks Beach, *Life of Sir Michael Hicks Beach, Earl St. Aldwyn* (London: Macmillan and Co., 1932), I: 209–276; Alfred E. Gathorne-Hardy, ed., *Gathorne-Hardy, First Earl of Cranbrook: A Memoir* (London, Longmans, Green, and Co., 1910), II, Diary, July 23, 1886–August 2, 1886, pp. 253–258; Harold E. Gorst, *The Fourth Party* (London: Smith, Elder, and Co., 1906). For Lord John Manners's firsthand narrative of the making of Salisbury's first ministry, see Charles Whibley, *Lord John Manners and His Friends* (Edinburgh and London: William Blackwood and Sons, 1925), II: 307–313. The newly published Nancy E. Johnson, ed., *The Diary of Gathorne Hardy, later Lord Cranbrook, 1866–1892: Political Selections* (Oxford: Clarendon Press, 1981), does not alter the account given here.

43. Salisbury to Lady John Manners, May 1884, quoted in Cecil, *Marquis of Salisbury*, III: 88.

such a relationship must have been a strain on Salisbury, and was a high price to pay for Churchill's dramatic performances in the House of Commons.[44]

The informal tone of the correspondence suggests, however, that the relationship was not merely a political burden which Salisbury shouldered with distaste. The tolerant way in which he encouraged Churchill to vent his feelings points to Salisbury's own empathy with the younger man.[45] For Churchill could and did reveal emotions that echoed the annoyance and resentment Salisbury had felt two decades earlier. Though the ideological commitments of the two were often poles apart, their stances of embattled independence were comparable. To be sure, Salisbury had always been cautious in expressing such feelings or in acting on them; yet he guessed at a distant fellowship in Churchill. Thus while he maintained a respectful demeanor toward the older generation of Tory leaders and grieved over Northcote's displacement, he did not rebuke Churchill for his impatience and thinly veiled contempt.

In the short parliamentary session of September 1886, the newly installed leader conducted himself adroitly and won high marks from even those most skeptical of his elevation. Yet scarcely had the House adjourned before he began to interfere in the work of his colleagues. His interventions were so varied, ranging over all aspects of government affairs, that it is impossible to discern a fixed purpose in his behavior. The first to suffer from his intrusiveness was Salisbury himself. While the prime minister sought to aid his foreign secretary in charting a course through the Bulgarian maze, Churchill embarked on an Eastern policy of his own, leaving European diplomats in a state of bewilderment. Then, in turn, Churchill quarreled with the three most influential ministers who sat in the Commons and who had been his most loyal supporters, Sir Michael Hicks Beach, W. H. Smith, and Lord George Hamilton. Intermittently but sharply he criticized Beach's performance in Ireland, and by insisting on reductions in military spending, he came into conflict with Smith at the

44. For Salisbury's relations with Churchill during his first ministry, see ibid., III: 125–164, 262–292; George Earle Buckle, ed., *The Letters of Queen Victoria*, 2nd Series (London: John Murray, 1926–1928), III, Salisbury to Queen Victoria, July 20, 1885, pp. 688–689; British Cabinet Papers, Cab. 41/19/49, August 11, 1885, and Cab. 41/-20/1, January 17, 1886; Winston Churchill, *Lord Randolph Churchill*, pp. 192–220.

45. See, for example, the letter from Lady Frances Balfour to Gerald Balfour, undated [late December 1886 or early January 1887]: "Arthur was surprised when I told him Uncle Robert had said to me 'In many ways he had found Randolph very attractive.' " Lady Frances Balfour, *Ne Obliviscaris*, II: 76.

War Office and Hamilton at the Admiralty. In short, when his attacks on the common enemy were in abeyance, he started assaulting his own colleagues.[46]

Almost from the beginning, then, the cabinet, in Salisbury's words, was "not a happy family."[47] Churchill found the source of this unhappiness in his colleagues' refusal to contemplate the "constructive" legislation he was advocating. Alone amidst a group of unrepentant Tories, he pitied himself for the constant and wearying struggle he was forced to wage.[48] The other ministers viewed the situation in similarly personal terms. For them the difficulty lay in Churchill's unwillingness "to yield his opinion, or mould it so as to cooperate with his colleagues."[49] As Smith remarked, if Churchill was "in a Government, he must be Chief, Supreme, a Bismarck."[50] It was Churchill's Bismarckian behavior, his determination to lead the orchestra in playing music he chose, rather than any single issue, that threatened to disrupt the British cabinet. By virtue of his office the prime minister bore the responsibility for curbing this demonic force and defining what was acceptable conduct between colleagues. When Lord Cranbrook, lord president of the council, wrote to Salisbury at the end of November, he spoke for others besides himself:

> It is indeed to you I look to harmonise our views and bring about liberty of action. You must forgive me for saying you have too much self-renunciation for a Prime Minister, and that you have rights which you forgo in guiding our deliberations. . . . My great desire is that we should not fall to pieces. . . . The position requires your distinct lead and your just self-assertion.

46. For the most detailed account of Churchill's activity from August 1886 to January 1887, see Winston Churchill, *Lord Randolph Churchill*, pp. 438–585. For Churchill's interventions in foreign affairs, see Cecil, *Marquis of Salisbury*, III: 318–322; *The Letters of Queen Victoria*, 3rd Series, I, Salisbury to Queen Victoria, September 7, 1886, pp. 201–203, and Salisbury to Queen Victoria, September 22, 1886, pp. 211–212; C. J. Lowe, *Salisbury and the Mediterranean, 1886–1896* (London: Routledge and Kegan Paul, 1965), pp. 1–8. For his quarrels with his Commons colleagues, see Lord George Hamilton, *Parliamentary Reminiscences and Reflections, 1886–1906* (London: John Murray, 1922), pp. 28–45; Viscount Chilston, *W. H. Smith* (London: Routledge and Kegan Paul, 1965), pp. 92–111.

47. *The Letters of Queen Victoria*, 3rd Series, I, Queen Victoria quoting Salisbury in her journal, December 16, 1886, p. 229; see also Queen Victoria to Salisbury, November 25, 1886, pp. 224–226, and Salisbury to Queen Victoria, November 26, 1886, pp. 226–227.

48. Churchill to Salisbury, November 6, 1886, quoted in Winston Churchill, *Lord Randolph Churchill*, p. 564.

49. Gathorne-Hardy, ed., *Cranbrook*, II, Diary, December 25, 1886, p. 270.

50. W. H. Smith to Balfour, December 23, 1886, quoted in Chilston, *W. H. Smith*, p. 227.

Salisbury was loath to accept this responsibility. His answer to Cranbrook was scarcely adequate:

> What you call my "self-renunciation" is merely an effort to deal with an abnormal, and very difficult, state of things. It arises from the peculiarities of Churchill. . . . He is wholly out of sympathy with the rest of the Cabinet: and being besides of a wayward and headstrong disposition, he is far from mitigating his resistance by the method of it. As his office of Leader of the House gives him a claim to be heard on every question, the machine is moving along with the utmost friction both in home and foreign affairs. My self-renunciation is only an attempt—a vain attempt—to pour oil upon the creaking and groaning machine.

How could the prime minister's self-renunciation have solved the problem which in the next paragraph he defined as "leading an orchestra in which the first fiddle" played "one tune and everybody else," including himself, wished "to play another"?[51] Though Salisbury was anxious to avoid a direct confrontation with Churchill, he was equally worried that the ministry would not survive in its current state. In November, when contention was at its height, he brought his nephew Arthur Balfour into the cabinet. Balfour himself noted his role as counterpoise to Churchill and then added: "But this I say, not as rating myself high (Heaven knows!), but as rating the rest of my colleagues from this point of view, low."[52] Yet until Salisbury was assured of his colleagues' complicity, and not merely their encouragement, he was hesitant to act. Churchill's attack on Smith a few weeks later offered a perfect opportunity: by resolutely defending the war minister's position, Salisbury could be firmness incarnate while denying any personal animus.

That the end should have come so suddenly and completely took everyone by surprise. Prepared, at last, to resist Churchill's attempts to dictate policy, Salisbury did not anticipate that the younger man would cut short the struggle by offering his resignation. Though Churchill had used such tactics before to get his own way, this time Salisbury proffered no concessions and held out no compromise. When the chancellor of the exchequer wrote on December 20 that unless Smith's budget requests were reduced, he must be allowed to retire from the government, Salisbury, after waiting two days, granted that permission. Instead of prevailing once again as he had

51. Gathorne-Hardy, ed., *Cranbrook*, II, Cranbrook to Salisbury, November 23, 1886, pp. 264–265, and Salisbury to Cranbrook, November 26, 1886, pp. 265–266.
52. Balfour to Salisbury, November 17, 1886, quoted in Blanche E. C. Dugdale, *Arthur James Balfour, First Earl of Balfour* (London: Hutchinson and Co., 1936), I: 118.

expected, Churchill found himself abandoned; much to his chagrin, few of his former colleagues—and no one of the first rank—gave him signs of continued friendly sentiments.[53]

Though relieved that Churchill was gone, Salisbury and his colleagues did not experience a sense of deliverance. When Churchill had been in the government, they had felt threatened by the hostile and subversive agent in their midst. Their conflict with him had made them personally more vulnerable, and in their exposed state they reacted with alarm to the news of his resignation. Beach, who might well have tried to reconcile Salisbury and Churchill if he had imagined that the latter intended to resign, proposed that the cabinet itself relinquish office.[54] Salisbury in fact made overtures to Lord Hartington, with the suggestion that the Liberal Unionist peer form a ministry. Hartington refused to take office; but his chief lieutenant, George Goschen, joined the Conservative cabinet in Churchill's old post as chancellor of the exchequer.[55] With Goschen's adhesion and W. H. Smith's appointment to the leadership of the House, the acute phase of the political crisis had been surmounted, and Salisbury could resume his efforts at cementing emotional ties between himself and his badly shaken colleagues.

■

It was not until early March that the reshuffling of the cabinet personnel was finally complete. Just as the public was learning of Churchill's resignation, Beach informed Salisbury that he could not go on much longer as chief secretary for Ireland. His eyesight was rapidly deteriorating under the administrative and parliamentary burdens of his office, which was certainly the most strenuous in the government. Salisbury despaired of finding a suitable replacement and urged the Irish secretary to stay on.[56] By early March, however, when Beach actually resigned, Salisbury was prepared with the name

53. For the most detailed account of Churchill's resignation, see Winston Churchill, *Lord Randolph Churchill*, pp. 557–586. See also Robert Rhodes James, *Lord Randolph Churchill*, pp. 281–315, and Lord George Hamilton, *Reminiscences and Reflections, 1886–1906*, pp. 40–53.

54. For Beach's reaction, see Lady Victoria Hicks Beach, *Sir Michael Hicks Beach*, I: 300–302. Cranbrook appears to have been less upset than his colleagues, but he was only indirectly involved in the resignation crisis: Gathorne-Hardy, ed., *Cranbrook*, II, Diary, December 29, 1886, p. 270.

55. Cecil, *Marquis of Salisbury*, III: 334–339; Memorandum by Sir Henry Wolff in Winston Churchill, *Lord Randolph Churchill*, pp. 796–808; Elliot, *Goschen*, II: 102–114; Thomas J. Spinner, Jr., *George Joachim Goschen: The Transformation of a Victorian Liberal* (Cambridge: Cambridge University Press, 1973), pp. 130–134.

56. Lady Victoria Hicks Beach, *Sir Michael Hicks Beach*, I: 300–316.

of Arthur Balfour. The appointment of someone so lacking in experience (and apparently in mettle too) was greeted by British politicians with surprise and concern lest Ireland once again undermine the health of its chief official. The Irish MPs gleefully asked: "We have killed Forster, we have blinded Beach. What shall we do to Balfour?"[57]

The fact that until his appointment as Irish secretary, Balfour had demonstrated little commitment to public affairs simply added to the sense of astonishment. Even as late as 1884, when Salisbury was asked what he thought his nephew "had most at heart, politics or philosophy, he replied without hesitation, philosophy!"[58] While recognizing that Balfour's inclinations led him toward Cambridge rather than Westminster, Salisbury had carefully steered him in the latter direction. Not only had he successfully urged the younger man to enter Parliament—in 1874 Balfour was elected in a constituency where the Cecil influence was considerable—but he took him to the Congress of Berlin as his private secretary. In the 1880 parliament, as an intermittent member of Lord Randolph Churchill's fourth party, Balfour began to make his presence felt. His main concern, however, was to act as his uncle's eyes and ears in the lower house: he watched vigilantly Churchill's growing prominence in the Commons and in the Conservative party organization, offering Salisbury advice that bespoke his solicitude for the older man's authority. Nor was loyalty to his uncle simply repayment for past or future favors; it was the guiding force, the emotional impulse, at the center of Balfour's own political activities.[59]

Yet he did not wear his heart upon his sleeve. Far from it: he was invariably described as languid, and he assiduously cultivated a reserved and distant manner. He detested the display of emotion, not through coldness or want of feeling, but through fear: "fundamentally he was afraid of it—it was one of the few things of which he was afraid—and this coloured his reception of it in other people on all ordinary occasions."[60] And it was Balfour's need to protect the realm of feeling, to wall off a special sphere immune to the onslaught

57. Dugdale, *Balfour*, I: 126; for a slightly different version, see Cecil, *Marquis of Salisbury*, III: 347.

58. Lady Frances Balfour, *Ne Obliviscaris*, I: 422.

59. For accounts of Balfour's early political career, see Arthur James Balfour, *Chapters of Autobiography* (London: Cassell and Co., 1930), pp. 84–222; Dugdale, *Balfour*, I: 35–125; Kenneth Young, *Arthur James Balfour* (London: G. Bell and Sons, 1963), pp. 61–102; Sydney H. Zebel, *Balfour: A Political Biography* (Cambridge: Cambridge University Press, 1973), pp. 14–59. The most recent biography is Max Egremont, *Balfour: A Life of Arthur James Balfour* (London: Collins, 1980).

60. Dugdale, *Balfour*, I: 34.

of reason, that shaped his early philosophical work. That sphere he demarcated as ineffable and inexpressible.

Where Salisbury had erected a rough-hewn bulwark, both religious and intellectual, against his own despondency, his nephew's defensive strategy was more complex and involuted. To be sure, they wrote in different genres; Salisbury chose political articles, while Balfour labored on a treatise entitled *The Defence of Philosophic Doubt*, which was published in 1879. Whereas the emotional currents were not far below the surface in Salisbury's writings, passion was expunged from Balfour's dry analysis. Still, the young philosopher acknowledged that his work had been prompted by the hope that the results would buttress his profoundest beliefs.[61] In brief, by criticizing the philosophical assumptions of science, by demonstrating that those assumptions were not themselves susceptible to scientific verification, he arrived at the practical conclusion that religion was "no worse off than science in the matter of proof."[62] Freed from the necessity of providing a logical defense of religion, he could safely make a confession of faith:

> I and an indefinite number of other persons, if we contemplate Religion and Science as unproved systems of belief standing side by side, feel a practical need for both; and if this need is, in the case of those few and fragmentary scientific truths by which we regulate our animal actions, of an especially imperious and indestructible character—on the other hand, the need for religious truth, rooted as it is in the loftiest region of our moral nature, is one from which we would not, if we could, be freed.[63]

Thus by indirection Balfour skillfully defended the sanctity of his religious sensibility.

When viewed in the context of his early affective development, Balfour's emotional stance—a combination of personal reserve and abiding faith—gains in substance and depth. He began a fragmentary autobiographical account by denying any memory of the first eight years of his life, from 1848 to 1856. On the following page he confessed to a single recollection, one which he would have gladly put out of mind and which he hoped would not "be regarded as representative of the forgotten residue."[64] Yet the incident was from so crucial a point in his life, just before the death of his father, who for the

61. Arthur James Balfour, *A Defence of Philosophic Doubt*, new edition (London: Hodder and Stoughton, 1920), pp. 313-314. See also John David Root, "The Philosophical and Religious Thought of Arthur James Balfour (1848-1930)," *The Journal of British Studies* 19 (Spring 1980): 120-141.
62. Balfour, *A Defence of Philosophic Doubt*, p. 319.
63. Ibid., p. 320.
64. Balfour, *Chapters of Autobiography*, p. 3.

better part of two years had been seriously ill with tuberculosis, that one must disregard his wish.

> My "Uncle Charlie" Balfour ... took us children out for a sail in the roadstead. A squall struck the boat; it heeled over, and blue water began pouring into the well. I do not know whether we were in any serious peril, and I do not remember what the other children did. For myself, I lost no time in climbing on to the seat, where I incontinently burst into tears, weeping copiously till the situation was restored. So far as I remember, little or nothing was *said* by my elders about this inglorious exhibition, but I was left in no doubt as to what was *thought*; and the impression left was indelible.[65]

Though he could recall nothing of his father's death, the memory of his mishap at sea was pregnant with the impending loss that struck the family. Still more, it suggested not only Balfour's own terror but the uneasiness his feelings provoked in the adults around him. The experience and the lesson it taught were undoubtedly repeated, as his mother (Salisbury's sister), exhausted and distraught, lay ill after her husband's death: the boy's emotions were a burden both to himself and to her. To protect his mother, he had learned, the expression of feeling must be severely curbed.

Balfour left no doubt that she was the primary influence in his life, and members of the family noted how he came to resemble her. A description of her, before her husband became ill, underlines their affinities:

> In Blanche there is such a wonderful power of command and duty that to know her slightly you would think she was a healthy-minded, happy wife, a mother of children, doing all the good she could, and consequently at peace with God and man. But you never could suspect the intense funds of feeling, dashing and flashing and bursting and melting and tearing her at times to pieces. And she looks so quiet, and pure.... She is a glorious character.[66]

Though her health was shattered by years of childbearing—nine children in eleven years—and nursing her husband, up to the very time of her death in 1872 at the age of forty-seven, she "did not allow weakness or pain to interfere with the single remaining purpose of her existence—the training of her children."[67]

The warmth of her eldest son's response is suggested by an inci-

65. Ibid., p. 2 (emphasis in the original).
66. Lady Victoria Talbot to Lady Waterford, January 4, 1854, quoted in Dugdale, *Balfour*, I: 17.
67. Ibid., I: 17.

dent she recounted shortly after taking up this task: "Last night proverbs as usual. Arthur the questioner. He put himself astride my lap and gave his question: 'Can you tell me why I love you so much?' "[68] She did not record her answer. Balfour's later remarks that she was "amusing" and "brilliant" are obviously incomplete.[69] He might have pointed to his religious conviction, not only as evidence of shared faith, but as testimony to the quality of his bond to his mother. When he spoke of God, he meant:

> a God whom men can love, a God to whom men can pray, who takes sides, who has purposes and preferences, whose attributes, howsoever conceived, leave unimpaired the possibility of a personal relation between Himself and those whom He has created.[70]

His mother's belief in a personal deity was accepted by Balfour because her behavior confirmed the meaningfulness of that belief. In the setting she provided, Balfour could imagine God, not as a force he might control, but as an utterly reliable and interested presence.

But how could a child who had discovered self-restraint as a way of protecting the one he loved furnish the necessary clues to the emotional vicissitudes of his own life? Not unexpectedly the delicacy of Balfour's health, for which no organic cause was discovered, came to the rescue. Though he might feel debilitated by the lethargy and languor that frequently seized him, such attacks were undoubtedly accompanied by a relaxation of discipline and increased personal attention. Illness as a means of provoking sympathy and gaining adult companionship figured prominently in his first years at school.[71] Even when he was appointed Irish secretary, he had not yet abandoned the semiinvalid's attitude of passive importunity, the expectation that fortitude tinged with martyrdom would preserve emotional attachments.

For such a silent appeal to be effective, Balfour needed an audience. And that he always had. Though he remained a bachelor, never able to fill the void left by the loss of his mother and the death of May Lyttelton, the woman he had intended to marry, he was anything but a hermit. Unlike his uncle Salisbury, Balfour enjoyed entertaining, sparkled in company, and in the 1870s earned the title "King Arthur." While his manner could be aloof and even arrogant, his elegant and long-legged form exerted an undeniable charm on

68. Undated letter by Lady Blanche Balfour, quoted in ibid., I: 18.
69. Balfour, *Chapters of Autobiography*, pp. 10, 18.
70. Arthur James Balfour, *Theism and Humanism* (London: Hodder and Stoughton, 1915), p. 21.
71. Balfour, *Chapters of Autobiography*, pp. 5–6, and Dugdale, *Balfour*, I: 21–23.

women.[72] And he evidently appreciated the affection of the varied and lively group with which he surrounded himself.

At first glance the bond between Salisbury and his nephew reminds one of the Bismarcks, father and son. In both cases the older man turned to a close family member whose gratitude and loyalty could be counted on to buttress his political position. Yet as one examines these two relations more closely, it becomes clear that they bore little resemblance to one another. Where the German chancellor regarded his son as an emanation of himself without a voice of his own, Salisbury not only acknowledged that Balfour was a free agent, but consistently supported his nephew's efforts to stake out a place for himself. And it was Balfour's independent bearing, coupled, to be sure, with an unruffled demeanor which was the polar opposite of Herbert Bismarck's abrasive and brutal deportment, that elicited admiration and sympathy and facilitated mutual accommodation within the cabinet.

That Salisbury should have treated Balfour, eighteen years his junior, with courtesy and respect is not surprising. Toward his own children, his daughter commented, his manners, "whether he spoke in jest or in earnest, were unfailingly polished: 'My father always treats me as if I were an ambassador,' was the murmured reflection of a youth in his teens, 'and I *do* like it.' "[73] But good breeding alone does not account for Salisbury's ability to nurture his nephew's self-confidence. Balfour himself, in describing an incident in the mid-1860s that had left an indelible impression, revealed how much—apparently without conscious effort—his uncle had done for him:

> In itself it was nothing more than a chance conversation with my Uncle Robert . . . which sprang from nothing in particular, of which I remember no details. In what, then, lay its magic? Not surely in the fact that he said interesting things in a very interesting way, though this was part of the charm, but in the fact that he spoke as a man speaks to a man, and not as a man speaks to a boy. He permitted no flavour of patronage, no tactful manipulation of the subject-matter, to mar the impression of conversa-

72. On Balfour's relations with May Lyttelton, see ibid., I: 33–34. On his friendships, see Balfour, *Chapters of Autobiography*, pp. 223–234; Lucy Masterman, ed., *Mary Gladstone: Her Diaries and Letters* (London: Methuen and Co., 1930); Young, *Arthur James Balfour*, pp. 27–47. For a lively description of Balfour's personality and that of his mother by one of his friends, see Emma A. M. Asquith, Countess of Oxford and Asquith, *The Autobiography of Margot Asquith* (London: Thornton Butterworth, 1920–1922), I: 256–266. His niece portrayed the Balfour family circle: Blanche E. C. Dugdale, *Family Homespun* (London: John Murray, 1940), pp. 51–97.

73. Cecil, *Marquis of Salisbury*, III: 12 (emphasis in the original).

tional equality. If he asked a question it was not in the spirit of an examiner. If he gave information it was not in the spirit of a teacher. He assumed reciprocal comprehension; he looked for an intelligent response; and the result was a conversation whose effects on one of the speakers lasted long after its themes were forgotten by both.[74]

By the 1880s Balfour had long been an intimate in Salisbury's household: "his sympathetic wit, his delight in his uncle's verbal audacities and exact appreciation of what they stood for, put him into perfect touch with his company, while the challenge of his equal cultivation and lightning quickness of apprehension would rouse Lord Salisbury to a fuller exertion of his faculties."[75] But this very intimacy made Balfour fearful lest he forfeit his uncle's trust by a too rapid promotion up the political ladder. Though the dangers of the Irish post had the effect of muting charges of nepotism, Balfour's advancement had not been the reward for demonstrated prowess. Unlike Randolph Churchill, whose outstanding parliamentary success had won him a place in the government, Balfour could point to no comparable achievement. Indeed, he knew that his earlier performance as president of the Local Government Board, a post he had held during Salisbury's first ministry, had not been highly rated. Uncertain of his merit and his own political standing, at the start of his uncle's second ministry he had hesitated before accepting the secretaryship for Scotland:

> *Unless I can be of use* I do not wish to be mixed up in the formation of the new Government. One man has already written to me asking me to get him a place! Ludicrous as it is, seeing that I do not know that *my* services will be required in the new Administration, still no doubt his example will be followed. I feel no natural vocation for being a Great Man's Great Man, still less for being thought so.[76]

Only when Salisbury's eldest son had vouched for his father's confidence in and need for Balfour did he accept without further demur. Less than eight months later he again agreed when Salisbury asked him to take over as secretary of state for Ireland.

■

Balfour was in fact of great service to his uncle. He alone among the members of the cabinet carved out for himself a position as confi-

74. Balfour, *Chapters of Autobiography*, p. 22.
75. Cecil, *Marquis of Salisbury*, III: 24.
76. Balfour to Lady Frances Balfour, July 23, 1886, quoted in Dugdale, *Balfour*, I: 107 (emphasis in the original).

dant to the prime minister. The steadiness of Balfour's temper worked like a tonic for his uncle when the latter's spirits threatened to collapse.[77] Though the two were alike undemonstrative and reserved, the very fact that they had long since become accustomed to each other meant that their "continuous personal intercourse" was the emotional center of the cabinet.[78] In this sense their attachment resembled the bond between Gladstone and Granville. But Gladstone had found in Granville both a close friend and someone alive to the needs of others, who actively sought to reduce friction between his chief and their colleagues. Such personal diplomacy was not an undertaking congenial to a man of Balfour's cool detachment.

Though Balfour did not act as an emotional go-between, by his performance in Ireland, he set the tone for the entire cabinet. As he assumed his arduous assignment, iron seemed to enter his soul. With a determination and fearlessness which few had suspected he possessed, he managed to achieve a calm in that troubled island which for the better part of a decade had eluded his predecessors. It is not necessary to recount here his administrative activities, how his combination of suppressing disorder and attempting to ameliorate the conditions that he and his colleagues assumed lay at the root of Irish unrest, earned him not only the title "Bloody Balfour" but the respect of his adversaries. At no time did he expect to prevail by coercion alone:

> I shall be as relentless as Cromwell in enforcing obedience to the law, but, at the same time, I shall be as radical as any reformer in redressing grievances, and especially in removing every cause of complaint in regard to the land. It is on the twofold aspect of my policy that I rely for success. Hitherto English Governments ... have either been all for repression or all for reform. I am for both.[79]

Without the imaginative flair of Churchill, he accomplished the feat of both cutting a dramatic figure and accurately reflecting Conservative sentiment.

Once Irish matters were in the hands of a reliable co-worker who had acquired a stature of his own, the other members of the cabinet could turn to their individual administrative duties. Indeed in the

77. A case in point was the crisis produced by the discovery that the letters published by the *Times* accusing the Irish Nationalist leader Charles Stewart Parnell of condoning murder had been forged: see Curtis, *Coercion and Conciliation in Ireland*, pp. 289–290.

78. Cecil, *Marquis of Salisbury*, IV: 171.

79. Quoted in Curtis, *Coercion and Conciliation in Ireland*, p. 179. For the best discussion of Balfour's performance as chief secretary for Ireland, see ibid., pp. 174–410.

biographies and memoirs of cabinet members, the dominant impression is one of striving for administrative competence. And given Salisbury's aversion to personal contact and Balfour's example in handling Ireland, it is not surprising that such competence should have been the commonly shared goal and distinguishing feature of the ministry.[80] Though the prime minister's colleagues continued to seek his advice and counsel, he himself interfered as little as possible in affairs he considered to be outside his personal bailiwick. Instead he focused his attention on what most passionately engaged him, the business of his own department. In the cabinet reshuffle of January 1887, Salisbury had returned to the Foreign Office, combining that post with the prime ministership. When, in the Caretaker ministry, he had earlier held these two posts, the experiment had not been regarded favorably; his intense involvement in foreign affairs had been held partially responsible for his flaccid performance as prime minister. No such criticisms were voiced about the coupling of the two offices during the remainder of Salisbury's second ministry, and these were the years in which he most clearly demonstrated his masterly skill as foreign secretary.

If Balfour's feat in Ireland and the emphasis on management that it induced served to minimize interaction and friction, his performance in the House of Commons drew the cabinet together in a way that belies a depiction of it as simply a collection of administrators. The parliamentary situation confronting the Irish secretary was difficult indeed. Since 1880 the obstructive tactics of the Irish nationalist MPs had worked like a plague on government programs, devastating or crippling the legislative efforts of Liberals and Conservatives alike. Only in 1890 when Charles Stewart Parnell, disgraced by the exposure of his long-standing affair with Kitty O'Shea, refused to relinquish his position as Nationalist leader and thereby split his party, was the problem substantially eased. Through exhaustingly long sittings, Balfour served as beacon light for his cabinet and parliamentary colleagues; he provided the driving force that sustained and fortified members whose physical and emotional endurance was tried to the utmost.

A combination of lightning verbal assaults and an apparent invulnerability to personal abuse characterized Balfour's mode of operation and quickly earned him a commanding place in the House:

> If any member who had sat through a session or two of the Parliament of
> 1880 had fallen asleep in the library and had, on any night when the pres-

80. For a similar observation, see Cooke and Vincent, *The Governing Passion*, pp. 61–62.

ent House of Commons is sitting, returned to his old place, he would not know this still slim young gentleman who in Mr. Gladstone's Parliament was member for Hertford. . . . The dilettante stripling that used to lounge about the House, moved to . . . suffering the boredom of being interested when Lord Randolph Churchill was attacking somebody, has grown into the hardest-worked Minister of the Crown, the deviser and stern executor of an Irish policy as nearly Cromwellian as the prejudices of the nineteenth century will permit. . . .

In personal appearance and in manner no one could less resemble Cromwell than the present ruler of Ireland. To look at Mr. Balfour as he glides with undulous stride to his place in the House of Commons one would imagine rather he had just dropped in from an exercise on the guitar than from the pursuit of his grim game with the Nationalist forces in Ireland. His movements are of almost womanly grace and his face is fair to look upon. Even when making the bitterest retorts to the enemy opposite he preserves an outward bearing of almost deferential courtesy. Irish members may, if they please, use the bludgeon of Parliamentary conflict, for him the polished, lightly-poised rapier suffices for all occasions. The very contrast of his unruffled mien presented to furious onslaughts of excitable persons . . . adds to the bitterness of the wormwood and gall his presence on the Treasury bench mixes for Irish members. But if he is hated by the men some of whom he has put in prison, he is feared and, in some sense, respected. In him is recognized the most perfect living example of the mailed hand under the silken glove.[81]

Lord George Hamilton echoed this description in paying tribute to his colleague:

The history of the House of Commons for the next four years is really a record of Balfour's marvellous Parliamentary performances. How . . . he kept the whole Home Rule Party, even when officered by such giants as Parnell and Gladstone, first at bay and then in subjection, how in speech and tactics he beat them daily in every encounter they provoked, how he broke down lawlessness in Ireland, and in this achievement became the first man in Parliament, how he ridiculed and trampled underfoot as dung the foul personal allegations made against him, how his wonderful performance changed the malice and fury of the Irish members into first a feeling of respect and then of admiration and regard for his personality—these things are not written in the records of Parliament.[82]

81. Henry W. Lucy, *A Diary of the Salisbury Parliament, 1886–1892* (London: Cassell and Co., 1892), pp. 424–426. For other appreciations of Balfour's performance in the House of Commons, see *The Letters of Queen Victoria*, 3rd Series, I, W. H. Smith to Queen Victoria, September 16, 1887, p. 353; Extract from the Queen's Journal, February 7, 1890, p. 563; W. H. Smith to Queen Victoria, March 24, 1890, p. 588. See also John, Viscount Morley, *Recollections* (London: Macmillan and Co., 1917), I: 225–229.

82. Lord George Hamilton, *Reminiscences and Reflections, 1886–1906*, pp. 62–63.

As Balfour eased his colleagues' burdens, the other occupants of the front bench became emotionally involved in his parliamentary feats. Moved by the silent appeal of his unflinching attitude toward the kind of invective that had unmanned previous Irish secretaries, his colleagues watched the years of almost nightly combat leave their mark upon him:

> At the end of a fifth year this fighting habit tells upon a man. It is still possible to find Mr. Balfour's face lighted up by a swift gleam of an almost boyish smile. But when he sits on the Treasury bench in charge of a Government measure his face is both hardened and aged compared with the day when, amid doubtful smiles among friends and open jeers from enemies, he tripped up to the Treasury bench to take charge of Ireland.[83]

While Balfour himself commented that personal abuse had made his political fortune,[84] it had done so because his suffering had evoked, along with admiration and sympathy, a willingness to share his struggle. Hence he did not go into battle alone.

Without the help of W. H. Smith, Balfour, despite his parliamentary brilliance, would have been unable to secure the passage of essential Irish measures. When Smith had assumed the leadership of the House of Commons after Churchill's resignation, most observers regarded his appointment as a *pis aller,* as testimony to the weakness of the Conservative front bench in the lower house. It proved to be one of Salisbury's most successful moves. Though Smith was never an exciting speaker, his feats of endurance in remaining steadfastly in place to guide procedural and legislative proposals through enervating sessions transformed him into "a tower of strength to his colleagues and his party." W. H. Lucy, the parliamentary diarist, summed up the general view:

> Mr. Smith is no genius, but he is a man of business habits and is gifted with a certain shrewd insight into public affairs, which, in his position, is worth more than eloquence. He has a way of conciliating opposition and slipping through Government business not excelled by any of his more famous predecessors since the days of Peel. How astute in his management, and how considerable his personal influence, was not perceived till nearly a month ago he was obliged to take to his bed.

Indeed, Smith's health, rapidly deteriorating under the strain, caused his colleagues many anxious moments. Compelled by a sense of duty that was inordinately self-sacrificing, he stuck to his post until just before his death in 1891. Dubbed "Old Morality" because of his

---

83. Lucy, *Diary of the Salisbury Parliament,* p. 387.
84. Balfour to Margot Tennant, December 24, 1889, quoted in Young, *Balfour,* p. 109.

"utterance of common-places, and a disposition to cite little tags reminiscent of copybook ... literature," he could equally appropriately have been nicknamed "Old Reliable."[85] At his death, the succession to the leadership of the House naturally devolved on Balfour.

Smith had been the perfect complement to his dramatic and elegant successor. While Balfour had shouldered the main burden of offensive operations, Smith had made sure that aid was ready at hand. By their division of labor, the two had managed to keep emotion within bounds, Smith's tact reinforcing the restraint which Balfour's example inspired and which his exploits facilitated. Except for the ties between Salisbury and Balfour, the relationships between the other members of the cabinet had been respectful rather than close. Yet the harmonious atmosphere that had prevailed among them had provided precious emotional support for their individual endeavors.

No one valued the ensuing freedom "from quarrels among friends" more than Salisbury himself.[86] Responding to Lord George Hamilton's compliments on his management of the cabinet after the government's resignation in the wake of its defeat at the polls in 1892, Salisbury summed up his appreciation:

> I agree with you that the agreement and solidarity of our Cabinet have been quite remarkable—ever since Randolph left us. But I fear I cannot flatter myself that the cause is that which you are good enough to suppose. We have been fortunate in having had a very "straight" set of men; so that intrigue in the Cabinet was unknown.[87]

■

The implication was clear: personal preference or whim offered no excuse. Here one finds an ideal—and its observance—common to both Salisbury and Gladstone's cabinets: the encouragement of self-suppression and the belief that such selflessness was a sign of personal strength. Anthony Trollope captured this attitude in a letter he devised for the Duke of St. Bungay to write to another lofty peer and

85. Lucy, *Diary of the Salisbury Parliament*, pp. 416–418. For similar comments on Smith, see *The Letters of Queen Victoria*, 3rd Series, I, Salisbury to Queen Victoria, November 28, 1888, pp. 453–454, and Extract from the Queen's Journal, November 29, 1890, pp. 658–659; II, Extract from the Queen's Journal, October 6, 1891, p. 73, and Salisbury to Queen Victoria, October 7, 1891, p. 74; see also Gathorne-Hardy, ed., *Cranbrook*, II, Diary, January 12, 1889, pp. 300–301, and October 7, 1891, p. 326. The standard biography of Smith is Sir Herbert Maxwell, *Life and Times of the Right Honourable William Henry Smith, M.P.*, 2 vols. (Edinburgh and London: William Blackwood and Sons, 1893). For a more recent treatment, see Chilston, *W. H. Smith*.
86. Salisbury to McDonnell, August 26, 1892, quoted in Cecil, *Marquis of Salisbury*, IV: 407.
87. Salisbury to Lord George Hamilton, August 16, 1892, quoted in ibid., IV: 406.

former prime minister, the Duke of Omnium. Trying to convince the
sensitive and diffident Omnium that returning to office was his duty,
Trollope's other duke wrote:

> It is a work as to which such a one as you has no option. Of most of those
> who choose public life,—it may be said that were they not there, there
> would be others as serviceable. But when a man such as you has shown
> himself to be necessary, as long as health and age permits, he cannot re-
> cede without breach of manifest duty. The work to be done is so impor-
> tant, the numbers to be benefited are so great, that he cannot be justified
> in even remembering that he has a self.[88]

If Salisbury, for one, did not entirely forget that he had a self, the
restraint he exercised was nonetheless remarkable. Though this restraint derived from childhood hurt, rather than from the achievement of a theoretical and unattainable psychic maturity, one should
not on that account overlook the emotional resources it betokened.
Salisbury's early years had been bleak; but he had not found himself
totally bereft. The memory of nurture once bestowed lingered on,
and the trust thereby engendered eventually bore fruit. Salisbury's
determination and his diffidence—his angers and his fears—all testified to his wish to preserve that harvest. To that end he needed more
than self-control; he required tranquillity in the world around him.

Certainly Salisbury had little tolerance for friction, and for his
own peace of mind contention had to be kept at a distance. While he
might deem it noble to do battle against Gladstone and Home Rule,
strife among colleagues he found highly distasteful. With Irish policy
no longer a matter of cabinet dispute, in large measure due to Balfour's transforming it into administrative routine, Salisbury's position as prime minister was greatly eased. Though he never truly
enjoyed that office, in contrast to the foreign secretaryship, its burdens now become bearable. Neither Salisbury nor his nephew encouraged close attachments; yet the members of the cabinet learned
through their joint efforts to lend assistance to the man who served
them as both shield and sword that they could also depend on each
other. Thus among the Conservatives, the relative absence of both
discord and intense personal interaction—the low emotional tem-
perature—fostered mutual trust and reassurance.

Gladstone too had never wavered in his belief that colleagues
ought to band together and refrain from quarreling; at the very least
they should make every effort to keep differences within bounds. In-

88. Anthony Trollope, *The Duke's Children*, Oxford edition (London: Oxford
University Press, 1954), p. 171.

deed he conceived of politics as a form of discipline for holding self-seeking in check—his own and that of others. To that end he strove to accommodate his co-workers' firmly held convictions; to acknowledge what he regarded as the wellspring of self-esteem. At his best, then, Gladstone fostered an atmosphere of mutuality which encouraged the self-restraint indispensable to it.

The emotional bounty he had received as a child, coupled with the physical vulnerability of those who provided it, had made him alert to the damage his aggression might produce. He had long ago learned that scrupulousness served to safeguard those he loved. Still more, in his attempts to go beyond mere scrupulousness to a nurturing role, self-suppression remained an essential ingredient: an intrusive ego would have rendered such an attempt null and void.

Salisbury's judgment was far less sympathetic. During the struggle over the Second Reform Bill, he had accused Gladstone of self-seeking. The subsequent struggle over Home Rule would not have induced him to revise his opinion. In his view, the Liberal leader was guilty of self-deception: notwithstanding the sincerity of his beliefs, personal ambition drove him on. But even Salisbury might have been led to admit that Gladstone's was a curious form of self-seeking. In staking out a position for himself, the Liberal leader did not deprive others of their standing-ground. Instead of bullying his followers into subservience, he accepted with equanimity the severance of political ties.

Gladstone and Salisbury stood opposed. The one radiated confidence while the other remained encased in diffidence. Yet they inhabited the same emotional universe. For both of them an ingrained self-restraint marked their achievements as architects of political cohesion.

Chapter 5

Fabrication of a New "Authority Figure"

Power in Berlin at the End of the Century

What happened to those at the German political summit when their semidivine leader had been summarily ordered off stage and had taken his departure? How did they fabricate or accept a new authority figure who, pianissimo, replaced the fallen god? Before proceeding, it might be useful to restate briefly the argument up to now.

From the readiness with which those around Bismarck subordinated themselves to him, it was but a short step to deduce that his associates latched onto this colossus for their own psychological needs. Their fantasies or illusions of being necessary to him, not as mere tools but as indispensable adjuncts to his mission represented a tacit strategy for preserving a precarious sense of superiority—the strategy of replenishing self-esteem through the active incorporation of an authority figure. And as Bismarck lost his magic aura, as his political power was called into question by impending changes in the imperial succession, as his physical strength diminished and he came to rely almost exclusively on his son, his subordinates reacted with dread. The endemic infighting and nastiness of German political life became a personal threat that proved well-nigh intolerable. From this reconstruction of brittle relationships a crucial paradox remained: the apparent incongruity of psychological dependence on someone who provided so little personal reassurance and emotional support.

When, however, this paradox is viewed as a repetition or reenactment of tense and painful childhood experience, it disappears. In the earlier instance the needs of the child were so imperative that the relationship could not be severed, the child could not avoid accepting whatever tainted nourishment the mother had to offer. Though one might think a child would flee an unsatisfying mother, the psychological truth is otherwise. The infant clings to her for the simple reason that there is nothing else. The predisposition to submit again rather than to be cast adrift—indeed, the readiness to accept such a choice as the human condition—becomes firmly fixed. In such cases separation is hard to accomplish, and pseudoindependence, suffused with hostility, is prominent. Anger and rage, ostensibly directed toward breaking the tie, in fact serve as ways of maintaining it. In short, the Bismarckian paradox unravels as soon as one looks at the Iron Chancellor's symbolic function: his subordinates responded to him as if he were a "bad" mother.

"Bad" is, of course, an unacceptably vague term. What must be distinguished more precisely is the kind of maternal behavior that Bismarck—with the seduction of his power and the capriciousness of his favor—symbolically recreated. To judge from the biographies of the protagonists of the present study, Germany had its share of forceful mothers. Despite the convention of paternal dominance and maternal submissiveness, some women at least did not retreat into psychic numbness. Instead they determined to fulfill their own "masculine" strivings, made more intense by society's admiration for virility. To be sure they could do so only by indirection. The indirect means in question amounted to an appropriation of their sons. Male children served as surrogates, acting out unrealized maternal fantasies and providing compensation for the blows inflicted on their mothers. The possessiveness of such intrusive—or seductive—mothers was tantamount to rejection: they did not value their children as persons in their own right; they did not accord them the status of separate beings.

With mothering, once again, a starting point, one must chart a path through the vicissitudes of personal interaction to the establishment of a semblance of political cohesion.

I. A Haunted Gray Eminence

When Bismarck finally sent in his resignation on March 18, 1890—after William, through an aide, had demanded that the document be delivered forthwith—it was already clear that Herbert would not remain once his father had departed. Those intimate with the workings of the German Foreign Office could not fail to appreciate that the de facto directorship of the Wilhelmstrasse would pass to Friedrich von Holstein, privy councillor in the political department. For the next sixteen years, Holstein played a crucial role in German foreign policy. His contemporaries regarded him as a gray eminence who secretly wove the diplomatic threads. From the sinister undertones of this description historians have subsequently demurred, without, however, criticizing its substance.[1] Still more, it is apparent that in the first years after Bismarck's fall Holstein acted as a chief navigator, directing his superiors through the maelstrom of domestic as well as foreign affairs. The centrality of his position, the fact that he was the most important holdover from the Bismarckian regime, makes him the logical point of departure for assessing political relationships in the 1890s.

From the outset Holstein sought to avoid the limelight. According to his own account—his testimony is not corroborated elsewhere—he declined the state secretaryship of foreign affairs in 1890.[2] In that year he decided to refuse all promotion, and until near the very end of his career he held firmly to this resolve. By remaining in the shadows he protected himself against the exposure of either his sense of secret superiority or the painful self-doubt which it masked. He did not thereby forfeit real power. One might surmise that the position he had attained in 1890 would have buttressed his mental balance. This was not to be the case. The rupture with Bismarck, now complete and irrevocable, and the effort at emotional separation it entailed, proved a severe test of Holstein's equilibrium and necessitated a regrouping of his psychological defenses.

When the political connection between them snapped, Holstein ceased to fret over Bismarck's presumed mental and physical deterioration. Once the chancellor had resigned, he regained his luster in his former subordinate's eyes. Holstein no longer doubted Bismarck's latent power; he now lived in dread of a diabolical force which would wreak vengeance on its faithless underlings. Count Philipp zu Eulenburg-Hertefeld, the emperor's confidant, commented on the fear that haunted the Wilhelmstrasse and in particular its Gray Eminence:

1. For the most recent and thorough account of Holstein's political role, see Norman Rich, *Friedrich von Holstein: Politics and Diplomacy in the Era of Bismarck and Wilhelm II*, 2 vols. (Cambridge: Cambridge University Press, 1965).
2. Helmut Rogge, ed., *Friedrich von Holstein Lebensbekenntnis in Briefen an eine Frau* (Berlin: Ullstein, 1932), Holstein to Ida von Stülpnagel, January 5, 1895, p. 172.

I spent literally the whole day in the Foreign Office, which seems to me more and more like hell. Under old Bismarck one was disgusted by the terrified fluttering at the thought of Jupiter's approach, and the disagreeable capricious treatment of subordinates. But now the fear of "his" possible return ... dominates every councillor, secretary, understrapper.... My God, but Bismarck still has *that* crew under his coarse thumb!... Then there's Holstein, sitting like a ferret in the diplomatic cockroost, seeing spectres in every corner.[3]

For Holstein, Bismarck had lost none of his emotional significance. In repudiating his former chief, Holstein had exchanged a visible dominance for a frightening psychological presence which threatened to overwhelm him.

Fear of this sort, though it was considered pathological even by Holstein's contemporaries, is rarely without some foundation. And Bismarck provided his successors with ample reason for concern. The new chancellor, General Leo von Caprivi, had scarcely familiarized himself with his duties before Bismarck began what was to develop into a full-scale campaign against the government. In press interviews he discoursed freely on foreign policy, leaving little doubt that he considered those currently in charge less than adequately equipped for their posts. Nor did Bismarck restrict himself to personal declarations. By keeping in touch with followers of long standing—together they constituted the so-called Bismarck Fronde—he made his opinions reverberate in the political arena. Clearly, then, the emperor and his ministers faced a nerve-wracking task in finding an antidote to the fallen chancellor's venom. For Holstein this assignment gave a new coherence to his multiple endeavors.[4]

The first imperative was to keep Caprivi afloat. One need not recapitulate here the stormy political issues which threatened to drown the government or the trimming and tacking which managed to prolong its voyage. What should be stressed is the part played by the complex network of personal relations that Holstein pieced together

3. Memorandum by Philipp Eulenburg, quoted in Johannes Haller, *Aus dem Leben des Fürsten Philipp zu Eulenburg-Hertefeld* (Berlin: Gebrüder Paetel, 1924), trans. Ethel Colburn Mayne as *Philipp Eulenburg: The Kaiser's Friend* (New York: Alfred A. Knopf, 1930), I: 182–183.

4. For a brief summary of Bismarck's attacks on the government in 1890 and 1891, see J. Alden Nichols, *Germany After Bismarck: The Caprivi Era, 1890–1894* (Cambridge, Mass.: Harvard University Press, 1958), pp. 101–106. For a detailed account of his activities throughout the 1890s, see Hermann Hofmann, *Fürst Bismarck, 1890–1898*, 3 vols. (Stuttgart: Union Deutsche Verlagsgesellschaft, 1913–1914); see also Otto Gradenwitz, *Bismarcks letzter Kampf, 1888–1898* (Berlin: Verlag von Georg Stilke, 1924), pp. 195–272. For a recent description of Bismarck as patriotically motivated, see Wolfgang Stribrny, *Bismarck und die deutsche Politik nach seiner Entlassung, 1890–1898* (Paderborn: Ferdinand Schöningh, 1977).

and supervised with an obsessive and sometimes hysterical solicitude. To be sure, his exertions served to safeguard his own position. But it was the terror inspired by Bismarck which both drove him on and gave him confidence that his own advice would be welcomed and followed.

The new chancellor was himself a mere beginner in politics. Until 1882 he had had an honorable military career, marked by distinction during the war of 1870 and steady advancement thereafter. Then, abruptly, he had been transmuted into a vice-admiral and put in charge of the German navy. Six years later, with equal suddenness, he had brought this interlude to a close by resigning over William's interference in naval affairs. From the army command to which he had returned, the stubborn and strong-willed Caprivi found himself ordered into a major battle for which he had no prior training or experience.[5]

Nor could he turn to the man who took over as state secretary for foreign affairs, Baron Adolf Marschall von Bieberstein. An expert on jurisprudence and former state prosecutor, Marschall had been minister to Prussia from his native Baden. As the link between Berlin and Karlsruhe, his position had turned out to be crucial during the months before Bismarck's dismissal. In constant touch with Holstein, he had been privy to the day-by-day development of the conflict between chancellor and emperor. And it was Holstein who played the leading role in Marschall's subsequent appointment to Herbert Bismarck's post. The new state secretary's oratorical talents equipped him to lead the defense in the Reichstag against onslaughts from the Bismarckian forces; he in turn counted on Holstein to provide him ammunition. In short, if the Gray Eminence exercised a kind of thraldom over Caprivi and Marschall, it was not simply because as Bismarck claimed, "Among the blind of the Foreign Office ... the one-eyed man" was "king." Rather the fact that Bismarck lay in wait with such aphorisms compelled his successors to rely on the man he distinguished as the least incompetent among them.[6]

The second imperative, which followed logically from the first, was to assure that the emperor supported his own chancellor. This

5. For a biographical portrait of Caprivi, see Heinrich Otto Meisner, "Der Reichskanzler Caprivi: Eine Biographische Skizze," *Zeitschrift für die gesamte Staatswissenschaft* 3 (1955): 669–752. The best account of Caprivi's tenure in office is Nichols, *Germany After Bismarck*. For brief characterizations of all of Bismarck's successors, see Hugo Graf Lerchenfeld-Koefering, ed., *Erinnerungen und Denkwürdigkeiten von Hugo Graf Lerchenfeld-Koefering, 1843 bis 1925* (Berlin: E. S. Mittler, 1935), pp. 368–398.

6. On Marschall's relations with Holstein from the mid-1880s until 1897, see J. C. G. Röhl, *Germany Without Bismarck: The Crisis of Government in the Second Reich,*

assignment taxed Holstein to the utmost. As opposed to the stolid and predictable Caprivi and the pliable and self-effacing Marschall, William was volatility itself. He kept escaping from the fantasy role that Holstein had fabricated for him, and in so doing reduced Holstein to desperation.

Prior to Bismarck's dismissal, the Gray Eminence had repeatedly stressed the necessity of William's becoming a "political factor," and of his acquiring a "personal position" in addition to the one which was his birthright. Only then would Holstein permit himself to believe that Bismarck could be dispensed with and that the role he had played would no longer be essential to the Reich's well-being. Though Holstein never imagined that William would be a second Bismarck, he did hope that the young emperor would eclipse the Iron Chancellor—at least in the public eye.[7] His consistent concern that William back up Caprivi should not be construed, then, as a desire for a strong chancellor and hence an aversion to the so-called personal rule of the emperor.[8] Rather Holstein considered both a sturdy chancellor and a sturdy monarch as protective cover.

In consequence, what was of prime concern to Holstein were his own relations to William. Holstein's preference for the shadows was demonstrated in its starkest outline by the fact that only once, in November 1904, did the Gray Eminence actually meet the emperor.[9] And it was no easy matter to induce him to appear before His Majesty. Nor could Holstein substitute written communication for personal contact, simply adding William to the long list of diplomats and politicians with whom he carried on an extensive private corre-

---

1890–1900 (Berkeley and Los Angeles: University of California Press, 1967). On Marschall's performance as state secretary, see Lamar Cecil, *The German Diplomatic Service, 1871–1914* (Princeton, N.J.: Princeton University Press, 1976), pp. 260–281; see also Ludwig Raschdau, *Unter Bismarck und Caprivi: Erinnerungen eines deutschen Diplomaten aus den Jahren 1885–1894* (Berlin: E. S. Mittler, 1939), pp. 110–372. For excerpts from Marschall's reports to the Grand Duke of Baden on the chancellor crisis of 1890, see Gradenwitz, *Bismarcks letzter Kampf*, pp. 120–150. For Bismarck's remark, see Gerhard Ritter and Rudolf Stadelmann, eds., *Otto von Bismarck: Die gesammelten Werke*, IX: *Gespräche* (Berlin: Deutsche Verlagsgesellschaft, 1926), conversation with Poschinger, October 3–5, 1892, p. 255.

7. John C. G. Röhl, ed., *Philipp Eulenburgs Politische Korrespondenz*, I: *Von der Reichsgründung bis zum Neuen Kurs 1866–1891* (Boppard am Rhein: Harald Boldt Verlag, 1976), Holstein to Eulenburg, November 5, 1889, p. 365, and Holstein to Eulenburg, January 27, 1890, p. 422.

8. The expression is Erich Eyck's: *Das Persönliche Regiment Wilhelms II: Politische Geschichte des deutschen Kaiserreiches von 1890 bis 1914* (Erlenbach-Zürich: Eugen Rentsch Verlag, 1948). Eyck's line of argument was substantially adopted by Röhl, *Germany Without Bismarck*.

9. Rogge, ed., *Friedrich von Holstein*, Holstein to Ida von Stülpnagel, November 26, 1904, pp. 236–237.

spondence. The emperor had little taste for reading and writing. So Holstein was compelled to rely on a go-between. The appropriate intermediary was not hard to choose: Philipp Eulenburg. As soon as Holstein learned of Eulenburg's growing intimacy with the young prince, this apparently obscure secretary of the Prussian Legation in Munich began to receive personal letters from the Gray Eminence. Eulenburg quickly became the crucial link between Holstein and William, and until 1894 Holstein expressed himself as substantially satisfied thereby. With commendable fidelity Eulenburg passed on opinions and advice, duly acknowledging Holstein as the fount of wisdom. Along this wire William flashed his own message of appreciation:

> "I rely on H. and look on him as a tower of strength even though I do not know him personally. I am glad Caprivi relies on him so firmly. I am sorry not to know H. personally, but I have no wish to disturb his habits and force myself upon him. He has arranged his life after his own fashion. No doubt he has his own good reasons for it."[10]

In the same letter Eulenburg had reported the emperor's readiness to defend Holstein unto the last: "Anyone who attacks Holstein attacks me," was William's phrase. But the changeable young man did not remain fixed in that blessed state of mind. When *Kladderadatsch*, a satiric political journal published in Berlin, began a series of attacks on Holstein in December 1893, when the elaborate network of relationships with which he had defended himself against the Bismarckian nightmare came under assault, he found no emperor at his side. Where Holstein had expected that a combination of indirect prods and rebukes would keep William at the post he had assigned him, he now beheld the painful spectacle of a partial reconciliation between emperor and fallen chancellor—a reconciliation which in the end failed to lead to the dire consequences the Gray Eminence had foreseen. But in the meantime Holstein had occupied an exposed position. While the terror inspired by Bismarck never lost its grip on his own mind, it proved insufficient to induce others to come to the rescue of the stricken man.

For those around Holstein fear of Bismarck was eclipsed by a sadistic delight in watching the Gray Eminence squirm. He writhed and raged under the accurate shots that continued to assail him from *Kladderadatsch* until the end of April. In the form of a parody the

10. Norman Rich and M. H. Fisher, ed., *The Holstein Papers*, III: *Correspondence 1861–1896* (Cambridge: Cambridge University Press, 1961), Eulenburg quoting the emperor in a letter to Holstein, August 1, 1890, p. 354.

articles described a permanent card game being played in Berlin, where the participants concocted nefarious designs for redeploying friend and foe alike within the German diplomatic service. The disguises in which they slunk to their meetings merely served to make their identities unmistakable: Holstein, Eulenburg, and Holstein's closest associate in the Foreign Office, Alfred Kiderlen-Wächter. Apparently Holstein did not suspect that he had been betrayed by two denizens of the Wilhelmstrasse itself; yet it was clear that only those intimate with the workings of the Foreign Ministry could have given firing orders right on target. In his efforts to track down the traitors, who he presumed to be in Bismarck's camp, Holstein turned for help to his co-belligerent, Philipp Eulenburg.[11]

Unlike Holstein, Eulenburg soon discovered the identity of at least one of *Kladderadatsch's* informants. Without enlightening his comrades-in-arms, he proceeded to negotiate a separate peace. Though the attacks on Eulenburg were broken off, he did not immediately decamp. Instead, like an honest Iago, he let his distraught friend pour out his anger and hurt, all the while nourishing a secret contempt. In subsequently describing Holstein, Eulenburg struck again the note of scorn:

> Together with the shrewdness of his political ideas, the intensity of his desires and anxieties, there emerges a certain excess of feeling—which I might go so far as to call effeminate. Take it for all in all, undeniably a most interesting psychological type.

The pathology obviously fascinated Eulenburg:

> My friendship for this Holstein had two foundations. The highest admiration—not so much for his infinite craftiness as for his subtle intelligence, his eminent political and literary learning, his undeniable gift of divination; but more than this, the deepest compassion for that self-tormenting, evasive, even craven nature, subjected to the psychical sway of neurotic tendencies that were not to be denied by any observer.[12]

And what a chance for observation Eulenburg now enjoyed as a half-crazed Holstein struggled to unmask his enemies and prove his own valor!

11. For the most complete account of the Kladderadatsch affair, see Helmut Rogge, "Die Kladderadatschaffäre," *Historische Zeitschrift* 195 (August 1962): 90–130. For Philipp Eulenburg's summary of his own role, see Eulenburg to Kuno Moltke, June 15, 1895, Eulenburg Papers/35, pp. 433–438. See also Otto Hammann, *Der neue Kurs* (Berlin: Verlag von Reimar Hobbing, 1918), pp. 58–66; Raschdau, *Unter Bismarck und Caprivi*, pp. 320–326; Rich, *Holstein*, I: 403–415.

12. Philipp Eulenburg, "The Real Privy Councillor Fritz von Holstein," quoted in Haller, *Eulenburg*, II: 291, 294. Compare Eulenburg to Wilhelm II, February 27, 1896, Eulenburg Papers/40, pp. 101–107.

Convinced that legal action would simply produce more dirt without offering any guarantee that the malefactors would be punished, and disappointed by efforts to exert pressure on *Kladderadatsch* through unofficial channels, Holstein came to the conclusion that only one course remained: he must challenge personally those he assumed to be the instigators of the press attacks. He singled out Herbert Bismarck and on two occasions demanded explanations and statements from him. These were forthcoming, and Holstein was obliged to let his quarry go. Before he had found a suitable alternative candidate, the third "card-player," Kiderlen, entered the lists. In the early weeks of the *Kladderadatsch* campaign, Kiderlen, unlike Holstein, had found the descriptions of himself a source of amusement. When his reserves of humor were exhausted, he too issued a challenge; this time it was taken up, and Kiderlen fought a duel with the editor. Though he shot his man, the wound was neither fatal nor did it halt the press attacks.[13] By then Holstein had chosen his second target, Count Guido Henckel von Donnersmark, a member of the Bismarck Fronde. Once again the intended victim got away; Holstein had to accept as technically satisfactory statements which left his thirst for blood unslacked.[14] Yet with this last round he found his quietus; his performance had finally evoked a sign of approbation from the emperor.

Holstein had not anticipated that such a sign would be so long in coming. The preceding December he had counted on its imminent appearance to put an end to a torture which had in fact barely begun. To Eulenburg he had expressed his sense of urgency:

> I must say . . . that I don't think my patience will last long.
>
> If in my friendless existence I still have to see His Majesty looking on and smiling coldly while I am having filth thrown at me . . . then he cannot be surprised if in the near future I turn over my cards to someone else—anybody who wants them—and no longer take part in the little three-handed game that is vexing *Kladderadatsch*.
>
> It isn't the wretched attacks that annoy me. I am hurt by the attitude of His Majesty who doesn't lift a finger, but rather seems pleased when a lot of nastiness is unleashed.[15]

Only after Holstein had twice proved himself willing to defend his

13. On Kiderlen's role, see Ernst Jäckh, ed., *Kiderlen-Wächter der Staatsmann und Mensch: Briefwechsel und Nachlass* (Stuttgart: Deutsche Verlags-Anstalt, 1924), I: 96–99.

14. For Holstein's efforts to obtain satisfaction, see Holstein, *Correspondence 1861–1896*, pp. 461–473.

15. John C. G. Röhl, ed., *Philipp Eulenburgs Politische Korrespondenz*, II: *Im Brennpunkt der Regierungskrise 1892–1895* (Boppard Am Rhein: Harald Boldt Verlag, 1979), Holstein to Eulenburg, December 28, 1893, p. 1173.

honor in single combat did William cease being a passive spectator. When Eulenburg reported the second episode, the Emperor signaled his delight at the performance the Gray Eminence had put on:

> H.M. said after I had read him the telegram: "Bravo! that is my old Holstein! Plucky and won't stand any nonsense! He is now well out of it: a declaration from Herbert, one demanded of Henckel—who will now hang anything on him? Telegraph him immediately that I am *very* glad."[16]

If William's approval enabled Holstein to continue at his post, it did not erase the painful impression created by its long delay. The *Kladderadatsch* affair simply confirmed Holstein's deep-rooted distrust of those around him. It had shattered the desperate hope he had entertained that a common fear of Bismarck would allow him a free hand to spin his own fear-inspired political webs. And though both Eulenburg and William had been prepared to recognize his superiority, to bestow on him the code word "indispensable," it had a hollow ring when unaccompanied by any gesture of solidarity.[17]

In Holstein's eyes, the emperor's tardiness in offering support convicted William of "political adultery."[18] This was a serious charge indeed; it echoed accusations of "political bigamy" Holstein had leveled against Bismarck a half-decade earlier.[19] In both cases the imagery referred to marital infidelity, and it was as a betrayal of the most intimate sort that Holstein experienced the sadism of his associates. Now that he had proved his manhood, he was in a position to appreciate what Bismarck must have realized long ago—that in the world in which these two moved, manliness brought with it the menace of cuckoldry. Conformity to the demands of manhood had provided no release from torment: on the contrary, chancellor and councillor alike had found the reality of their haunting inner worlds confirmed.

II. An "Orphaned" William

> If only because the inferiority complex has become so popular, I will venture to entertain you here with a short digression. A historical personality of our own days . . . suffers from a defect in one of his limbs owing to an injury at the time of his birth. A very well-known contemporary writer

16. Holstein, *Correspondence 1861–1896*, Eulenburg to Holstein, April 5, 1894, p. 469 (emphasis in the original).

17. See, for example, Röhl, ed., *Philipp Eulenburgs Korrespondenz 1892–1895*, Eulenburg to Wilhelm II, January 23, 1894, pp. 1193–1196.

18. Ibid., Holstein to Eulenburg, March 22, 1894, p. 1264.

19. See, for example, Norman Rich and M. H. Fisher, eds., *The Holstein Papers*, I: *Memoirs* (Cambridge: Cambridge University Press, 1955), p. 128.

who is particularly fond of compiling the biographies of celebrities has dealt, among others, with the life of the man I am speaking of. Now in writing a biography it may well be difficult to suppress a need to plumb the psychological depths. For this reason our author has ventured on an attempt to erect the whole of the development of his hero's character on the sense of inferiority which must have been called up by his physical defect. In doing so, he has overlooked one small but not insignificant fact. It is usual for mothers whom Fate has presented with a child who is sickly or otherwise at a disadvantage to try to compensate him for his unfair handicap by a superabundance of love. In the instance before us, the proud mother behaved otherwise; she withdrew her love from the child on account of his infirmity. When he had grown up into a man of great power, he proved unambiguously by his actions that he had never forgiven his mother. When you consider the importance of a mother's love for the mental life of a child, you will no doubt make a tacit correction of the biographer's inferiority theory.[20]

Thus Sigmund Freud rebuked Emil Ludwig, underlining the crucial influence of the Empress Frederick—familiarly called Vicky—on her son, the future William II. Whether this transplanted English princess can be viewed as a characteristic Prusso-German mother is a thorny question. She always considered herself an Englishwoman and was so regarded in Prussia; she never forgot or was allowed to forget that her origins were different from and alien to those of the ruling house and the Prussian landowning class. Still, if blood lines have any relevance, which they don't, she could well be looked upon as German. Her mother, Queen Victoria, was predominantly of German stock, while her father, Prince Albert, came of the house of Coburg. More to the point, she grew up in a bilingual household in which German affairs were of consuming interest; subsequently as Prussian crown princess she found herself swept up in the nationalist fervor generated by three victorious wars.[21] In brief, the question allows no simple answer.

What is crucial here, and can safely be said, is that Vicky's experi-

20. Sigmund Freud, "Dissection of the Personality," in *New Introductory Lectures on Psycho-Analysis*, Standard Edition, trans. James Strachey (London: Hogarth Press, 1964), XXII: 66. As a further indication of the fascination William has exerted on psychoanalysts, see Heinz Kohut, "Thoughts on Narcissism and Narcissistic Rage," *The Psychoanalytic Study of the Child* 27 (1972): 372–373.

21. The most informative biography of the Empress Frederick is Egon Cesar, Count Corti, *Wenn ... Sendung und Schicksal einer Kaiserin* (Graz: Verlag Styria, 1954), trans. E. M. Hodgson as *The English Empress: A Study in the Relations between Queen Victoria and her Eldest Daughter, Empress Frederick of Germany* (London: Cassell and Co., 1957); see also E. F. Benson, *Queen Victoria's Daughters* (New York: D. Appleton-Century Co., 1938), and Daphne Bennett, *Vicky, Princess Royal of England and German Empress* (London: Collins and Harvill Press, 1971).

ence helps illuminate how noxious surroundings can pervert a hope-
ful and affectionate nature. Buffeted by psychological shocks when
still a very young wife and mother, she was particularly vulnerable
to the distrust and hostility she encountered in Berlin. It is this mental anguish—produced by the interplay of environment and personality—that must be taken into account. Only then can the simple
and harsh judgment Freud rendered be replaced by a more nuanced
assessment both of her behavior and of her relationship with her son.

The correspondence between the crown princess and her mother
sheds a retrospective light on the special pains which had been taken
in molding the high-strung and intelligent girl.[22] In that process her
father had played the leading role, and to him she felt permanently
indebted. That the prince consort should have sought in her, his eldest child, an intellectual and political disciple, she considered an
honor to be forever treasured. Her father remained the polestar in
her emotional life, the embodiment of ideal qualities and precepts, a
standard for her own behavior and that of others. What she "most
cared for in all the world was a word of praise or a look of satisfaction" from her "darling Papa"; she "used to feed on it for days."[23]

Rather than representing a breach with her mother, Vicky's devotion to Albert bore witness to the sturdiness of the earlier bond,
which was amply demonstrated in the correspondence between the
two women. Vicky was not fleeing her mother; her mother shared
and actively participated in her adoration of Albert. And whatever
jealousy the queen may have felt about the closeness between father
and daughter was muted by the delight with which she watched the
girl develop into "beloved Papa's child."[24] Thus to emulate her father became the surest way for the young Vicky to win the approval
of both her parents.

Having been nourished on Albert's liberal political principles,

22. Selections from the correspondence of the Empress Frederick were first pub-
lished in Sir Frederick Ponsonby, ed., *The Letters of the Empress Frederick* (London:
Macmillan and Co., 1929). The correspondence between mother and daughter has
been more extensively published in Roger Fulford, ed., *Dearest Child: Letters between
Queen Victoria and the Princess Royal 1858–1861* (London: Evans Brothers, 1964);
Roger Fulford, ed., *Dearest Mama: Letters between Queen Victoria and the Crown
Princess of Prussia 1861–1864* (London: Evans Brothers, 1968); Roger Fulford, ed.,
*Your Dear Letter: Private Correspondence of Queen Victoria and the Crown Princess of
Prussia 1865–1871* (London: Evans Brothers, 1971); Roger Fulford, ed., *Darling
Child: Private Correspondence of Queen Victoria and the Crown Princess of Prussia
1871–1879* (London: Evans Brothers, 1976).

23. Fulford, ed., *Your Dear Letter*, the Crown Princess to Queen Victoria, August
5, 1866, p. 86.

24. Fulford, ed., *Dearest Child*, Queen Victoria to the Princess Royal, April 27,
1859, p. 187.

Vicky had arrived in Prussia in 1858 as the bride of Prince Frederick William, with dreams that together they might transform the reactionary kingdom. The eventual nightmare—the ninety-nine day reign of her cancer-stricken husband in 1888—is well known. By then Vicky and Fritz had experienced thirty years of frustration and disappointment. The state of siege, both personal and political, had begun even before Bismarck's appointment as minister-president foreclosed the future. In the crown princess's correspondence one can trace oscillations in mood. Yet above all one is impressed by her resilience, her toughness, her refusal to admit defeat.

That resilience was tested to the utmost by the sudden death of her father in December 1861:

> I feel so discouraged at times. It is very wrong but it is human; all the efforts that I made for doing my duty here in this position, which is no easy one, were made in hopes of pleasing Papa.... I felt so full of determination and courage and high spirits....
>
> I am but beginning life and the unerring judgment on which I built with so much security and so much confidence for now and for the future is gone! Where shall I look to for advice? I am only 21 and things here wear a threatening aspect![25]

This loss was not the only one she suffered. Less than five years later death claimed her third son, Sigismund, the one who, in her mind at least, most closely resembled her adored "Papa." If the world had worn a "threatening aspect" when her father had died, it proved equally menacing when—in her own words—her "pride," her "joy," her "hope" was gone.[26]

The gall and wormwood she was forced to swallow daily in Berlin exacerbated her sense of injury. In the atmosphere in which she lived, her efforts to do good—to make reparation for anger and assuage guilt—were stillborn: "I feel that I am getting more savage against people every day which is very wrong I know and I don't observe that all the difficulties I have to encounter great and small do me any good whatever!"[27] The hostility she met with in her adopted land—the contrast between it and the respectful attention she had earlier been accustomed to—bore in upon her her own helplessness.

25. Fulford, ed., *Dearest Mama*, the Crown Princess to Queen Victoria, December 26, 1861, p. 29.

26. Fulford, ed., *Your Dear Letter*, the Crown Princess to Queen Victoria, June 19, 1866, p. 77.

27. Fulford, ed., *Dearest Child*, the Princess Royal to Queen Victoria, May 3, 1861, p. 329.

> We are behind the scenes and know why the right things are not done, and it is hard work to keep one's intellect clear enough to understand this net of petty intrigues and considerations in which we are caught and well nigh smothered. . . . Sometimes I do wish I could be a man just for a few days![28]

To her mother, Vicky reported the Prussian view of what women were made for: "to have stupid compliments and flattery paid them and to have children."[29] No wonder, then, that gasping for breath, she grasped onto her husband and her eldest son to validate her claim to figure as "beloved Papa's child."

Vicky's attitudes toward both her designated paladins bore a striking similarity. She expected of husband and of son the same fortitude which she herself felt compelled to demonstrate. More than that, she set the pace:

> I know what a responsibility I take upon myself in taking advantage of my husband's reliance on my judgment and in giving any advice as positively as I can.
>
> Until I find the person whose judgment I can feel greater confidence in than in my own, I shall go on with might and main trying to assist Fritz in pursuing the only road I consider right and safe.
>
> It is very disagreeable to me to be thought meddling and intriguing. Mixing in politics is not a ladies' profession. I should like to conciliate all parties and particularly to live in peace with all those by whom we are surrounded, whose affection I know I could gain if I sought it by having no opinion of my own. But I should not be a free-born Englishwoman . . . if I did not set all those things aside as minor considerations. I am very ambitious for the country, for Fritz and the children and so I am determined to brave all the rest![30]

With Bismarck ever on the alert for nefarious "petticoat influence," Fritz's attachment to his wife was widely interpreted as a lack of manliness.[31] Yet the harmony and understanding between the couple were not disturbed thereby. In the case of her son William, however, Vicky's intrusiveness was to prove their mutual undoing.

28. Ibid., the Princess Royal to Queen Victoria, March 30, 1860, p. 242. For Fritz's own experiences, see Heinrich Otto Meisner, ed., *Kaiser Friedrich III: Tagebücher von 1848-1866* (Leipzig: Verlag von K. F. Koehler, 1929).

29. Fulford, ed., *Dearest Child*, the Princess Royal to Queen Victoria, August 4, 1859, p. 205.

30. Fulford, ed., *Dearest Mama*, the Crown Princess to Queen Victoria, July 3, 1863, pp. 242-243. See also the Crown Princess to Queen Victoria, December 17, 1862, quoted in Corti, *The English Empress*, p. 100.

31. See, for example, Fulford, ed., *Dearest Child*, the Princess Royal to Queen Victoria, April 5, 1860, pp. 244-245.

Under constant assault, within and without, the young mother—
she was only eighteen when, in January 1859, she gave birth to
William—was scarcely in a position to offer her child the "superabundance of love" that Freud was to prescribe after the fact. But
she did not withdraw from him, as Freud implied. On the contrary
she was a devoted, indeed possessive, mother, who at the same time
had resolved not to spoil her son. The traces of her symbiotic tie to
her infant, which Queen Victoria described in Trollope's phrase as
"baby worship," never disappeared.[32] How could she have let him go
when she regarded his future success as both compensation and vin-
dication?

> The education of sons is an awful responsibility and a great anxiety and it
> is bitter indeed if they do not repay one for one's care and trouble—it
> makes me tremble when I think of my little William and the future![33]

The very difficulties under which Vicky and her husband labored
could only add to the burdens she placed on little William's shoul-
ders:

> Maybe I shall be able to instil our British feeling of independence into
> him, together with our broad English common sense—so rare on this side
> of the water; the Prussians will not hate me for that in the end—however
> jealous they may now be of my foreign influence over him and Fritz at
> present.[34]

Vicky refused to heed her mother's warning about the dangers of
"too great care, too much constant watching."[35] Her doubt whether
William would prove up to the mark simply sharpened her keenness
in "acting the policeman" to her son:

> Not one person in the house has as quick a perception of all the little
> failings that ought to be prevented from increasing, and my fear of their
> never being corrected made me perhaps see them in a stronger light than
> necessary, as my lively imagination dwelt on the consequences which
> might arise from them.[36]

Had Vicky felt safe herself, she might have grieved less over

32. See ibid., Queen Victoria to the Princess Royal, November 17, 1858, pp. 143–
144, and Queen Victoria to the Princess Royal, March 16, 1859, pp. 167–168.
33. Fulford, ed., *Dearest Mama*, the Crown Princess to Queen Victoria, December 29, 1861, p. 32.
34. Fulford, ed., *Your Dear Letter*, the Crown Princess to Queen Victoria, January 11, 1865, pp. 15–16.
35. Ibid., Queen Victoria to the Crown Princess, February 10, 1871, p. 319.
36. Ibid., the Crown Princess to Queen Victoria, December 10, 1866, p. 112.

William's celebrated withered arm. "Oh!" she exclaimed, "were dearest Papa here to appeal to on every question" she "would not care for two lame arms!" The more uncertain she became of her own (and her husband's) standing-ground, the more she clung to the idealized image of her father—and the more her son suffered by comparison:

> He is a dear promising child—lively and sweet-tempered and intelligent; it is a thousand pities he should be so afflicted; he would really be so pretty if it were not for that; it disfigures him so much, gives him something awkward in all his movements which is sad for a prince; though you know I would rather he was straight in mind than in body but I cannot help thinking of dear Papa who was perfect in both, and it is hard that it should be our eldest that has this misfortune.[37]

If Vicky was sympathetic to the suffering William endured at the hands of ignorant medical practitioners, she did not allow compassion to outweigh what was "necessary for his good"; it seemed "so cruel to torment the poor child, still it would be no kindness to save him inconvenience now at the expense of causing him much greater hereafter."[38] The same willingness to sacrifice the present for the future guided her choice of George Hinzpeter as tutor to the seven-year-old boy. Though the rigid asceticism of this "not very bright" nor socially polished man offered nothing to soothe or comfort a child, the crown princess thought she had found in him a trustworthy and methodical ally in counteracting William's defects.[39] With Hinzpeter standing watch, she allowed herself to hope that her son could navigate the critical "passage from childhood to manhood." It never occurred to her that her own relationship with William might not survive the process:

> I am happy to say that between him and me there is a bond of love and confidence, which I feel sure nothing can destroy.[40]

---

37. Ibid., the Crown Princess to Queen Victoria, May 31, 1865, p. 28, and the Crown Princess to Queen Victoria, May 17, 1865, p. 26.

38. Fulford, ed., *Dearest Mama*, the Crown Princess to Queen Victoria, April 28, 1863, pp. 203–204.

39. Fulford, ed., *Your Dear Letter*, the Crown Princess to Queen Victoria, August 17, 1866, p. 92; see also ibid., the Crown Princess to Queen Victoria, December 10, 1866, pp. 111–112.

40. Ponsonby, ed., *The Letters of the Empress Frederick*, the Crown Princess to Queen Victoria, January 28, 1871, pp. 119–120; see also ibid., the Crown Princess to Queen Victoria, September 1, 1874, pp. 135–136.

And what of William's feelings? How did he respond to his mother's intrusive concern? Only by examining his early hurts and vulnerabilities and the defensive strategies he adopted for coping with them can his portrait acquire coherence. To be sure, William is not an unknown character. Certain descriptive tags are commonplace—his mental instability, his alternation between grandiose poses and nervous prostration. But when these bits and pieces are lumped together without discrimination, all that emerges is a titillating collection of neurotic symptoms, to which William's notoriously hostile relations with his mother figure as an idiosyncratic addendum. In fact, his experience of his mother is the foundation for everything else. With that in position, priority and order can be assigned to prominent features of his personality.

The crown princess's running account of the deterioration of her relationship with her son, though scattered through her correspondence, is straightforward. The lament began quietly enough with accusations of neglect when William joined the military milieu in Potsdam.[41] Along with criticizing her son, she blamed his new associates. This pairing remained constant. In the mid-1880s, when a series of political differences separated parents and child, she held Bismarck responsible for the widening gulf between them. Both mother and father saw in their son a newly acquired instrument of their archenemy. Both responded to William's admiration for the Iron Chancellor by charging him with immaturity and condemning his political intelligence as worthless:

> He is not sharp enough or experienced enough to see through the system, nor through the people, and they do with him what they like.... The malady must take its course, and we must trust to later years and changed circumstances to cure him! Fritz takes it profoundly *au tragique,* whilst I try to be patient and do not lose courage![42]

Did she ever lose courage? After her husband's death her faith certainly wavered. It was only when widowhood made her subject to her son's authority that she tasted the full bitterness of mortification. Fritz had scarcely breathed his last before William showed himself

41. Fulford, ed., *Darling Child*, the Crown Princess to Queen Victoria, August 29, 1877, pp. 260–262. Among the biographies of William, the most helpful is Michael Balfour, *The Kaiser and His Times* (Boston: Houghton Mifflin Co., 1964). See also Tyler Whittle, *The Last Kaiser: A Biography of Wilhelm II, German Emperor and King of Prussia* (London: Heinemann, 1977), and Alan Palmer, *The Kaiser: Warlord of the Second Reich* (London: Weidenfeld and Nicolson, 1978).

42. Ponsonby, ed., *The Letters of the Empress Frederick*, the Crown Princess to Queen Victoria, April 22, 1887, pp. 214–215.

the master with a blatant disregard for the feelings of his grief-
stricken mother. Her recitation of the indignities she suffered at that
time and in the months following need not be repeated here; her
account of the bare facts has remained unchallenged. Of the motives
behind William's behavior she rarely spoke. For the most part she
stuck to her conviction that his mind had been poisoned against
her.[43] She preferred this explanation to believing that her firstborn
had rejected her on his own.

It was an explanation with which William himself might have
agreed—giving it, however, a different twist. What his mother labeled treason, he called duty.[44] In invoking duty, William was not
simply sounding a conventional and hollow note; for him duty stood
as the polar opposite of tender emotions. Such a dichotomy figures
prominently in William's account of his education at the hands of
Hinzpeter. By him, William claimed to have been taught "the big-
gest lesson a man can learn—to work and do his duty."[45] At the same
time as he expressed gratitude for such instruction, he deplored the
system by which it had been instilled:

> To me it seems that an education from which all joy is excluded is psycho-
> logically false. Joyless as the personality of this dry, pedantic man, with his
> gaunt meagre figure and parchment face, grown up in the shadows of Cal-
> vinism, was his educational system; joyless the youth through which I was
> guided by the "hard hand" of the "Spartan idealist."[46]

Yet William had accepted as valid the stern imperative thus decreed
(without, however, acquiring the requisite self-discipline): he must
aggressively subdue early and deep-seated yearnings. And it was this
imperative that gave substance to his formal explanation of his conduct.

Although William did not voice it with utter clarity, the same pre-
cept governed his emotional attachments to women—notably to his
wife, whose company he could endure only for short periods.[47] How

43. For the fullest account, which quotes amply from her correspondence, see
Corti, *The English Empress*, pp. 282–333.
44. Wilhelm II, *Aus meinem Leben* (Berlin and Leipzig: Verlag von K. F.
Koehler, 1927), translated as *My Early Life* (London: Methuen and Co., 1926), pp.
260–287; see also Wilhelm II, *Ereignisse und Gestalten* (Leipzig and Berlin: Verlag
von K. F. Koehler, 1922), trans. Thomas R. Ybarra as *The Kaiser's Memoirs* (New
York and London: Harper and Brothers, 1922), p. 12.
45. Wilhelm II, *My Early Life*, pp. 20–21.
46. Ibid., p. 19.
47. See, for example, Eulenburg to Holstein, August 4, 1890, Eulenburg Pa-
pers/12, pp. 519–520. For a description of William's behavior in private with his wife,
see Henry W. Fisher, *Private Lives of Kaiser William II and His Consort: Secret
History of the Court of Berlin*, 3 vols. (New York: J. R. Smith and Co., 1909).

did it come to exercise such sway? In his autobiography, William gave no direct account of maternal solicitude; instead he relied on Hinzpeter to depict a relationship he himself hesitated to recall:

> Hinzpeter told me that during the first ten years of her married life she was wrapped up in the husband she adored; she was the wife rather than the mother, and her three elder children had a stern upbringing. Not till the Crown Prince began to be drawn into politics did she turn to her nurseries. Her younger children, who knew her as a tender mother, idolised her.[48]

William's choice of informant was inappropriate. Hinzpeter had not belonged to the household when his future charge was a small child. He had not had occasion to observe the crown princess's intense involvement in her nurseries from the very start. One may surmise, however, that William experienced his mother's intrusiveness and appropriation as rejection—rejection of him as a person in his own right—crippled arm and all. If his mother had not in fact abandoned him, her son nonetheless feared she might do so. This was the message which his obsessive worrying about her as a seven-year old was apparently trying to convey:

> Master Willy said to me this morning in French "when I am grown up you will be dead. Is that not so?" Very civil was it not? He is continually occupied with when I shall die, and who will be his Mama.[49]

The more he longed for his mother, the more susceptible he was to such fear, and the only way he could conquer his fear was by repressing this longing.

What is striking in William's account of his father's death is the stark contrast he drew between his parents. Where he described his father as affectionate and eager to welcome him, he portrayed his mother as prepared, indeed determined, to prevent her son from gaining access to the dying man. Still worse, William blamed his mother for his father's death, ascribing it to her blind adherence to the British specialist called in to treat the crown prince:

> When one considers that, if the English doctor had not intervened my

---

48. Wilhelm II, *My Early Life*, p. 5. The Crown Princess viewed herself as the one sorely tried: "My three eldest children give me a good bit of anxiety in one way and another, and are not all I could wish . . . but my three youngest make up for all by their sweet womanly natures." Crown Princess Frederick to Marie Dönhoff, December 8, 1881, Bülow Papers/167.

49. Fulford, ed., *Your Dear Letter*, the Crown Princess to Queen Victoria, December 7, 1866, p. 111.

father would in all human probability have been saved, one will understand how it was that I took every opportunity of opposing the most violent resistance to this ostrich policy. That my mother could not free
herself from the Englishman's authority, even when the facts had become
fully clear to everyone else, had the worst possibly effect upon my relations with her.[50]

This stress on maternal guilt (which, from the medical standpoint,
was nonsense) allowed William to avoid fully recognizing his disappointment with his father—a disappointment he had hinted at earlier in his autobiography.[51] At the same time it was a confession of
helplessness: his mother, not he, exercised control over emotional sustenance.

What, then, was the nature of the salvation young William found
in his relationship with his grandfather, William I, king of Prussia
and first German emperor? Stressing their mutual affection—a
theme he repeated in describing his relations with his two grand-
mothers[52]—the younger William assigned his grandfather a predomi-
nant place in his emotional life:

> I looked up to him with awe, and was devotedly attached to him. He was
> in return a kind, friendly and loving grandfather, and in this spirit he kept
> his eye on the whole of my youthful development; above all, in my mili-
> tary career I owe everything to him. He had always the greatest confi-
> dence in me. . . .
>   Often . . . I was invited to dine alone with my grandfather. . . . I shall
> never forget those intimate hours together; all the love of a grandfather
> for his grandson was then fully expressed.[53]

Thus in speaking of himself as his grandfather's successor, William
was referring to more than the brevity of his own father's reign.[54] He
also revealed his unspoken wishes: the intervening generation had
not simply disappeared; he had banished it. And in his "orphaned"
state, he had installed his grandfather as a replacement for his unsatisfactory parents.

William's mention of his military career points to the boundaries
of that relationship. It was only as junior officer—a role hallowed by

50. Wilhelm II, *My Early Life*, pp. 276–277; see also Wilhelm II, *Memoirs*, p. 21.
For a contemporary report on William's relations with his parents during his father's
final illness, see Holstein, *Correspondence 1861–1896*, Radolinski to Holstein, March
2, 1888, pp. 266–268, and Radolinski to Holstein, March 6, 1888, pp. 269–271. See also
Crown Princess Frederick to Marie Bülow, December 3, 1887, Bülow Papers/170.
51. See, for example, Wilhelm II, *My Early Life*, p. 5.
52. See, for example, ibid., pp. 61, 85.
53. Ibid., pp. 81–82.
54. See, for example, Wilhelm II, *Memoirs*, p. 3.

royal convention, which he entered into at the age of ten—that he experienced the affectionate attention of his grandfather. When he was a small child, his mother had complained bitterly that the extended family looked "upon him half with pity and half with dislike."

> Our children are invariably pitied for . . . the great misfortune of having me for their Mama. It is supposed they cannot possibly turn out well; . . . I trust my children may grow up like my Fritz, like Papa, like you and as unlike the rest of the Prussian royal family as possible.[55]

That William's account of the military ethos shared by him and his grandfather was doubtless in great part a fiction does not detract from its importance. In cases such as his, fantasy may well be essential for maintaining psychological equilibrium. William's military romance provided him a means to reconcile conflicting inner needs. From it he derived a modicum of emotional support—indeed he frequently described the bonds between officers and men in maternal terms[56]—while resisting to the utmost his longing for his mother. So great was its significance for him that William never abandoned the image of himself as a member of the Prussian officer corps.

If his identification with his grandfather served to palliate the pain of his early ties with his mother, it by no means eradicated it. The young emperor did not rest content with imagining himself as one officer among many—a dutiful cog in an elaborate machine. Rather he embroidered the simple design which had satisfied his grandfather and fancied himself the actual driver of that machine—a position which, constitutionally at least, was his. Still more, he buttressed this grandiose notion by a notorious insistence on the divine right of Hohenzollern kings. William's infatuation with an anachronistic doctrine of political authority struck even a loyal court official as a sign of his tenuous grasp on reality:

> In many respects he lives in a mental atmosphere of his own, where nothing can influence him. . . . And then he is only too eager to seize every opportunity to glorify the Hohenzollerns; and from this ancestor worship he promises himself results that we are not likely to see.[57]

55. Fulford, ed., *Your Dear Letter*, the Crown Princess to Queen Victoria, August 17, 1867, pp. 148–149.

56. See, for example, Wilhelm II, *My Early Life*, pp. 151–152, and Wilhelm II, *Memoirs*, p. 224. See also Eulenburg's comments on William's attachment to and idealization of the officer corps: "Adjutatenpolitik," 1901, Eulenburg Papers/40, p. 126a.

57. Robert von Zedlitz-Trützchler, *Zwölf jahre am deutschen Kaiserhof* (Stuttgart: Deutsche Verlags-Anstalt, 1924), trans. Alfred Kalisch as *Twelve Years at the German Imperial Court* (London: Nisbet and Co., 1924), March 22, 1905, p. 138. See also Eulenburg's account of William's mental state during the annual cruise in 1903: Eulenburg to Bülow, July–August 1903, Eulenburg Papers/74, pp. 3–18.

That William's claim satisfied inner demands was suspected more than sixty years ago by the American psychologist Morton Prince:

> What counts ... is that the Kaiser believes that a Divine right is his prerogative. How, in this age, a man who has shown such marked ability in certain directions can be such a fool—I mean psychologically, of course—as to persuade himself to believe such stuff ... could probably be traced to subconscious wishes which have produced this conscious delusion, just as such subconscious processes determine the delusions of insane people.[58]

At first glance it would seem that William's assertion of divine right represented, in paradigmatic form, a quest for uncritical acceptance. But the very pomposity of his posture exposed him to further disapproval. Witness Queen Victoria's reaction four months after his accession:

> As regarding the Prince's [of Wales] not treating his nephew as Emperor; this is really too *vulgar* and too absurd, as well as untrue, almost *to be believed.*
>
> We have always been very intimate with our grandson and nephew, and to pretend that he is to be treated *in private* as well as in public as "his Imperial Majesty" is *perfect madness*! ... *If* he has *such* notions, he [had] better *never* come here.[59]

One should, then, beware of interpreting William's insistence on divine right simply as a defense against maternal rejection. The fact that it did not fulfill this putative defensive function points to his inability to block out that early experience. Though he might repudiate his mother, in the very act of so doing—that is, in inflating his Hohenzollern inheritance—he invited others to treat him as she had done.

It was precisely on this point—William's insistence on his monarchical position—that he came into conflict with Bismarck. One need not recapitulate here the issues which divided the two former allies. What is of interest is their differing perceptions of the psychological drama they enacted. In brief, Bismarck accused William of lacking the crucial quality that had cemented his relationship with the young emperor's grandfather: the loyalty of master to servant.

In the presence of Kaiser William II, I could not get away from the im-

58. Morton Prince, *The Psychology of the Kaiser: A Study of His Sentiments and His Obsessions* (Boston: Richard G. Badger, 1915), p. 45.

59. George Earle Buckle, ed., *The Letters of Queen Victoria*, 3rd Series (London: John Murray, 1930-1932), I, Queen Victoria to Salisbury, October 15, 1888, pp. 440–441 (emphasis in the original). See also E. F. Benson, *The Kaiser and His English Relations* (London: Longmans, Green, and Co., 1936).

pression of one-sided affection; the feeling which is the firmest foundation of the constitution of the Prussian army, the feeling that the soldier will never leave the officer in the lurch, but also that the officer will never leave the soldier in the lurch, a sentiment to which William I conformed in respect to his servants almost to exaggeration, cannot so far be recognized as entering, in any adequate degree, into the mentality of the young sovereign.[60]

In his *Memoirs,* William never answered the charge that had already appeared in print. He simply stated his distaste for and disapproval of "the open warfare" which acceptance of Bismarck's antisocialist proposals would have entailed.[61] From Philipp Eulenburg's correspondence one gets a more extensive, if indirect, view of the young emperor's inner turmoil. William saw himself desperately struggling to stave off bondage to Bismarck.[62] The many issues in dispute dissolved into one brutal question: Would he confess his helplessness and submit unconditionally to the Iron Chancellor? Would he grant Bismarck the status of indispensability and admit his utter dependence on the man he recognized as the "creator of the German Empire"? After months of mental anguish William gave his answer; though left, in his own words, an " 'orphaned' young Emperor," he severed the tie.[63]

He did not, however, admit to his own actions; rather he commented tersely that he had been "confronted by the unexpected retirement of Bismarck."[64] In effect, then, William returned Bismarck's charge of faithlessness with an accusation of abandonment. Charges and countercharges of this sort ran like a dark thread throughout William's reign; condemned for infidelity by political associates, he responded with indictments of desertion. Where does the psychological truth lie? It is clear that the emperor felt keenly the emotional isolation brought on by his own behavior. Yet he seemed to cling to, if not provoke, such painful experiences. He could not

60. Gerhard Ritter and Rudolf Stadelmann, eds., *Otto von Bismarck: Die gesammelten Werke,* XV: *Erinnerung und Gedanke* (Berlin: Deutsche Verlagsgesellschaft, 1932); I have quoted from the English translation of the last volume of Bismarck's memoirs: Otto von Bismarck, *The Kaiser vs. Bismarck,* trans. Bernard Miall (New York and London: Harper and Brothers, 1921), pp. 150–151.

61. Wilhelm II, *Memoirs,* p. 2.

62. For the clearest example, see Röhl, ed., *Philipp Eulenburgs Korrespondenz 1866–1891,* Eulenburg to Holstein, January 17, 1890, pp. 412–413. A brief summary of the crisis as related by the emperor is in Hajo Holborn, ed., *Aufzeichnungen und Erinnerungen aus dem Leben des Botschafters Joseph Maria von Radowitz,* II: *1878–1890* (Stuttgart and Berlin: Deutsche Verlags-Anstalt, 1925), March 20, 1890, pp. 215–217.

63. Wilhelm II, *Memoirs,* pp. 1, 54.

64. Ibid., p. 53.

escape the figure of his mother hovering in the background of these repetitive dramas. While William may have exiled Bismarck from the political stage, he had not succeeded in excising his mother from his emotional life.

III. Willy's Friend Phili

Among the emperor's associates, Philipp zu Eulenburg-Hertefeld stands out as his loyal friend, as the person who claimed to provide William the emotional comfort he so sorely required. This friendship has long been considered central to the development, or perhaps more accurately retardation, of German political institutions in the 1890s. To put the argument simply: Eulenburg's success in securing key positions for his own friends, men who shared his admiration for William, made possible the emperor's "personal regime"; these appointments marked the defeat of Holstein and his fellow bureaucrats who in their struggle to restrain the monarch figure as the forces of political responsibility; finally, with William in control, the way lay open for the *Weltpolitik* and naval building which made the last years of the century so fateful for German and world history.

What is offered here is not another discussion of institutions and policies. It is rather an analysis of Eulenburg's relation to William, of the quality of his devotion to his sovereign. Eulenburg's appreciation of and sympathy for William's psychological vulnerability—despite the cloying sentimentality of the effusions in which he indulged—is beyond question. Yet he was unable to provide the steady sustenance from which his royal friend might have developed an integrated sense of self. What, then, in the German emotional universe did it mean to be a loyalist par excellence?

If Eulenburg has been an elusive character in historical accounts, it is in large measure owing to the fact that he seems so very different from those with whom he had political dealings. According to his official biographer, Johannes Haller, Eulenburg's artistic temperament ill fitted him for the demands of bureaucratic routine. More than that, it turned his life in the political arena into one of torment and self-abnegation. If Haller had been less intent on hagiography, he might well have put equal stress on Eulenburg's homoerotic proclivities as a personal trait which eventually brought him public woe.[65] Does Eulenburg, then, stand as a solitary figure at odds with the world around him? The remarkable surefootedness in treach-

65. For the most thorough review of the evidence on these two points, as well as a brief biographical account, see the editor's introduction by Röhl, *Philipp Eulenburgs*

erous terrain which he demonstrated for the better part of a decade suggests that the answer should be no. Yet the obvious difficulty of describing him leads one to surmise that Eulenburg represents a variant of what, up to now, has emerged as dominant.

In his memoirs, Eulenburg gives pride of place to Bismarck.[66] That the Iron Chancellor should have loomed so large was in part the consequence of Eulenburg's decision to refrain from publishing material on his own activities in the 1890s. If, despite this reticence, the memoirs were to shed light on German politics at all, Bismarck's personality had to become the focal point. In addition, Eulenburg knew whereof he spoke: from his childhood he had been well acquainted with the entire Bismarck family and had had ample opportunity to observe the majestic "Jupiter" in an informal setting. As a fledgling diplomat, Eulenburg had formed an intimate friendship with Herbert Bismarck, which he strenuously denied having betrayed in the crisis of 1890 that led to the departure of both father and son. Still more, Bismarck's presence was crucial for Eulenburg's claim to lofty understanding: Eulenburg had the audacity to pose as a foil to the Iron Chancellor, thereby elevating himself to the most exalted sphere.

Hence Eulenburg did not venture to belittle the founder of the Second Reich. On the contrary he acknowledged an uncanny or perhaps divine fit between Bismarck and the mission which had been his: "That nature created a Bismarck for Germany should be conceived of as decisive for the development of a people which needed in hard, realistic labor a person of this type."[67] Yet the fact that Bismarck had stamped his own personality on his creation made the defects of that personality a continual source of regret and lamentation. What Bismarck lacked, above all, was an appreciation for art. Eulenburg's criticism should not be dismissed as frivolous. In his mind, art stood not only for cultural artifacts of distinction, but for the sympathetic temper which he assumed must infuse such work. In short, the new German state had been deprived of its soul:

> Something was lacking, and more than that, something was lost through this lack. There was sealed, so to speak, . . . an estrangement of Germany

---

Korrespondenz 1866–1891, pp. 9–53. Aside from Haller, the most frequently cited biography is Reinhold Conrad Muschler, *Philipp zu Eulenburg: Sein Leben und seine Zeit* (Leipzig: Verlag von Fr. Wilh. Grunow, 1930). See also Isabel Virginia Hull, "The Entourage of Kaiser Wilhelm II, 1888–1918 (Die kaiserliche Umgebung)" (Ph.D. dissertation, Yale University, 1978), pp. 68–231.

66. Johannes Haller, ed., *Aus 50 Jahren: Erinnerungen, Tagebücher und Briefe aus dem Nachlass des Fürsten Philipp zu Eulenburg-Hertefeld* (Berlin: Verlag von Gebrüder Paetel, 1925).

67. Ibid., p. 57.

from its true culture: a turn toward political-military "culture," which I feel signifies decline rather than rise.[68]

In contrast to the military ethos that Bismarck had fostered, Eulenburg saw himself as a repository of artistic values. Though his memoirs were put together after the First World War, this view did not simply reflect his country's defeat. His had been a long-standing discontent with what he considered the dominant and even suffocating pressure of Prussianism. He had found relief in music and felt his spirit breathe freely in the song cycles and ballads he composed. Of all his works, Eulenburg judged his *Skaldengesänge*, derived from the Nordic Sagas, as his best. Certainly they figured prominently in the musical entertainment he provided his friends. Though the emperor took delight in these performances, to the modern reader the lyrics, at least, seem devoid of both originality and literary grace.[69] Quite obviously Eulenburg did not possess sufficient talent to rise to the level of his musical-poetic hero, who was none other than Richard Wagner.[70]

In Eulenburg's mind, introducing artistic qualities into politics went hand in hand with injecting emotional sensitivity into the world of public affairs. Here again he underlined a striking difference between himself and Bismarck. One need not recapitulate his account of Bismarck's wrath and how deep-seated antagonisms shaped the Iron Chancellor's politics. What is of interest is Eulenburg's depiction of Bismarck as relentlessly bludgeoning sovereigns and subordinates alike, unable to perceive an emotional reality other than his own. It was precisely in the realm of psychological observation that Eulenburg professed mastery—a mastery he attributed to the passivity and weakness which he regarded as the feminine aspect of his nature.[71] He cherished this weakness, enshrining it as a discrete and sacred part of his personality. By thus accepting and indeed accentuating the conventional opposition of male and female, Eulenburg highlighted his own special form of prowess: his ability to enter the hearts and minds of those around him by adopting a womanly posture.

How did Eulenburg account for this extraordinary capacity? Again he pointed to differences between Bismarck and himself, or

68. Ibid., p. 58.

69. Philipp Graf zu Eulenburg, *Skaldengesänge* (Braunschweig: George Westermann, 1892). William was particularly fond of "König Eriks Genesung," pp. 2–5, and "Atlantis," pp. 34–36: Eulenburg, *Erinnerungen*, pp. 147, 202, and Wilhelm II, *My Early Life*, p. 186.

70. Eulenburg, *Erinnerungen*, p. 57.

71. Ibid., pp. 247–248.

rather between Bismarck's mother and his own. Of the former, the already familiar picture of a clever and cold woman emerges. In sharp contrast to the psychological deprivation Eulenburg suggests that Bismarck experienced, he describes his own family as cultivating a rich emotional life.[72] Under his mother's affectionate protection, his sympathies expanded. Where Bismarck had been blighted, he blossomed. To phrase Eulenburg's contention more crisply than he could have managed to do himself: his attachment to his mother equipped him to supplement and complete the work of Bismarck.

What was the nature of the bond between mother and son? Eulenburg's testimony is clear. According to Haller, "His peculiar relation to her was the keynote of his whole life. He loved her, adored her, shared everything with her, as did she with him, so long as she lived; even when at a distance they kept up an almost daily correspondence."[73] When in 1902 he finally lost her, he was desolate: "something had bound me to her since childhood," he wrote, "something which came from heaven and is incomparable with anything else."[74] And it was something which he would have liked to possess entirely. In writing to a colleague, he insisted on her total devotion to him:

> You ... have learnt to know my good mother's character. She is simply sacrificing herself for me, and I am in the distressing position of being able to find no way out from all these problems which affect me so deeply.[75]

How much of this mutual devotion was wishful thinking and how

72. Ibid., pp. 73–75. See also Eulenburg, "Ich selbst: Betrachtungen, die meinen Kindern gewidmet sind, 1900–1902," Eulenburg Papers/73.

73. Haller, *Philipp Eulenburg*, I: 8–9. Compare Eulenburg's own comment: "Es war eben nicht Ehrgeiz, sondern nur Phantasie, die in meinem Leben herrschte. Nicht vermag ich mit Worten die Macht zu schildern, welche die Phantasie in meiner Kindheit, in meiner Jugend, auf mich ausübte. Sie war so stark, dass sich das äussere Leben in einen Widerspruch zu ihr stellen *musste,* zu einem Widerspruch, der sich als *Unzufriedenheit* und *innerliches Unbehagen* äusserte. . . . Nur in der Liebe meiner Mutter und in meiner Liebe zu ihr, fand meine Phantasie einen entsprechenden, gewissermassen realen Ausdruck. Darum wurde auch diese Liebe zu einer Vergötterung. Ich habe noch heute die Empfindung, dass niemals ein Sohn seine Mutter so geliebt hat als ich." Eulenburg, "Phantasie und Ehrgeiz," May 1901, in "Ich selbst," Eulenburg Papers/73 (emphasis in the original). See also Eulenburg to Wilhelm II, May 11, 1902, Eulenburg Papers/59, pp. 53–54.

74. Eulenburg to Auguste Viktoria, October 21, 1902, Eulenburg Papers/59, p. 96. See also Röhl, ed., *Philipp Eulenburgs Korrespondenz 1866–1891,* Eulenburg to his mother, September 10, 1881, pp. 128–129, and Eulenburg to his mother, March 26, 1895, Eulenburg Papers/35, pp. 202–203. Extracts from his mother's diary, which cover periods she spent with Eulenburg and his family, and which make abundantly clear her intense involvement in her son's life, are to be found throughout "Eine preussische Familiengeschichte 1886–1902": Eulenburg Papers/1–60.

75. Eulenburg to Heinrich VII Prinz Reuss, October 18, 1893, Eulenburg Papers/25; also quoted in Haller, *Philipp Eulenburg,* I: 180.

much reality? The very intensity of Eulenburg's attachment makes one doubt his testimony; one suspects that it sprang from a demand for maternal love that had not been fully met. Or better, its bestowal had been accompanied by possessiveness on his mother's part as well—a possessiveness which he complied with by adopting a feminine identity. Yet the very qualities with which he claimed his mother had endowed him—and which made him the ideal complement to Bismarck—threatened to undermine his well-being. He portrayed himself as condemned to hover on the edge of despair. From this destiny he apparently never wanted to escape.

In short, pain rather than satisfaction attended his expressions of emotional need. And it is this combination of yearning coupled with suffering that sets Eulenburg apart—but as a variant and not an exception. Though he disavowed the usual imperative to vanquish his deepest longings, the torment that accompanied them bespoke the familiar world of scant reassurance.

What, then, was the psychological significance of Eulenburg's feminine stance? In an extremely condensed form it represented a set of interrelated positions. In the first instance, it reflected his fixation on his mother. In the second instance, its self-aggrandizing function counteracted the suffering produced by that symbiotic relationship. Looking ahead, one would expect themes of fusion and its dangers to recur in the series of relationships Eulenburg entered into to consolidate his precarious emotional balance.

■

Eulenburg and William met in the summer of 1886, at a time when the prince, the younger of the two by twelve years, was allied with Bismarck and doing battle with his own parents. William's published comments on this encounter and the ensuing friendship are brief but appreciative:

> I have to thank Eulenburg for many things connected with art, science, and literature, and no less for his delightful companionship. Whenever he came to our Potsdam home, it was like a flood of sunshine shed on the routine of life. Such a friend as he then was to me he remained through decades of unchanging loyalty. . . . For my part I shall always hold him in grateful remembrance.[76]

In William's memory, at least, art rather than politics served as the nodal point of the relationship. From Eulenburg's account it is

76. Wilhelm II, *My Early Life*, p. 187.

clear that William's enthusiasm for his friend's ballads acted like a magic potion inducing a state of ecstacy in the author.[77] No wonder he discerned in the young prince a reflection of his own personality:

> He has his ... special charm in ... intimate contact. His officer's tone vanishes, and with the whole liveliness of his intelligence he pursues without reserve every theme which is touched on. His whole being breathes strength and understanding. All his expressions are characteristic and unusual. ... But what endows his strong-willed being with a peculiar fascination is a gentle, mystical bent that determines his view on many things. It is a trust in God in the guise of *Kismet*, a readiness to be propelled by the force of fate, with a slight flavor of the tragic about it.[78]

That Eulenburg's friendship should have been colored with exclusiveness was merely the psychological corollary of the fusion he evidently desired:

> I thought of Potsdam, of our sledge-driving, our intimate communion, and a sense of such deep friendship came over me that all of a sudden I felt the glitter around me as an unbearable oppression. How human is our relation—and how I suffer from the thought that the social abyss between us, bridged by our friendship, must widen and deepen more and more when the Imperial Crown is on your head.[79]

To keep the outside world from interfering, Eulenberg was prepared to sacrifice his own person. He pictured himself as renouncing his earthly well-being in order to relieve the burdens of his beloved emperor. When he asks, "Why did God give me this deep, this sacred sense of Friendship?", it becomes apparent that a fantasy of himself as Jesus crowned with thorns is not far below the surface.[80] For Eulenburg, merger and masochism went hand in hand.

Sadism was not far behind. In sending William a small momento— a peasant knife with a trite inscription about the necessity of joy in

77. See, for example, Eulenburg, *Erinnerungen*, p. 135.

78. Ibid., p. 222. See also Röhl, ed., *Philipp Eulenburgs Korrespondenz 1866–1891*, Eulenburg to Wilhelm II, September 11, 1888, p. 312; Eulenburg to Bülow, April 5, 1894, Eulenburg Papers/29, p. 351; Eulenburg to Holstein, December 17, 1895, Eulenburg Papers/39, pp. 888–889.

79. Eulenburg to Prinz Wilhelm, January 10, 1888, Eulenburg Papers/3, p. 2; also quoted in Haller, *Philipp Eulenburg*, I: 42.

80. Eulenburg's diary, late 1896, quoted in Haller, *Philipp Eulenburg*, II: 124. Under the stress of the legal proceedings in 1908, Eulenburg expressed this fantasy explicitly: "Sometimes I fancy that God must have given me my imagination and my talents simply for the purpose of making it easier to bear the crown of thorns He has appointed for me—and which, for reasons that are hidden from me, I must wear." Diary entry, June 4, 1908, quoted in ibid., II: 357–358. Compare Eulenburg to Bülow, October 21, 1895, Eulenburg Papers/38, pp. 251–252.

life—he added the comment: "I should like at the same time to point out the significant circumstances that the motto is carved upon a *knife*. That means that we must stick anyone who disturbs our 'joy,' and that the sticking is another kind of 'joy' in itself!"[81] The aggression inherent in the threat of knifing requires further comment. Hate, it would seem, could take the place of love: it simply projected outward the masochism central to Eulenburg's attachment. It might be called forth by a dangerous world; it might even be called forth by William himself, should he try to alter the terms of what was an inherently unstable relationship. But so long as Eulenburg could regard his friend as emotionally in need and "with a slight flavor of the tragic," that peril could be avoided.

In fact Eulenburg was to be found only infrequently at William's side; prolonged contact had a deleterious effect on his nervous system. In the summer of 1889, when Eulenburg first accompanied the young emperor on a Norwegian cruise, he succumbed to an attack of shingles, abandoned ship, and took refuge in an extended cure. On subsequent voyages he fared better, though he never became an enthusiast for the sea.[82] It was in Munich, with its active artistic community, that Eulenburg felt in his element, and after brief stays in Oldenburg and Württemberg he was delighted to return there in 1891 as Prussian minister. He regarded his elevation three years later to the post of German ambassador in Vienna as a mixed blessing. Above all, he wanted to avoid Berlin. Fearful that constant attendance upon the emperor would both diminish his influence on his friend and increase his dependence on Holstein, he refused to seek an appointment at court.[83]

Absence from Berlin, however, proved no bar to political commu-

81. Eulenburg to Prinz Wilhelm, July 19, 1887, Eulenburg Papers/2, pp. 44-45; also quoted in Haller, *Philipp Eulenburg*, I: 45.

82. For Eulenburg's remarks on what he had suffered during his first cruise, see Röhl, ed., *Philipp Eulenburgs Korrespondenz 1866-1891*, Eulenburg to Holstein, August 6, 1889, pp. 345-347. To Friederike von Bujak he commented even more forcefully in a letter dated December 29, 1889: "Ich blicke auf das vergangene Jahr wie auf schwere Krankheit, wie auf ein Erlöschen meiner Individualität und glaube wirklich schwer krank zu sein." Ibid., p. 397. For a running account of his annual cruises, mostly in the form of letters to the empress, see Fürst Philipp zu Eulenburg, *Mit dem Kaiser als Staatsmann und Freund auf Nordlandsreisen*, 2 vols. (Dresden: Carl Reissner Verlag, 1931).

83. Röhl, ed., *Philipp Eulenburgs Korrespondenz 1892-1895*, Eulenburg to Bülow, November 7, 1894, p. 1401; Eulenburg to Holstein, November 7 and November 8, 1894, pp. 1402-1403; Bülow to Eulenburg, November 10, 1894, pp. 1404-1405; Eulenburg to Wilhelm II, November 14, 1894, pp. 1409-1411; Bülow to Eulenburg, November 16, 1894, pp. 1411-1412; Eulenburg to Wilhelm II, January 23, 1895, pp. 1447-1448. See also Haller, *Philipp Eulenburg*, II: 125-127.

nication. Once Holstein had become aware of Eulenburg's friendship with William, he fostered a close alliance with him by mail and telegraph. Keeping the line open to the emperor was more problematical. Eulenburg wrote, but William rarely reciprocated with a written reply. Verbal exchanges filled the gap. In addition to the Norwegian cruises in July, Eulenburg joined the emperor on shooting and hunting expeditions in spring and fall.[84] And in times of crisis Eulenburg would be summoned to Berlin to hold the hands of both William and Holstein. The protracted crisis leading to Bismarck's dismissal had given this triangular arrangement its baptism of fire. After such a rite of passage it was well-equipped to withstand the buffeting of the next three years.

By early 1894, however, the bond between Eulenburg and Holstein was fast dissolving.[85] Their common fear of Bismarck, which had kept them in tandem for more than four years, was losing its force. Though Bismarck never ceased to terrorize Holstein, Eulenburg appears to have grown immune to the fear the Iron Chancellor inspired—or rather, Eulenburg may have imagined that Bismarck would prove susceptible to his own variety of charm. In keeping with his self-proclaimed feminine sensibility, Eulenburg came to believe that the former chancellor could be seduced into lending his support to those now dominant in Berlin. It was this notion of a reconciliation with Bismarck that most gravely eroded relations between Holstein and Eulenburg.[86] Had the Gray Eminence found Eulenburg and William utterly reliable on this score, it is doubtful that he would have fired his ideological volleys at their friendship.

84. Haller, *Philipp Eulenburg*, I: 133.
85. On this dispute, see Rich, *Holstein*, II: 484–525. For Eulenburg's defense, see Haller, *Philipp Eulenburg*, I: 297–388. The main features of the dispute can be traced in the Eulenburg Papers in the following letters: Holstein to Eulenburg, November 27, 1894, 33/pp. 920–922; Eulenburg to Holstein, December 2, 1894, 33/pp. 933–938; Holstein to Eulenburg, December 4, 1894, 33/pp. 938–940; Eulenburg to Holstein, December 5, 1894, 33/pp. 940–942; Eulenburg to Bülow, December 10–12, 1894, 33/pp. 962–964; Eulenburg to Bülow, December 25, 1894, 33/pp. 997–998; Holstein to Eulenburg, December 24, 1894, 33/pp. 998–1000; Eulenburg to Holstein, December 27, 1894, 33/pp. 1001–1003; Holstein to Eulenburg, January 1, 1895, 34/pp. 8–10; Bülow to Eulenburg, January 5, 1895, 34/pp. 17–21; Eulenburg to Holstein, January 11, 1895, 34/pp. 25–26; Holstein to Eulenburg, February 17, 1895, 34/pp. 115–117; Bülow to Eulenburg, August 25, 1895, 37/pp. 572–576; Eulenburg to Bülow, November 12, 1895, 39/pp. 810–812; Holstein to Eulenburg, December 17, 1895, 39/pp. 908–909; Holstein to Eulenburg, December 26, 1895, 39/pp. 944–946; Holstein to Eulenburg, February 9, 1896, 40/pp. 55–57; Eulenburg to Holstein, February 14, 1896, 40/pp. 89–91. Five of these letters are reprinted in Röhl, ed., *Philipp Eulenburgs Korrespondenz 1892–1895*, and another is reprinted in Holstein, *Correspondence 1861–1896*.
86. For Eulenburg's attitude toward a reconciliation with Bismarck, see the materials he included in his *Erinnerungen*, pp. 255–268. For evidence that fear of Bismarck

Though Eulenburg throughout those years had invited Holstein to bear witness to his special ties to the emperor, Holstein had never been an ideal spectator. Eulenburg's biographer, reflecting his protagonist's point of view, argues that Holstein saw the relationship as a political contrivance and failed to appreciate the human depths of Eulenburg's attachment. In short, the Gray Eminence threatened Eulenburg's joy with William, and in return Eulenburg prepared to stick Holstein with a knife.

Eulenburg did not, however, abandon Holstein until a replacement had been designated and measures taken to secure the new ally's advancement. In 1894 the Gray Eminence and the emperor's friend, working together, obtained the Rome embassy for the man on whom Eulenburg was counting for salvation, Bernhard von Bülow.[87] At one and the same time Eulenburg regarded Bülow as an alter ego and as another Bismarck. Though Bülow had no ear for music, Eulenburg believed that his new associate had caught the fine tuning of his own relationship to William. With Bülow as an appreciative third party, Eulenburg anticipated both the narcissistic gratification of a mirroring self-image and relief from too close an intimacy with his beloved monarch. In the end, when Bülow was finally installed in Berlin itself, he effectively deflated Eulenburg's fantasy of imposing a "feminine" element at the German political summit—a fantasy which had proved to be no more than a precarious variant of the familiar male stance of self-aggrandizement.

IV. The Artifices of Bülow

It took three years to move Bülow from Rome to Berlin. During that time the crucial political issue in the capital remained what it had been since the beginning of the crisis which had led to Bis-

---

assailed Eulenburg from time to time thereafter, see Eulenburg to Kuno Moltke, June 15, 1895, Eulenburg Papers/36, pp. 438–442. For Holstein's continuing anxiety, see, for example, Holstein to Eulenburg, October 23, 1894, Eulenburg Papers/32, pp. 810–811; Holstein to Eulenburg, October 28, 1894, Eulenburg Papers/32, pp. 839–840; Holstein to Eulenburg, October 29, 1894, Eulenburg Papers/32, pp. 840–842; Holstein to Eulenburg, November 11, 1894, Eulenburg Papers/33, pp. 884–885; Holstein to Eulenburg, December 4, 1894, Eulenburg Papers/33, pp. 938–940. Three of these letters are reprinted in Röhl, ed., *Philipp Eulenburgs Korrespondenz 1892–1895*.

87. On Eulenburg's relations with Bülow, see the following letters in ibid., Eulenburg to Bülow, October 6, 1894, pp. 1368–1370; Bülow to Eulenburg, October 6, 1894, pp. 1370–1373; Bülow to Eulenburg, October 15, 1894, pp. 1383–1385; Eulenburg to Wilhelm II, February 14, 1895, pp. 1463–1464. See also the following documents in the Eulenburg Papers: Eulenburg to Wilhelm II, February 18, 1895, 34/pp. 118–121; Eulenburg to Bülow, February 1895, 34/pp. 121–122; Eulenburg, "Promemoria für meine Privat-Akten," December 3, 1895, 39/pp. 871–872; Eulenburg to

marck's resignation, the relations between emperor and chancellor. That this issue was not insoluble had been amply demonstrated by Bismarck's long tenure in office. It was equally obvious that the failure of his successors to soothe William's restless temperament had allowed the monarch to nourish pretensions to rule. Hence the problem facing a future chancellor was not one of consolidating the "personal rule" of the emperor, but rather one of gaining William's "allegiance" in order to induce him to withdraw from center stage.

Indeed to speak of a "personal regime" is doubly misleading.[88] First, such an interpretation fails to draw the logical conclusion from the emperor's temperamental inability to undertake the burdens of autocratic rule; in this respect he was no different from most monarchs in Europe's history. Second, it underestimates the role of the bureaucracy. The institutional line of cleavage did not run between monarchical absolutism and "responsible" government; rather it ran between bureaucratic cum monarchical administration and a parliamentary regime. Under these circumstances—with a parliamentary solution an unrealistic option—it is not surprising that the struggles of the 1890s had so little institutional significance.

At the outset General Caprivi had taken upon himself the task of transforming the German political temper while keeping intact the Bismarckian constitutional system. To summarize briefly: he had hoped to follow a national policy and to rule with the support of the Reichstag. But he had made no concerted attempt to cement together a reliable majority. Instead he had cemented the special interests of Prussian conservatism in opposition to himself. In 1892 he had felt obliged to relinquish his position in Prussia by separating the office of Prussian minister-president—which went to Botho zu Eulenburg (Philipp's cousin)—from that of chancellor of the Reich. Caught between the Prussian Landtag and the German Reichstag, defeated in one and uncertain of support in the other, Caprivi had fallen back upon the bureaucracy. In so doing, he had been brought again face to face with his dependence upon the crown. In October 1894, after ten serious crises in four and a half years, William dis-

---

Bülow, December 6, 1895, 39/pp. 881–884; Wilhelm II to Eulenburg, December 25, 1895, 39/pp. 940–941; Bülow to Eulenburg, December 25, 1895, 39/pp. 947–951. See also Haller, *Philipp Eulenburg*, II: 3–41.

88. On this issue, see Eyck, *Wilhelm II*; Röhl, *Germany without Bismarck*; Hull, "The Entourage of Kaiser Wilhelm II." See also Ekkehard-Teja P. W. Wilke, *Political Decadence in Imperial Germany: Personnel-Political Aspects of the German Government Crisis 1894–97* (Urbana, Ill.: University of Illinois Press, 1976). Wilke takes issue with Eyck and Röhl's claim that William succeeded in establishing a personal regime; instead he portrays the emperor as having become ensnared by his friend Eulenburg and Eulenburg's satellite Bülow.

missed Caprivi and Botho Eulenburg. At the very least these crises testified to Caprivi's failure—not surprising in view of the magnitude of the assignment—to depersonalize German politics.[89]

Caprivi's successor, Prince Chlodwig zu Hohenlohe-Schillingsfürst, a mediatized Catholic princeling from Bavaria, was a man of more modest goals. Despite a distinguished diplomatic career, including, in the 1870s, the embassy in Paris, where he had formed a lifelong association with Holstein, Hohenlohe is generally considered to have been a nonentity as chancellor.[90] Indeed it was with the expectation that the seventy-five year old grand seigneur would be pliable that William had appointed him. In the course of the following six years, Hohenlohe, who was distantly related to the emperor and whom William called "Uncle," proved that his "nephew's" judgment had been accurate.

Above all, Hohenlohe tolerated "the decisive lurches in German policy" that are associated with the end of the century.[91] Or, to put it another way, he simply stayed in office as the political course veered back in a Bismarckian direction. One need not elaborate here the comparisons which have been recently drawn between the policies of the late 1870s and those of the late 1890s and the label "social imperialist" which has been applied to the full range. In the broadest sense, it is clear that the social-structural problems of the late 1870s—the tension between a preindustrial landowning ruling elite and a modern industrial economy—remained a central feature of the Second Reich. On that particular level of abstraction, politics appears to derive from underlying social fissures, and human actors are in danger of being reduced to mere puppets.[92]

89. Nichols, *Germany After Bismarck*, p. 374; see also A. J. P. Taylor, "The Ruler in Berlin," in his collection of essays *From Napoleon to Stalin* (London: The Right Book Club, 1950), pp. 78–79.

90. For information on Hohenlohe's relationship with Holstein and correspondence between the two, see Helmut Rogge, ed., *Holstein und Hohenlohe* (Stuttgart: Deutsche Verlags-Anstalt, 1957). For insight into Hohenlohe's experience, see Karl Alexander von Müller, ed., *Fürst Chlodwig zu Hohenlohe-Schillingsfürst: Denkwürdigkeiten der Reichskanzlerzeit* (Stuttgart and Berlin: Deutsche Verlags-Anstalt, 1931); see also Alexander von Hohenlohe-Schillingsfürst, *Aus meinem Leben* (Frankfurt: Frankfurter Societäts-Druckerei, 1925), pp. 223–333.

91. Taylor, "The Ruler in Berlin," p. 79.

92. The recent emphasis in German historiography on socioeconomic developments and tensions was stimulated in part by the revival of interest in the path-breaking work of Eckart Kehr. See his *Schlachtflottenbau und Parteipolitik 1894–1901* (Berlin: Verlag Dr. Emil Ebering, 1930), translated by Pauline R. Anderson and Eugene N. Anderson as *Battleship Building and Party Politics in Germany, 1894–1901* (Chicago, Ill.: University of Chicago Press, 1975), and his collected essays, edited by Hans-Ulrich Wehler, *Der Primat der Innenpolitik* (Berlin: Walter de Gruyter and Co., 1965) which have been translated by Grete Heinz and edited by Gordon A. Craig

The focus of this study has been and must continue to be on those human actors and their personal relations. What is of primary concern here, then, is how Bülow as state secretary for foreign affairs and Hohenlohe's successor-designate imposed himself as an authority figure. Though Bülow's stature never approached Bismarckian dimensions—even after his elevation to the chancellorship in 1900—Philipp Eulenburg's hopes for his protégé were not entirely misplaced. An explanation of Bülow's comparative success should shed light on the deep-seated psychological instability of a ruling elite which remained "feudal" and militaristic even as it sought to bring into its orbit the new industrial element in German society.

■

From Bülow's memoirs one would hardly suspect that he had been a statesman of the first rank. His "name is weighed down" by what A. J. P. Taylor judges to be "the most trivial record ever left by a man who has occupied high position."[93] The original reaction in Germany, where the four volumes of memoirs appeared in 1930 and 1931 shortly after Bülow's death,[94] had been similar. Though "trivial" was not a term applied by German readers unlikely to have dismissed out of hand Bülow's critique of his country's diplomacy in 1914, his memoirs were deemed nevertheless to have damaged his reputation forever. But it was not his testimony on the question of war guilt that alone came under attack. Nor was the outrage confined to those who were themselves the targets of the former chancel-

---

as *Economic Interest, Militarism, and Foreign Policy: Essays on German History* (Berkeley and Los Angeles: University of California Press, 1977). Among the generation of German historians trained after the Second World War, it has been Wehler who has taken the lead in developing Kehr's line of argument and turning it into a complex social-scientific model: *Bismarck und der Imperialismus* (Köln and Berlin: Kiepenheuer and Witsch, 1969). For the most convenient summary of views Wehler has repeatedly presented, see his *Das deutsche Kaiserreich 1871–1918* (Göttingen: Vandenhoeck and Ruprecht, 1973). For a comparable set of judgments, see the essays in Michael Stürmer, ed., *Das Kaiserliche Deutschland: Politik und Gesellschaft 1870–1918* (Düsseldorf: Droste Verlag, 1970).

93. Taylor, "The Ruler in Berlin," p. 79. On Bülow's years in power, see Volker R. Berghahn, *Der Tirpitz Plan: Genesis und Verfall einer innenpolitischen Krisenstrategie unter Wilhelm II* (Düsseldorf: Droste Verlag, 1971); Barbara Vogel, *Deutsche Russlandpolitik: Das Scheitern der deutschen Weltpolitik unter Bülow 1900–1906* (Düsseldorf: Bertelsmann Universitätsverlag, 1973); Peter Winzen, *Bülows Weltmachtkonzept: Untersuchungen zur Frühphase seiner Aussenpolitik 1897–1901* (Boppard am Rhein: Harald Boldt Verlag, 1977).

94. Franz von Stockhammern, ed., *Fürst von Bülow Denkwürdigkeiten*, 4 vols. (Berlin: Ullstein, 1930–1931), trans. F. A. Voigt and Geoffrey Dunlop as *Memoirs of Prince von Bülow*, 4 vols. (Boston: Little Brown and Co., 1931–1932). For the manuscript version of the *Denkwürdigkeiten*, which was shortened but not substantially altered for publication, see Bülow Papers/139–146.

lor's venom. To be sure, historians were suitably horrified by Bülow's inaccuracies, while loyal biographers came to the defense of their subjects. Beyond such predictable responses, people reacted against a tone considered offensive in its combination of vanity and calumny.[95] If Bülow had intended his memoirs to assure his place in history, he had failed utterly.

Such may have been his conscious intent when he finally began dictating these volumes in 1921. Yet the work was shaped, in ways he may not have fully appreciated, by what he and his country had undergone since his dismissal in 1909.[96] Obviously the experience of war and defeat had left their traces. More specifically they had heightened both Bülow's sense of injury that he had not been recalled to power and his estimation of the services he believed that he alone could have rendered his country. In addition his method of composition—his reliance on epigrammatic notes kept in fragmentary fashion over the years and in which he had vented his spleen—ensured that spite and nastiness should be much in evidence. Do the memoirs, then, simply betray the corrosive effects of disappointments suffered during the previous decade and a half? Or do the vanity and taste for calumny they display cast a retrospective light on the man who by his own account deftly managed personal relations so long as he was securely ensconced at the German political summit?

The second question comes closer to the mark. Two motifs dominate the memoirs in an overlapping fashion. On the one hand Bülow presents himself as the rightful heir to Bismarck, and it is as one so destined that he lays claim to his inheritance. Scattered throughout the memoirs are reports of prophecies which foretold his future position. Bismarck himself appropriately figures as one of the prophets. And in stressing his steadfast loyalty to the Iron Chancellor, Bülow testifies to his own fitness for the highest office.[97] The Bismarckian chord epitomizes his effort to sustain his cherished fantasy of himself as a *Glückskind.*

Yet his self-image falters. So much is indicated by the prominence

95. See, for example, Friedrich Thimme, ed., *Front wider Bülow: Staatsmänner, Diplomaten und Forscher zu seinen Denkwürdigkeiten* (Munich: Verlag F. Bruckmann AG, 1932); Friedrich Thimme, "Fürst Bülow und Graf Monts," *Preussische Jahrbücher* 231 (March 1933): 193–219, 232 (April 1933): 17–34; Karl Bonhoeffer, "Zur psychopathologischen Beurteilung der Denkwürdigkeiten des Fürsten Bülow," *Berliner Monatshefte* 9 (June 1931): 601–603.

96. Friedrich Freiherr Hiller von Gaertringen, *Fürst Bülows Denkwürdigkeiten: Untersuchungen zu ihrer Entstehungsgeschichte und ihrer Kritik* (Tübingen: J. C. B. Mohr, 1956), see especially pp. 27–115.

97. See, for example, Bülow, *Memoirs*, I: 243; ibid., IV: 5, 284, 558, 680.

of a second motif: Bülow as the master of psychological manipulation. If he fancies his achievements as foreordained, he also pictures them as the result of his own adroitness. The emphasis does not fall on steady work, but on steady nerves and superior insight into human nature.[98] Nor did Bülow parade such skill only late in life; his pride in it emerges from letters written early in his career.[99] Above all, he kept insisting, it was his psychological agility that permitted him to master German politics—to thread his way in an environment where, as he described it, personal susceptibilities were the dominant reality. At one and the same time this quality set him apart from less successful officials and diplomats and enabled him to acquire visible distinction. In short, he achieved by his own dexterity what he had already claimed as his birthright.

At first glance these twin perspectives on his success appear to accomplish the single purpose of self-aggrandizement. Yet clearly he protests too much. One may infer that his mastery was no more than an artful contrivance, an inherently unstable posture which depended upon a manic control of his inner world—epitomized by the *Glückskind* motif—and, through psychological manipulation, of the outer world as well. And when his artful contrivance collapsed, he was overcome by rage; an emotion, one suspects, that had long simmered just below the surface.

What bits and pieces about Bülow's childhood do the memoirs provide? Though his testimony on his parents is fragmentary, his own rejection of them is clear. His father is depicted as the very model of an able bureaucrat who ordered his life according to the maxims of industry and sobriety.[100] A man abhorring excess of any sort, he clung to the conviction that the safest course was also the wisest. Despite such virtues the elder Bülow did not enjoy a career marked by steady progress. Initially he served in Denmark's diplomatic service: as that country's delegate to the Diet of the German Confederation, he began a long and eventually fruitful association with Bismarck. In 1862 he relinquished his post in Frankfurt and accepted ministerial office in Mecklenburg (Strelitz), returning thus to the North German region from which his family had originally come. Out of this obscurity he was lifted by the Iron Chancellor. Having served as Mecklenburg (Schwerin)'s representative in Berlin from

98. See, for example, ibid., IV: 7, 490, 587, 681.
99. See, for example, Röhl, ed., *Philipp Eulenburgs Korrespondenz 1866–1891*, Bülow to Eulenburg, March 2, 1890, pp. 466–474.
100. See, for example, Bülow, *Memoirs*, IV: 7, 84; see also the elder Bülow to his son, July 30, 1867, quoted in ibid., IV: 111–112.

1866, the elder Bülow seven years later was appointed Reich state secretary for foreign affairs. If diligence had offered scanty rewards up to then, his wise choice of allegiance finally brought him the ample compensation he enjoyed until his death in 1879.

Despite conventional tokens of filial respect, his son did not disguise his own contempt for the merely safe. When war hovered on the horizon in 1870, the younger Bülow, who was suffering at the time from a throat ailment, dismissed his father's injunction to remain in the rear. The quotation from Theodor Körner with which he closed his answer to the elder Bülow's plea epitomized his disdain: "Shame on you, fellow behind the stove, hiding behind skirts, clinging to apron strings."[101] And when, in accordance with his father's wishes, young Bülow left the army and entered the diplomatic service, he scorned the security this new course might offer. In notes jotted down for his memoirs but not actually published, he indicated, in the form of a dialogue with himself, the perils he sought:

> You had a choice between two paths: a small existence (consul-general in Cairo or Sofia; minister to Athens or the Hague; undersecretary; at the best, finally several years as ambassador; then retirement as simply Herr von B. with very little wealth, spending the evening of your life in Bonn or Venice in modest circumstances); or cabinet minister, prince, rich, ... a historical figure. The latter not possible without attacks, enemies, battles.[102]

The choice he made promised not only greater glory, but greater emotional distance from his father.

He disengaged himself from his mother's apron strings as well. Though Bülow says little about her, the picture that emerges is of a strong-minded woman. Her son compared her with Bismarck's wife Johanna, who was notorious for her bloodthirsty defense of her Otto. Indeed Bülow likened Johanna to "the women of the Goth and the Franks ... when the horns of battle were blown."[103] If he did not imply that his own mother displayed the wrath of barbarian invaders, he did suggest that she could be fiercely stubborn in her righteousness. Above all, Bülow noted, his mother and Frau von Bismarck were "united by a deep, sincere Evangelical piety."[104] Unlike

101. "Pfui über dich Buben hinter dem Ofen, unter den Schranzen und unter den Zofen!": ibid., IV: 136.

102. Quoted in Hiller, *Fürst Bülows Denkwürdigkeiten*, pp. 37–38. Compare Bülow, *Memoirs*, IV: 282–283.

103. Ibid., IV: 183.

104. Ibid., IV: 5–6.

Johanna, however, Frau van Bülow had not been reared in a pietist milieu. Rather she came from a patrician Hamburg family—comparable to Thomas Mann's Buddenbrooks—and her son delighted in their high station and luxurious lifestyle.[105] One cannot know why she turned to religion nor the particular significance of her faith. What is clear is that she used her religiosity to set limits to the affection for her children which her son described in conventional terms as "unbounded love."[106] With a convert's alertness to their frailties, she demonstrated no corresponding awareness of their feelings.

To this strict woman four sons had been born in the space of four years—Bernhard, the eldest, in 1849. It was with his brothers that the most distressing event of his childhood had occurred. When Bülow was five years old, the youngest of the four died. The death of a younger sibling is never without moment in a child's life. And in Bülow's case this happened under harrowing circumstances:

> I was playing with my brothers, who were one, two, and three years younger than I, Adolf, Alfred and Waldemar, in our nursery. On the table in the middle of the room was a large jug of boiling water which a servant-girl had carelessly put there. The youngest of us, Waldemar, tugged at the tablecloth in childish ignorance. The jug was upset, and the water scalded the poor boy, who was only two years old. His pitiful screaming still sounds in my ears, I still see before me the pain and dismay of my parents when they returned . . . a few hours later.

After two days of "terrible torment" the child was dead.[107] Though Bülow did not lay bare his feelings, one can well imagine the horror that gripped him. To have so narrowly escaped destruction oneself was frightening enough. If he had also unconsciously wished for the death of his brother—and fratricide alone promised permanent relief from the little intruders who had invaded his private domain—then his narrow escape had been from the consequences of his own violent emotions. While the fulfillment of fratricidal fantasies may be a not uncommon occurrence, for Bülow the shock was magnified by his mother's response.

An event which occurred fifteen years later sheds retrospective light on what that response had been. In referring to the death of his twelve year old sister, Bülow commented tartly on his mother's attitude: "She believed with the firmness of a rock that her child was

105. Ibid., IV: 28–36.
106. Ibid., IV: 6.
107. Ibid., IV: 22–23.

better in Heaven, than on this earth. Every dispute with Providence seemed a sin to her. 'Thy will be done, oh Lord!' "[108] Her rocklike demeanor had no doubt intensified little Bernhard's emotional hunger, converting it into angry need. And the religious diet she tried to force upon him he found unpalatable. He did not abide by his mother's faith:[109] despite the religious quotations which abound in his memoirs, Bülow's parade of piety strikes a false note.[110] In short, he sought by subterfuge to evade his mother's watchful eye.

Where, then, did Bülow find his salvation? He gave his answer in a litany sung in praise of his Italian-born wife, Marie. Throughout the memoirs he repeatedly refers to the transformation wrought by his attachment to her. The marriage itself constituted an act of daring, if not defiance. In a letter to Holstein written in 1884, Bülow outlined the secret life he had been leading for the better part of a decade.[111] In 1876 he had met Marie, who was then married to a German diplomat, Count Karl Dönhoff. Though she and Bernhard had frequently been separated geographically, their liaison continued. In 1883, after years of urging by her lover, she obtained a divorce, thereby forfeiting custody of her two children. Throughout that extended period Bülow had "regarded it as [his] duty . . . to preserve the *dehors*," and he had succeeded in keeping their names from being openly linked.[112] In brief, his situation resembled the one in which Herbert Bismarck had found himself when Elisabeth Carolath had divorced her husband on his account. Whereas Herbert had abandoned his beloved, Bernhard stood fast.

Herbert had withered before the stern disapproval of his father; Bülow triumphed over that of his mother. On religious grounds she

108. Ibid., IV: 128-129.

109. The extremes to which this faith could extend are suggested by a few sentences (in characteristically defective Italian) in which Crown Princess Frederick described Bülow's mother to his future wife: "La madre di B. m'ha fetto una visita l'altro giorno, e *molto* molto pia! Mi domanda si io no credeva che e possibile d'intendere qualche volta la voce dei morti? Che sentiva la lora presenza—e poteva imaginare *tutte* le gioie del cielo! I fear my assent was very faint—I do *not* quite feel this, being of too terrestrial a nature—please burn this letter." Crown Princess Frederick to Marie Dönhoff, July 28, 1880, Bülow Papers/167 (emphasis in the original).

110. On this point, see Reinhold Conrad Muschler, "Bülow als Literat," in Thimme, ed., *Front Wider Bülow*, pp. 366-383.

111. Holstein, *Correspondence 1861-1896*, Bülow to Holstein, April 18, 1884, pp. 110-113.

112. Ibid., p. 112. Those privately in the know included Crown Princess Frederick, who expressed favorable feelings about Bülow and offered Marie advice on how he should behave: Crown Princess Frederick to Marie Dönhoff, August 26, 1885, Bülow Papers/169.

strenuously opposed his choice—Marie was Catholic (although prepared to convert)—and it was not until the couple had become man and wife that the mother could reconcile herself to the *fait accompli*.[113] Bülow triumphed over career difficulties as well. In the same letter to Holstein, he confronted the problem of gaining official consent to his proposed marriage, without which he would be forced to leave the diplomatic service. To smooth the way toward such consent he sought to allay whatever suspicions his future wife might have aroused:

> I take this opportunity of remarking that you must not think that Countess D. is politically unreliable because she is friendly with the Crown Princess. To tell the truth, up to now she understands very little of politics, but of course she will never have any political views other than my own.[114]

It was no mean feat, then, for Bülow to bring his prize to port, to free himself from "years of uncertainty,"[115] and to rescue Marie from the ugly gossip that was finally beginning to surround her name.[116] In so doing he had demonstrated an adroitness which surpassed that of all the king's horsemen and all the king's men; he had put the world back together again.

Bülow's saccharine and sentimental expressions, however, make it difficult to uncover the reality of this world. That Marie proved to complement her husband socially in a brilliant fashion, entertaining with grace and elegance, is clear from contemporary comment. Her mother, too, Donna Laura Minghetti, the widow of a former Italian prime minister, added glitter to Bülow's establishment; among her

113. See Röhl, ed., *Philipp Eulenburgs Korrespondenz 1866–1891*, Eulenburg to Bülow, March 3, 1884, pp. 143–145; Eulenburg to Herbert Bismarck, May 14, 1885, pp. 152–153; Eulenburg to Herbert Bismarck, January 13, 1886, pp. 158–159; Bülow to Eulenburg, January 22, 1886, p. 159. See also Crown Princess Frederick to Marie Dönhoff, May 27, 1884, Bülow Papers/167; Crown Princess Frederick to Marie Dönhoff, December 1, 1885, Bülow Papers/169; Crown Princess Frederick to Marie Dönhoff, December 27, 1885, Bülow Papers/169.

114. Holstein, *Correspondence 1861–1896*, Bülow to Holstein, April 18, 1884, p. 111.

115. Ibid., p. 112.

116. Crown Princess Frederick to Marie Dönhoff, January 9, 1884, Bülow Papers/167; see also Karl Friedrich Nowak and Friedrich Thimme, eds., *Erinnerungen und Gedanken des Botschafters Anton Graf Monts* (Berlin: Verlag für Kulturpolitik G.M.B.H., 1932), pp. 153–154. For the assertion that Holstein had damaging information about Marie Bülow with which he could blackmail Bülow, see Eulenburg, "Pathologische Politik," 1913, Eulenburg Papers/77, p. 151; see also Ludwig Raschdau, "Meine Beziehungen zu Fürst Bülow," in Thimme, ed., *Front wider Bülow*, p. 29, and Johannes Haller, "Bülow und Eulenburg," in ibid., p. 45n.

many admirers figured none other than Holstein.[117] At the very least, Bülow acquired in Marie someone equipped to set off his own incandescence. Writing to Eulenburg shortly after his wedding, he expressed his satisfaction with his married state:

> I feel increasingly how excellently my wife suits me; she doesn't interfere with my individuality, aims, interests, views, and yet possesses what I entirely lack. She is also a rare being in that she combines ease and good nature with spirit and depth, joins together the good sides of the Italian and German, knows how to step out in society without eccentricities, free yet profoundly moral and serious.[118]

One cannot help being struck by the apparent contrast between Bülow's praise of his wife and the contemptuous attitude toward women he betrayed in society and in his memoirs. Baroness Hildegard von Spitzemberg was quick to see through his glib conversation: "He is one of those who seldom speak seriously to women, but rather pour a shower of compliments over them, and these indeed of so direct a kind that tasteless is scarcely too strong a word for them."[119] Tasteless would also be the word to describe his references to women in the fourth volume of his memoirs. Though published last, this volume is the first in chronological order, covering the years before Bülow reached the political summit. Here he exposed another side of his personality, or rather he showed himself in another role, that of Don Juan.[120] One need not stress his infidelity to Marie during their years of adulterous courtship, nor his thoughtless treatment of the women he seduced. Such behavior might well have been standard practice—even if it would not have earned the approval of his mother. What is significant is a boastfulness which clearly betokens something more than a conventional effort to deny the impotence of old age. It suggests that beneath an outer show of personal domination and satisfaction lurked the corresponding impotence of the child's angry need.

117. Rogge, ed., *Friedrich von Holstein*, Holstein to Ida von Stülpnagel, March 19, 1898, p. 189; Holstein to Ida von Stülpnagel, December 24, 1898, p. 191; Holstein to Ida von Stülpnagel, December 30, 1901, p. 200; Holstein to Ida von Stülpnagel, July 28, 1902, p. 209. See also Bogdan Graf von Hutten-Czapski, *Sechzig Jahre Politik und Gesellschaft* (Berlin: E. S. Mittler, 1936).

118. Röhl, ed., *Philipp Eulenburgs Korrespondenz 1866–1891*, Bülow to Eulenburg, May 29, 1886, p. 164.

119. Rudolf Vierhaus, ed., *Das Tagebuch der Baronin Spitzemberg* (Göttingen: Vandenhoeck and Ruprecht, 1960), June 2, 1898, p. 370.

120. See, for example, Bülow, *Memoirs*, IV: 119–120, 145–146, 206–207, 290–291, 345, 359–365, 408–411, 495–496.

■

What conditions did Bülow have to fulfill in order to be recognized as leader? How did he deal with those who brought him to power and on whom he depended for his continuance in office? From the portraits presented, which so far as possible have laid stress on each individual's childhood experience of his mother, one may deduce the expectations of the men eagerly awaiting him. What emerges is cohesion as escape—or possibly cohesion as a last resort.

Eulenburg's hopes have already been touched upon. He had long since undertaken the mission of installing Bülow as William's paladin-in-chief. In 1893 he had written to the man he regarded as his alter ego:

> Because I judge you as I do (and I only wish I was as sure of everything!) I have only one thought—namely, to smoothe your way and remove any snags with which the envy and dislike of petty natures may have encumbered your path. I have already a good many successes of this kind to point to—and my friendship exults in the thought of them![121]

Eulenburg had no inkling that his relations with his royal friend would be disturbed by Bülow's entrance onto the Berlin stage. On the contrary, once Bülow was added to the cast, Eulenburg felt convinced that his own role could be tailored to conform more perfectly to his fantasies. Relieved from the too close intimacy with William which more than once had brought him to the verge of nervous collapse, he could again enjoy wholeheartedly his performance as the emperor's friend.

Eulenburg was ecstatic over Bülow's success. At last, Eulenburg felt, he had steered the emperor's ship into a "safe harbourage."

> Perhaps it is presumptuous to call myself the steersman in this instance. But if I honestly ask myself whether the ship of state would have reached the harbor without my help . . . , I am bound to answer NO.
>
> For never in my difficult and responsible office of friendship have I deviated from the straight line of keeping the Emperor in touch with his instrument of government—by which I mean his legalised, established organs of administration. . . . Essentially it was a psychological work of art—one might even say a feat of manipulation—which was required of me. . . .
>
> These tasks I have now consigned to the skilful hands of Bülow. . . . I

121. Röhl, ed., *Philipp Eulenburgs Korrespondenz 1892–1895*, Eulenburg to Bülow, February 28, 1893, p. 1032.

need scarcely say that to him, as to the Emperor—being the trusted friend of both—I shall, now as then, give my counsel in any thorny question or situation. For I have never failed in friendship, not even when it was inseparable from serious inconveniences or actual perils.[122]

In the end Eulenburg turned out to be superfluous. In introducing Bülow, whom he regarded as his "sovereign's last card,"[123] Eulenberg in effect dealt himself out of the game. Once in Berlin, Bülow found he could dispense with this particular triangular relationship. Yet Eulenburg's eclipse was so gradual that he was only dimly conscious that his part was being excised from the play. The stark revelation of his fate did not occur until 1908. When he was forced to take legal action to silence charges of homosexuality and found no William at his side, he collapsed physically and emotionally.[124] Still, he never suspected that Bülow had been among those who betrayed him.[125] In his handling of Eulenburg, Bülow clearly vindicated his claim to psychological dexterity.

In Holstein's eyes, too, Bülow represented a last resort. As a subordinate in the Foreign Office when the elder Bülow had been state secretary, Holstein had had ample opportunity to know the son personally and to observe his professional development.[126] That Bernhard Bülow imparted to Holstein his marital hopes betokened a readiness to recognize the older man as an auxiliary in the world he was constructing. Not until a decade later, however, did the Gray Eminence begin to view Bülow in a similar light—that is, after his own relations with Eulenburg had deteriorated. During the years Bülow was serving in Rome, Holstein came to depend on him to repair the line to Eulenburg and thus to William. And as his reliance on Bülow increased, so too did his estimation of the younger man's abilities. Whereas in 1890 Holstein had threatened to resign should Bülow be named state secretary, seven years later, when the appoint-

122. Eulenburg's diary, 1898, Eulenburg Papers/50, pp. i–iii; also quoted in Haller, *Philipp Eulenburg*, II: 39–41. See also Eulenburg to Bülow, December 18, 1897, Eulenburg Papers/49, pp. 713–714, and Eulenburg to Bülow, August 23, 1902, Eulenburg Papers/59, pp. 72–72b.
123. Eulenburg to Bülow, May 2, 1899, Eulenburg Papers/53, p. 78; also quoted in Haller, *Philipp Eulenburg*, II: 37.
124. See Eulenburg's diary, April 21–June 24, 1908, reprinted in Haller, *Philipp Eulenburg*, II: 336–377.
125. On this point see the editor's introduction by Helmut Rogge, *Holstein und Harden* (Munich: Verlag C. H. Beck, 1959), pp. 8–15. See also Harry F. Young, *Maximilian Harden, Censor Germaniae: The Critic in Opposition from Bismarck to the Rise of Nazism* (The Hague: Martinus Nijhoff, 1959), pp. 82–125.
126. Holstein's attitude toward the elder Bülow was far from favorable. In his diary he commented: "When I was Bülow's immediate subordinate at the Foreign

ment finally materialized, he stayed at his post and prepared to lend his support.[127]

The cordial relations between Holstein and Bülow over the next twelve years have both fascinated and puzzled historians. To the question of who dominated whom, the answers have differed. Eulenburg, for one, urged Bülow to rid himself of Holstein as soon as possible and was dismayed when the Gray Eminence remained comfortably ensconced in the Wilhelmstrasse.[128] According to Eulenburg's biographer, Bülow became transformed into Holstein's creature, carefully executing orders handed down to him.[129] In this view Holstein, not Bülow, figures as Bismarck's true heir, and the Gray Eminence is credited with a capacity for ordering the reality of others—a capacity which he did not possess. Holstein's most recent biographer is closer to the mark when he claims that his protagonist surrendered "without a struggle and with apparent relief" the influence he had exercised in domestic affairs during the previous seven years.[130] How, then, did Bülow exorcize the demons that haunted Holstein?

Ministry, he did all he could to plague me, right up to the end. But after he had his stroke he sent for me, bade me farewell and entrusted his sons to my care." Norman Rich and M. H. Fisher, eds., *The Holstein Papers*, II: *Diaries* (Cambridge: Cambridge University Press, 1957), April 18, 1885, p. 187.

127. Holstein's relationship with Bülow can be traced in his *Correspondence 1861–1896*: Holstein to Hatzfeldt, November 10, 1886, pp. 194–196; Holstein to Eisendecher, March 26, 1890, p. 332; Bülow to Holstein, January 15, 1895, p. 490; Holstein to Bülow, January 23, 1895, pp. 491–492; Holstein to Bülow, February 21, 1895, pp. 499–502; Bülow to Holstein, March 10, 1895, pp. 508–509; Bülow to Holstein, January 3, 1896, pp. 582–583; Bülow to Holstein, January 16, 1896, pp. 586–587; Bülow to Holstein, March 19, 1896, pp. 598–599; Bülow to Holstein, April 3, 1896, p. 603; Bülow to Holstein, June 12, 1896, pp. 617–618. For the influence of the *Kladderadatsch* affair on Holstein's last minute decision to swallow Marschall's resignation without protest, see Eulenburg to Bülow, June 9, 1897, Bülow Papers/76 (also in Eulenburg Papers/47, pp. 328–332).

128. Eulenburg to Bülow, August 17, 1897, Eulenburg Papers/48, pp. 449–450, and Eulenburg to Bülow, August 23, 1897, Eulenburg Papers/48, pp. 466–468; see also Eulenburg to Hohenlohe, February 15, 1895, quoted in C. Hohenlohe, *Denkwürdigkeiten der Reichskanzlerzeit*, p. 41. Before entering office Bülow had seemed determined to dismiss Holstein: "Ich kann und will nicht Staatssekretär werden mit Holstein im Amt. Als Botschafter, vom Auslands aus komme ich vortrefflich mit Holstein aus . . . aber als Staatssekretär im Amte ginge es nun und nimmermehr!" Röhl, ed., *Philipp Eulenburgs Korrespondenz 1892–1895*, Bülow to Eulenburg, December 3, 1894, p. 1417; see also Bülow to Eulenburg, September 28, 1895, Eulenburg Papers/38, p. 672.

129. See, for example, Haller, *Philipp Eulenburg*, II: 99, 119. See also Eulenburg's marginal note, May 12, 1902, Eulenburg Papers/59, p. 46, and his "Pathologische Politik," 1913, Eulenburg Papers/77.

130. Rich, *Holstein*, II: 548; see also Winzen, *Bülows Weltmachtkonzept*, pp. 12–13, 427.

If demons were laid to rest, their quiescence cannot be attributed to Bülow. Rather nature took its course. In 1898 Bismarck finally died, thus relieving Bülow of the burden borne by his predecessors of defending against thunderbolts hurled by the Iron Chancellor. By the same token, Holstein's terror lost its principal object. Yet for the Gray Eminence, Bismarck had been, in large measure, a surrogate demon who derived his force from fears generated in Holstein's childhood. Bülow could not eradicate the traces of such experiences. What he could do was to validate the stratagems Holstein had long ago devised to battle his sense of impending catastrophe.

Without question Bülow recognized Holstein's aid as indispensable to his handling of foreign affairs. His reliance on Holstein as his adviser-in-chief continued until the Gray Eminence's death in 1909, shortly before Bülow's dismissal from the chancellorship. Even after Holstein himself had been forced out of the Wilhelmstrasse in 1906—an act for which Bülow was responsible, though Holstein, like Eulenburg, never suspected their mutual friend of betrayal—Bülow did not cease to consult the Gray Eminence. He passed on to him vital documents, keeping Holstein fully abreast of developments in his former bailiwick. To be sure, there had earlier been occasions when Holstein's advice was not followed and when he had resorted to threats of resignation to vent his annoyance. But such outbursts had been rare.[131] In short, Holstein's general mood of satisfaction testified to the aptness of the judgment he had passed on Bülow in 1885:

> Bernhard Bülow is clean-shaven and pasty, with a shifty look and an almost perpetual smile. Intellectually plausible rather than penetrating. Has no ideas in reserve with which to meet all contingencies, but appropriates other people's ideas and skilfully retails them without acknowledging the source. In this way he often flatters the originator of the idea.[132]

Bülow, however, was not alone in considering Holstein indispensable. In the 1890s that code word had been freely bestowed on the Gray Eminence and had been an accurate reflection of reality. Hence Bülow's estimate of Holstein's importance for foreign policy, since it had been voiced by so many others, cannot in itself explain why Holstein accepted Bülow as significant for his own emotional well-being. The crucial element for Holstein—and for Eulenburg too—was Bülow's relationship with William. By acting as a buffer

---

131. Rich, *Holstein*, II: 547–554; see also Raschdau, "Meine Beziehungen zu Fürst Bülow," in Thimme, ed., *Front wider Bülow*, pp. 21–29.

132. Holstein, *Diaries*, April 8, 1885, p. 188.

and muting the alarums and excursions of an excitable monarch, Bülow reestablished a semblance of order. Such order allowed Holstein to reduce his contacts with the external world—contacts which in the previous seven years had proved emotionally exhausting. He preferred to live in a restricted world so long as he was convinced that nothing important was going on outside it. Of this Bülow assured him, just as Bismarck had done.

What, then, was the nature of Bülow's relationship with William? Was Bülow nothing more than a crass flatterer who kept his sovereign in good humor by feeding his vanity? Many contemporary observers would have followed General Field Marshal Alfred Count von Waldersee in answering yes:

> Bülow's position with the Emperor is in my opinion unshaken. He is pleasing to the monarch because he never openly contradicts him. Thus he necessarily leads the exalted personage to overrate his own capacities and burdens himself with a heavy responsibility.[133]

For the better part of eleven years Bülow kept the allegiance of the emperor, who delighted in their cordial relations:

> When I was in Berlin, scarcely a day went by without my taking a long morning walk with the Chancellor. . . . I often had a meal with him, his amiable wife and a group of the most interesting men, in choosing whom [Bülow] was a master. He was likewise unsurpassed in skilfully conducting conversation and in the witty handling of the various topics that arose. To me it was always a pleasure to be in the company of the Chancellor and enjoy his bubbling wit.[134]

Was William simply taken in by Bülow's clever psychological manipulation? What is striking in his memoirs is how little he actually says about Bülow. In the chapter ostensibly devoted to the chancellor with whom he looked forward to sharing a common purpose, in part because they belonged to roughly the same generation, the emperor's subject largely disappears from view. Where one expects him to describe Bülow, one finds instead that William has launched into a

---

133. Heinrich Otto Meisner, ed., *Denkwürdigkeiten des General-Feldmarschalls Alfred Grafen von Waldersee*, III: *1900–1904* (Stuttgart and Berlin: Deutsche Verlags-Anstalt, 1923), December 1901, p. 176, and November 16, 1903, p. 220. See also Zedlitz-Trützschler, *Twelve Years at the Imperial German Court*, Summer 1903, pp. 27–28; November 3, 1904, p. 93; March 1906, p. 167. Compare Bülow to Eulenburg, December 26, 1897, Eulenburg Papers/49, pp. 725–726.

134. Wilhelm II, *Memoirs*, p. 96; see also Hutten-Czapski, *Sechzig Jahre Politik und Gesellschaft*, pp. 393–394. Through his mother, William had met Bülow's future wife in 1878 and had been charmed by her. She preserved his youthful letters to her: Bülow Papers/173.

tirade against the secret power of Holstein. Only when he comes to the *Daily Telegraph* Affair—when an indiscreet interview he had given appeared in the London newspaper—does the emperor comment at length, candidly revealing the wounds inflicted by his chancellor's failure to defend him from the ensuing public criticism.[135] William's curious substitution of Holstein for Bülow, coupled with his openness about his own subsequent humiliation, suggests that the denouement of his relations with his chancellor did not take him completely by surprise.

But the break—like similar ruptures in the past—was accompanied by nervous prostration. Though William might fail to husband his emotional strength, experience had taught him that his psychological constitution was far from robust. If he nevertheless continued to stir up storms, he also appreciated the personal risks he incurred thereby. His partial recognition of his own self-destructiveness had facilitated the task Bülow called "mental massage."[136] It had made William reluctant to call his chancellor's bluff, to test the sincerity of a pretended devotion in a naked contest of wills. Eulenburg perceived this hesitancy and commented on it to Bülow: the emperor, he wrote, had "a mixture of respect and fear" for his chancellor, "on account of his more or less distinct consciousness" that he could not "get on without" him.[137]

Hence flattery is too simple a description of Bülow's "massage." In giving advice on how to handle his royal friend, Eulenburg indicated both the complexity of the assignment and the course that Bülow ostensibly followed:

> If you want to attain something, if you want to serve and help your country, the Emperor must grow fond of you. You are a captivator, a great *charmeur;* you have enchanted many people in your lifetime; now strive to enchant the Emperor. *Pro Patria esto!* You can contradict the Emperor very well when it is necessary, but contradict him only in private and don't vex him unnecessarily over trifles. If the Emperor doesn't have the impression that you like him, that you love him and admire him, then nothing is to be done with him. You were a Hussar; you are a good rider; the Emperor is a horse which goes only if it is led with a light hand, if it feels pressure on its flank, but its mouth is not torn and it gets the spur not too often, if above all it gets a lump of sugar now and then or even frequently. Don't forget the sugar; without the sugar this nag can't be

135. Wilhelm II, *Memoirs*, pp. 119–120.
136. Bülow, *Memoirs*, I: 666.
137. Eulenburg to Bülow, August 9, 1903, Eulenburg Papers/74, pp. 14–15; also quoted in Haller, *Philipp Eulenburg*, II: 161. See also Eulenburg to Bülow, July 14, 1899, Eulenburg Papers/54, pp. 166–167.

brought over any fence, can't be prevented from breaking away, can't be ridden at all.[138]

If in contrast to Bismarck, Bülow used a light rein on the emperor—and fed him sugar—he still kept a whip in reserve. The brutality with which he treated William in his memoirs reflects not despised love, but rather a destructive temper freed at last. And clearly Bülow knew where his sovereign could be hurt. Through his wife, who was a long-standing and intimate friend of the Empress Frederick, he was fully informed of the gulf that separated mother and son. In his memoirs he referred repeatedly to the strained relations between them, depicting the Empress Frederick as a Cassandra uttering dark prophecies of the harm her son would wreak[139] and William as determined to defy someone "whom at certain moments, he even loved (he certainly loved her more than she loved him)."[140] To remind the emperor of his mother's forebodings, and in so doing to treat him as she had done, was thus for Bülow at once a temptation and a threat held in readiness.

In short, for more than a decade William had been willing to grant Bülow the upper hand. But the fear which went along with this dependence and which Bülow had it in his power to activate at any time betrayed how artificial was the world Bülow had fabricated for his royal master.

■

Still, a semblance of political cohesion, in the form of a series of personal contrivances, had been created. It was clearly a fragile balance, which Bülow could not solidify by a string of successes comparable to Bismarck's. By the same token, the cohesion achieved by these two statesmen has explicitly and intentionally been viewed from different but complementary angles. In the discussion of the founder of the Second Reich, the emphasis fell on the erosion of his authority, on the transformation of his subordinates' hostile dependence into panicky disavowal. In the discussion of Bülow, on the other hand, the central concern has been to delineate the individual dilemmas which added up to a readiness to accept a new authority

---

138. Eulenburg to Bülow [1897], quoted in Friedrich Thimme, "Fürst Bülow und Kaiser Wilhelm II," in Thimme, ed., *Front wider Bülow*, pp. 7–8. Compare Eulenburg to Bülow, December 29, 1895, Eulenburg Papers/39, p. 963.

139. Bülow, *Memoirs*, I: 92, 245–246, 315–316; see also Crown Princess Frederick to Marie Dönhoff, October 21, 1885, Bülow Papers/169, and Empress Frederick to Marie Bülow, March 26, 1889, Bülow Papers/170.

140. Bülow, *Memoirs*, IV: 171; see also ibid., IV: 172, 175–176, 219–220, 306.

figure. In both cases that figure emerged as a force for order and stability who himself manipulated or appropriated those about him in an effort to reinforce his own emotional equilibrium.

The brittleness of the cohesion achieved suggests the perils which lay ahead. For haunted men—men with threatening inner landscapes—the outer prospect remained correspondingly hostile. An internal world run on fear produced an external world run on hate.

Chapter 6

A Younger Generation Taking Over

The Heirs of Gladstone and Salisbury

In the course of the 1890s the two stars that had illuminated the British political firmament, Gladstone and Salisbury, began to fade. Gladstone's bright glow was at last extinguished when he retired in 1894; Salisbury's light grew dimmer even while he continued to occupy high office. Thus those who remained confronted a problem comparable to that of their German counterparts: how to regroup in the face of the loss of a leader. With what pangs did they separate themselves from figures whose power was waning? Did they succeed in fashioning anew the type of relationships, characterized by personal restraint and mutual respect, which they had enjoyed under Gladstone and Salisbury?

Unlike the German case the relationships themselves have given rise to no glaring paradox. Did Gladstone and Salisbury, then, serve no symbolic function derived from the experience of childhood? Or did that very experience make such a function less obvious? One is thus led to wonder whether or not these British leaders symbolically recreated a kind of "good" maternal behavior which stood in sharp contrast to Bismarck's.

"Good" is an even more treacherous term than "bad." Psychoanalysts, as one might anticipate, have concentrated on the havoc wreaked by maternal failure, with the result that the good mother emerges from much of their writing as the woman who somehow manages to tread the narrow path between the pitfalls of too much and too little. A few markers are, nonetheless, discernible: a heightened sensitivity which makes adaptation to the infant's needs possible, followed by a reassuring constancy which holds the world steady for the growing child. Such is the protective figure capable of providing "good-enough" mothering.

The current psychoanalytic notion of "good-enough" represents an effort to refashion the ideal type of a good mother.[1] All mothers are to some extent bad, and hence no man or woman grows up without fearing his or her mother and without internalizing her as a frightening figure. What is meant, then, by "good-enough" is a mother who can also be internalized as a reassuring presence and thus counteract her own negative image. Emotional separation remains a difficult task; yet since infantile dependence has proved safe as well as frightening, the child is in a position to approach the outer world in a spirit of trust. To put matters very simply: a "good-enough" mother welcomes and sustains—and little by little corrects—the picture her child has conceived in order to satisfy his own longings.

The child of the "good-enough" mother does not develop without ambivalence. But in this case aggression, instead of helping to keep alive an attachment, is experienced as dangerous to self and loved one. (The ensuing efforts to put a damper on anger may take the form of deep-seated and ramifying inhibitions. At a time when it has become fashionable to consider only the detrimental effect of thwarting sexual or aggressive impulses, it is easy to overlook the compensations which derive from restraint.) Once that danger has been allayed, reassurance is at hand: defusing hostility and making reparation for it set a "benign circle" in motion again. When angry memories and experiences have been sorted out, when a safe internal world has been recovered, a person can accept nurture and offer it too.

In earlier discussions of Gladstone and Salisbury and their colleagues, motifs of this sort have already appeared. Is there reason, then, to believe that "good-enough" mothers dominated the British landscape? One might be tempted to venture an uncertain yes; there is no need, however, to push this matter beyond conjecture. Rather, as in the German case, the task at hand is to trace the varying for-

---

1. This line of thought reflects the influence of D. W. Winnicott—more particularly "The Capacity to be Alone," "The Theory of the Parent-Child Relationship," and "The Development of the Capacity for Concern," in his *The Maturational Processes and the Facilitating Environment: Studies in the Theory of Emotional Development* (London: Hogarth Press, 1965), pp. 29–55, 73–82; and "Transitional Objects and Transitional Phenomena," and "The Depressive Position in Normal Emotional Development," in his *Through Pediatrics to Psycho-Analysis* (London: Hogarth Press, 1975), pp. 229–242, 262–277.

tunes of human alliances to the renewal of political cohesion—with mothering as the point of departure.

I. The Ironies of the Great Mother: Queen Victoria and Her Male Maternal Surrogates

In a study designed to bring a domestic sensibility to bear on political history, it is curious that the chief proponent of domesticity has not yet made a grand entrance. Except as glimpsed through her daughter the Empress Frederick, Queen Victoria has remained behind the scenes. By the early 1890s she had become not only the mother of royalty, but the grandmother and great-grandmother as well. Fertility, however, offers no guarantee that one can provide "good-enough" mothering. Paradoxically the reigning matriarch, whose domestic tranquillity contributed substantially to fostering a reverent British attitude toward motherhood, represents an exception to the ideal type. She also stands as an example of how environment may improve mediocre material. This matter is of such thematic interest as to warrant an excursus—an excursus that should elucidate Victoria's performance as a mother in the light of her prior experience as a daughter.

When Victoria's mother died in March 1861, the forty-one-year-old queen was prostrate. Writing to her daughter Vicky six weeks after the Duchess of Kent's death, Victoria dwelt on her melancholy:

> I cried constantly yesterday and the grief and yearning and almost despair which at times comes over me are dreadful! I find even that gets worse than better.... It seems very long since I saw her—and heard from her—and so it must go on for the rest of my life! It seems a fearful thought.[2]

For months thereafter, the queen remained shrouded in gloom. Even in an age which granted more scope for mourning than present practice permits, her breakdown excited comment—and hence invites interpretation.[3]

2. Roger Fulford, ed., *Dearest Child: Letters between Queen Victoria and the Princess Royal 1858–1861* (London: Evans Brothers, 1964), Queen Victoria to the Princess Royal, April 26, 1861, p. 324.

3. See, for example, A. L. Kennedy, ed., '*My Dear Duchess': Social and Political Letters to the Duchess of Manchester 1858–1869* (London: John Murray, 1956), Clarendon to the Duchess of Manchester, March 27, 1861, and April 14, 1861, pp. 141, 148; Dean of Windsor and Hector Bolitho, eds., *Letters of Lady Augusta Stanley: A Young Lady at Court 1849–1863* (London: Gerald Howe, 1927), pp. 185–223. See also Elizabeth Longford, *Queen Victoria: Born to Succeed* (New York and Evanston: Harper and Row, 1964), pp. 290–292.

Indeed the outside observer would have judged Victoria well situated to cope with a trial that at some point everyone must undergo. Though she had not anticipated the actual timing of her mother's death, she had had ample opportunity during the previous two years, in which she had tended her ailing parent, to prepare herself for such an eventuality. Still more, Victoria, watched over by her adored husband, appeared securely ensconced in her own family. Yet in this crisis she derived no comfort from her children's solicitude, and even Albert's affection offered inadequate compensation for her loss. To account for her grief, Victoria invoked the convention of the imcomparability of a mother's love:[4] what her grief really expressed was a yearning for reunion. At its deepest level that reunion implied emotional fusion. In burying her mother, Victoria was overwhelmed by a fantasy of merger between parent and child which was profoundly self-destructive. The persistence of such a fantasy provides an ironic commentary on her lifelong effort to defend herself against too close an identification with the mother she mourned.

By Victoria's own account hers had been a melancholy childhood.[5] Her father had died when she was an infant, leaving his widow in uncertain financial and social circumstances far from her German homeland. The unremitting battle the Duchess of Kent subsequently waged against the unregenerate British royal family anticipated the experience of her granddaughter Vicky in Prussia forty years later.[6] And just as Vicky was to try to influence and mold her son in order to acquire a standing-ground of her own, so too did the Duchess of Kent determine to appropriate and control her child. The fact that Victoria was a daughter allowed the duchess to intrude to an extent that Vicky never could have managed with her Willy. In one sentence Victoria evoked a childhood devoid of privacy: "I was brought up very simply—never had a room to myself till I was nearly grown up—always slept in my Mother's room till I came to the throne."[7]

4. Arthur Christopher Benson and Viscount Esher, eds., *The Letters of Queen Victoria, 1837–1861* (London: John Murray, 1907), III, Queen Victoria to the King of the Belgians, March 16, 1861, March 26, 1861, March 30, 1861, April 9, 1861, pp. 435–439; see also Theodore Martin, *The Life of His Royal Highness the Prince Consort* (London: Smith, Elder, and Co., 1875–1880), V: 318–319.

5. See extract from Queen Victoria's reminiscences of her early childhood, 1872, in *The Letters of Queen Victoria, 1837–1861*, I: 10–14. See also Fulford, ed., *Dearest Child*, Queen Victoria to the Princess Royal, June 9, 1858, pp. 111–112.

6. For Queen Victoria's comment on this point, see *Dearest Child*, Queen Victoria to the Princess Royal, March 9, 1858, pp. 72–73.

7. Queen Victoria's reminiscences, in *The Letters of Queen Victoria, 1837–1861*, I: 11.

If as a child she could not escape her mother's manipulation, as an adolescent she could not escape her mother's sexuality. Whether or not the relations between the Duchess of Kent and Sir John Conroy, the head of her household, extended to physical intimacy has been much debated; clearly Victoria found their familiarity painful.[8] In an effort to retreat from this environment—to find a way out of the "imprisonment" she "had to endure"[9]—she took refuge in a precarious self-sufficiency which both repudiated her female body and denied her emotional needs.

As she struggled to blot out what was intolerable and to take charge of her own inner life, Victoria found an ally in Baroness Lehzen. "Governess" is the term usually applied to the woman who "was placed about" Victoria when the child turned five;[10] yet it is inadequate to describe Lehzen's position as confidante, mentor, and disciplinarian—a position she occupied until Albert forced her withdrawal in 1842. To Victoria she appeared the one fixed point in an uncertain world:

> *Dear good* Lehzen takes such care of me, that I shall never be able to repay her sufficiently for it but by my love and gratitude. I never can sufficiently repay her for all she has *borne* and done for me. She is the *most affectionate, devoted, attached,* and *disinterested* friend I have, and I love her most *dearly. . . .*[11]

Such were the terms of praise the princess bestowed upon her faithful servant—for servant rather than friend she remained. Victoria always demonstrated a marked awareness of her own status as royalty, and certainly by the age of five this form of class consciousness had taken root in her mind. Lehzen might be useful and trust-

8. Lytton Strachey and Roger Fulford, eds., *The Greville Memoirs 1814-1860* (London: Macmillan and Co., 1938), II, September 6, 1831, p. 194, and IV, August 15, 1839, p. 199; Longford, *Queen Victoria,* pp. 118-119.

9. *The Letters of Queen Victoria, 1837-1861,* I, Princess Feodore to Queen Victoria, 1843, p. 18.

10. Queen Victoria's reminiscences, in ibid., I: 14.

11. Viscount Esher, ed., *The Girlhood of Queen Victoria: A Selection from Her Majesty's Diaries between the Years 1832 and 1840* (London: John Murray, 1912), I, November 5, 1835, p. 138 (emphasis in the original). In line with Victoria's customary assertion that those around her were "attached" to her—striking evidence of her emotional need—she expressed similar sentiments, with far less warmth, about the nurse who had taken care of her before Lehzen's arrival: "Received the news of the death of my poor old Nurse, Mrs. Brock, which took place the day before yesterday. She was not a pleasant person, and undoubtedly had, as everybody has, her faults, but she was extremely attached to and fond of me, having been with me from my birth till my fifth year, therefore it is impossible, and it would be very wrong if I did not feel her death." Ibid., I, May 22, 1836, p. 159.

worthy, but her psychological significance for Victoria lasted only as long as she stayed by her charge's side. The social distance between them prevented Lehzen from sundering a mother's emotional hold: she was not the stuff out of which the regal Victoria could fabricate an ideal self-image. In this, as in other less exalted cases, difference of social class safeguarded the predominance of a mother who was not obliged to stoop to the daily grind of childrearing.

When Victoria ascended the throne in 1837, she staggered observers by her poise and self-command.[12] To her ministers she appeared as a solitary majestic figure. Though Lehzen stood close at hand, the new queen shunted her mother aside and got rid of Conroy. Had she in fact achieved an emotional balance of her own devising? The vicissitudes of the first years of her reign indicate that the answer is no. Her regal bearing belied her want of instruction for the office she gladly assumed. Nor had she been adequately prepared for the role which is of interest here—that of woman and mother. Her pseudo-independence and precocious self-management betokened an unstable equilibrium rather than an integrated psychic structure.

■

The story of Victoria's tutelage under her first prime minister, William Viscount Melbourne—her gradual, if incomplete acceptance of her constitutional duties—is well known.[13] The psychological function Melbourne fulfilled has been less clearly delineated. To be sure, it is common knowledge that he was very good to, and very fond of, the young queen, and that theirs quickly became a close and confidential friendship. Beyond this, it will be argued, Melbourne played a role comparable to that of a psychotherapist: in her relationship with him, Victoria dramatically reworked her strategy for dealing with deep-seated emotional needs. Here, as in the political realm, much remained undone. Yet it is Melbourne who deserves the credit for Victoria's relative success as wife and mother. If she still fell short of the ideal type of "good-enough" mother, thanks to Melbourne she came closer to it than one would have anticipated from knowledge of her childhood alone.

The prime minister's own attachment to Victoria was intense.

12. *Greville Memoirs*, III, June 21, 1837, pp. 372–376.
13. On Melbourne, see W. M. Torrens, *Memoirs of the Right Honourable William Second Viscount Melbourne*, 2nd ed., 2 vols. (London: Macmillan and Co., 1878); Lloyd C. Sanders, ed., *Lord Melbourne's Papers* (London: Longmans, Green, and Co., 1889); Lord David Cecil, *Melbourne* (Indianapolis and New York: Bobbs-Merrill Co., 1954); Philip Ziegler, *Melbourne: A Biography of William Lamb 2nd Viscount Melbourne* (London: Collins, 1976).

While an analyst is never without feelings for his patient, the quality of Melbourne's affection brings to mind a fictional character closer to the period—George Eliot's Silas Marner. The elegant and sophisticated statesman might bear little physical resemblance to Eliot's broken-down artisan, but like the wretched weaver whose life was transformed by the motherless babe he discovered on his hearth, Victoria's psychological fragility evoked in Melbourne a rush of tenderness and concern that had long been submerged. As one contemporary noted: he was "passionately fond of her as he might be of his daughter if he had one, and the more because he [was] a man with a capacity for loving without having anything in the world to love."[14] For Melbourne (unlike Marner), relations with women had always been central to his emotional being. At the age of fifty-eight he found a new object on which to bestow his solicitude; another chance was given him to protect and nourish a susceptible creature. For the next four years he devoted himself to the child who had come into his life.

The change in Melbourne's mode of existence did not go unobserved:

> It is ... marvellous that he should be able to overcome the force of habit so completely as to endure the life he leads. Month after month he remains at the Castle [Windsor], submitting to this daily routine: of all men he appeared to be the last to be broken in to the trammels of a Court, and never was such a revolution seen in anybody's occupations and habits. Instead of indolently sprawling in all the attitudes of luxurious ease, he is always sitting bolt upright; his free and easy language interlarded with "damns" is carefully guarded and regulated with the strictest propriety, and he has exchanged the good talk of Holland House for the trivial, laboured, and wearisome inanities of the Royal circle.[15]

This metamorphosis enabled Melbourne to spend more hours with Victoria "than any two people, in any relation of life, perhaps ever" passed together. For long periods he was "at her side for at least six hours everyday—an hour in the morning, two on horseback, one at dinner, and two in the evening."[16] Scarcely a day went by without a personal interview of roughly an hour and several exchanges in writing. What transpired during that time? In the published portion of Victoria's journals, which extend to her marriage in 1840, she has provided an almost daily report on their hours together. Its very

14. *Greville Memoirs*, IV, September 12, 1838, p. 93; for Greville's obituary judgment on Melbourne, see ibid., VI, November 29, 1848, pp. 129–136.
15. Ibid., IV, December 15, 1838, p. 110.
16. Ibid., IV, December 15, 1838, pp. 109–110; see also Esher, ed., *The Girlhood of Queen Victoria*, I, January 20, 1838, p. 259.

artlessness makes it touching: the unaffected recitation of trivia is juxtaposed with expressions of deep feeling—a feeling centered on Melbourne. It was with him that for the first time Victoria enjoyed steady protection:

> *He alone* inspires me with that feeling of great confidence and I may say *security,* for I feel *so safe* when he speaks to me and is with me; what he says is all so kind and good, and he never says anything which could alarm or hurt me.[17]

Above all, by providing an emotional haven for Victoria, Melbourne allowed her to relax her strenuous and anxious efforts at self-sufficiency. His reliability, his constancy, permitted a controlled regression and the rediscovery—without fear—of dependency needs. No one—not even Victoria's uncle, King Leopold, who had been an important but fleeting figure in her childhood—had adhered so scrupulously to Melbourne's prescription of patience and quiet as "the only way in which a man can have any power with a woman."[18] In the safe harbor of her relationship with Melbourne, Victoria succeeded in doing what she had not been able to accomplish as a child, to fabricate and to confirm an image of a soothing parent.

The hardest task Melbourne had to face was relinquishing his charge. The political world which had brought them together would one day divide them: Melbourne could not remain forever prime minister, and indeed his government stood in constant danger. Meditating on the prospect of an eventual separation from Victoria, he took comfort in the thought of her marrying: "a woman cannot stand alone for long, in whatever situation she is," he remarked.[19] As the wedding date drew near, he strove to reassure the nervous bride by promising her that he would dine with the royal couple on their return from their two-day honeymoon.[20] In similar fashion, when a year and a half later his resignation could no longer be postponed, he urged the queen to bestow on Albert the confidence which he himself had earlier enjoyed. The departing statesman had filled an emotional space whose existence Victoria had not suspected, and his last gift to her was to prepare the way for his successor.[21]

---

17. *The Girlhood of Queen Victoria,* I, January 9, 1838, p. 254 (emphasis in the original).

18. Ibid., II, January 21, 1839, p. 103.

19. Ibid., II, October 14, 1839, p. 267.

20. Ibid., II, February 7, 1840, pp. 315–316.

21. On this point, see *The Letters of Queen Victoria, 1837–1861,* I, Memoranda by Mr. Anson, May 4, 1841, p. 268, May 5, 1841, pp. 269–270, and August 31, 1841, p. 311; Viscount Melbourne to Queen Victoria, August 30, 1841, p. 306, and September 2, 1841, p. 315.

■

To what kind of man had he entrusted his treasure?[22] Though both Melbourne and Albert were handsome—and Victoria never ceased to marvel at the beauty of the young prince (and cousin) she had chosen—Albert did not replicate the older figure. If Melbourne has often been portrayed as a holdover from the nonchalant eighteenth century, Albert has seemed the embodiment of nineteenth-century moral earnestness. But such generational distinctions have a specious quality and obscure a most striking difference that obeyed no rules dictated by age: the difference in the two men's ease with women. Where Melbourne sought the company of women and found life empty without a female figure to light his way, Albert felt uncomfortable in their presence and shunned their society. His experience with his own mother had marked him profoundly. Incompatibility with her husband, misery over his sexual adventures, had driven her, when Albert was only five, to elope with another man. The child never saw his mother again. Yet he cherished her memory; for him memory became more precious—and safer—than physical reality. Nor did Albert forget the ravages caused by licentiousness and marital infidelity. Melbourne misspoke when he hinted to Victoria that the bridegroom might some day deviate from the highest standards of sexual morality.[23] So far as one can tell, this never occurred. Moreover, Albert's restrained behavior undoubtedly alleviated Victoria's fears about union with a man.

His restraint displayed itself in the unassertive way in which he acquired ascendancy over his wife. His relationship with his older brother had given him long practice in exercising influence without pushing himself into the foreground. The two boys, one year apart in age, had been reared as twins. Not until Albert had turned twenty-one was he separated from his sibling. It was only then—and much to his chagrin—that he gave up "the custom of saying *we*" and took

22. The two official biographies of Prince Albert, composed with Queen Victoria's assistance, are: Charles Grey, *The Early Years of His Royal Highness The Prince Consort*, 3rd ed. (London: Smith, Elder, and Co., 1865), and Martin, *The Prince Consort*; see also the reminiscences of Albert's political mentor: F. Max Müller, ed., *Memoirs of Baron Stockmar by his son Baron E. von Stockmar*, 2 vols. (London: Longmans, Green, and Co., 1872). More recent biographies are: Roger Fulford, *The Prince Consort* (London: Macmillan and Co., 1949), and Daphne Bennett, *King without a Crown: Albert Prince Consort of England 1819–1861* (London: Heinemann, 1977). Among the biographies of Queen Victoria, the following are particularly illuminating on her relations with her consort: Lytton Strachey, *Queen Victoria* (New York: Harcourt, Brace, and World, 1921), and Longford, *Queen Victoria*.
23. Esher, ed., *The Girlhood of Queen Victoria*, II, January 19, 1840, p. 299.

to using the word "*I*," which sounded "egotistical and cold."[24] Albert might chafe in what appeared the anomalous position of a young husband who was not master in his own house, but he knew how to endure it patiently until such mastery became his.

Clearly Victoria's reliance on Albert compensated for the loss she experienced with the disappearance of Melbourne. So much she made plain in a letter to her Uncle Leopold shortly after her first prime minister left office:

> It has been indeed a sad time for me, and I am still bewildered, and can't believe that my excellent Lord Melbourne is no longer my Minister. . . . After seeing him for four years, with very few exceptions—*daily*—you may imagine that I *must* feel the change; and the longer the time gets since we parted, the *more* I feel it. *Eleven days* was the *longest* I ever was without seeing him, and this time will be elapsed on Saturday, so you may imagine what the change must be. I cannot say what a comfort and support my beloved Angel [Albert] is to me, and how well and how kindly and properly he behaves.[25]

A year later Victoria's mourning was over, and she had relegated her relationship with Melbourne to the past. A footnote she added to her diary entry of March 22, 1839—an entry in which she had expressed her unbounded confidence in her first prime minister—bears witness to the change:

> Reading this again, I cannot forbear remarking what an artificial sort of happiness *mine* was *then,* and what a blessing it is I have now in my beloved Husband *real* and *solid* happiness, which no Politics no worldly reverses *can* change; it could not have lasted long, as it was then, for after all, kind and excellent as Lord M. is, and kind as he was to [me], it was but in society that I had amusement, and I was only living on that superficial resource, which I *then fancied* was happiness! Thank God! for *me* and others, this is changed, and I *know what* REAL happiness is.[26]

Victoria had transferred her ideal of a parental figure to Albert and subsequently clung to this idealized image with feverish tenacity. No ambivalence was allowed to mar the worshipful attitude she

24. Prince Albert to the Dowager Duchess of Gotha, November 28, 1838, quoted and translated in Grey, *The Early Years of the Prince Consort,* p. 184 (emphasis in the original).

25. *The Letters of Queen Victoria, 1837–1861,* I, Queen Victoria to the King of the Belgians, September 8, 1841, p. 320 (emphasis in the original).

26. Esher, ed., *The Girlhood of Queen Victoria,* II, October 1, 1842, pp. 135–136n (emphasis in the original). For pictorial evidence of this happiness, see Marina Warner, *Queen Victoria's Sketchbook* (New York: Crown, 1979). See also Virginia Surtees, *Charlotte Canning: Lady-in-Waiting to Queen Victoria and Wife of the First Viceroy of India 1817–1861* (London: John Murray, 1975), pp. 59–165.

adopted toward him. His official biographers—with her assistance and prompting—struck the proper note in their paeans: an Albert possessed of clear perception and cool judgment, endowed with discretion, forbearance, discipline, and calm, shines forth from their pages. Idealization and identification went hand in hand; Albert was, in Victoria's mind, her own better self. She might still shelter a poorer, lesser self, one that drew sustenance from the angry thoughts she could not bear to direct toward her husband. With Albert firmly ensconced, to paraphrase her words, as guide, protector, father, even mother, as well as husband, Victoria again found a safe harbor.[27] But this new allegiance inhibited further growth; rather it soon hardened into a rigid posture.

The disappearance of Melbourne cannot alone account for Victoria's inflexibility—for an imcomplete "therapeutic" experience which offered relief, though not the achievement of an elusive "maturity." If Melbourne paved the way for the young queen's reliance on her husband, it was the stress of motherhood, coinciding with his own departure, that made Victoria's need so urgent and overwhelming. Pregnancy and birth, even when daily child care is delegated to nursemaids, act as powerful stimulants to revive the mother's own childhood experience.[28] In the face of this regressive pull—spontaneous and frightening—Victoria's identification with Albert provided the only ballast available to her.

While the queen's relationship with her husband was crucial to her emotional equilibrium, that relationship itself had to be safeguarded against the psychic assaults of her children, especially the first two. Victoria could not help but perceive Vicky, born in November 1840, and Bertie, who appeared almost exactly a year later, as intruders and hence potentially dangerous. With neither of them, as she wrote Vicky's future mother-in-law, did she find "intimate intercourse . . . agreeable or easy."[29] In her mind emotional distance offered a measure of protection against what amounted to sibling rivalry with them. In the case of Vicky this peril was mitigated by the girl's ability to sustain the role her mother had assigned her, that of Albert's child. Her precocious development bore witness to the virtues of beloved Papa, and she was early inducted into the cult of

27. Fulford, ed., *Dearest Child*, Queen Victoria to the Princess Royal, June 9, 1858, pp. 111–112.

28. Compare D. W. Winnicott, "Primary Maternal Preoccupation," in his collection of papers *Through Pediatrics to Psycho-Analysis*, pp. 300–305.

29. Hector Bolitho, ed., *Further Letters of Queen Victoria: From the Archives of the House of Brandenburg-Prussia*, trans. Mrs. J. Pudney and Lord Sudley (London: Thornton Butterworth, 1938), Queen Victoria to Princess Augusta of Prussia, Octo-

her father. In their common identification with Albert, mother and daughter found a way to communicate with each other.

It was far otherwise with Bertie—the future Edward VII.[30] Though Vicky's high spirits and tempestuousness impeded her progress toward becoming "Albert's child," the unfortunate Bertie, despite pushing and prodding, stood condemned as scarcely capable of making a try. In intellectual endowment, there was never any question of which child had been more favored, and Bertie suffered as a consequence. While Victoria refused to bestow on her son the accolade of "Papa's child," she recognized him as hers—indeed as her "caricature."[31] With that phrase she summed up not only her disapproval of her son but her poor opinion of herself. Just as she thought it necessary to keep close rein on Bertie, so too she sought to hold her impoverished self in check.

Still more, the fact that he was the male heir to the throne made his intrusion well-nigh intolerable. Even before his birth Victoria had determined that a future Prince of Wales should not take precedence over his father, and the possibility of the boy's usurping what she considered her husband's place lingered in the queen's mind. It was Victoria who denied Bertie a taste of Oedipal victory, and she continued to do so after Albert's death. Beyond that there lurked the deeper danger of Bertie as heir, eventually usurping not only his father's dignity but her own.

So long as she held fast to Albert, Victoria could endure such slings and arrows. With her husband by her side, even her mother's company did not disturb her, and the Duchess of Kent, Albert's aunt as well as his mother-in-law, acquired a fixed position within the family circle. This reconciliation between mother and daughter, albeit on Victoria's terms, attested to the emotional security the queen enjoyed. And under the approving gaze of the world around her—far different from the hostile glances which were to be cast at Vicky in Berlin—she flaunted her domestic happiness. It was not surprising, then, that when Albert died in December 1861, Victoria, still unstrung by the death of her mother nine months earlier, should have felt totally bereft. Though her husband remained a living presence,

ber 6, 1856, p. 75. For comments on the upbringing of the children, see the letters of their governess: Mrs. Hugh Wyndham, ed., *Correspondence of Sarah Spencer Lady Lyttelton 1789–1870* (London: John Murray, 1912).

30. On Edward VII's childhood, see Sir Sidney Lee, *King Edward VII: A Biography* (London: Macmillan and Co., 1925–1927), I: 1–129, and Philip Magnus, *King Edward the Seventh* (New York: E. P. Dutton and Co., 1964), pp. 1–41.

31. Fulford, ed., *Dearest Child*, Queen Victoria to the Princess Royal, April 27, 1859, p. 187.

the passage of decades little by little blurred his messages from the beyond. In the end Victoria found herself forced back upon her royal dignity to withstand the uncertain sense of self her mother had bequeathed her.

II. Gladstone's Departure

Before one can examine the refashioning of political ties after the disappearance of Gladstone, one must take a look at the departure itself. Though the event occurred in March 1894, the process covered a longer time span. Throughout the last decade of Gladstone's career, observers constantly anticipated his imminent retirement from the political scene. While his opponents regretted that his resignation in 1874 had not been definitive, even among his supporters some regarded withdrawal as the surest means to safeguard his reputation. Was his behavior, in fact, such as to alter beyond recognition the features of his portrait already drawn? Did his reluctance to relinquish the leadership of his party cast him into the Bismarckian mold of an oppressive presence intent on controlling the world around him?

To this last question Queen Victoria would have responded with a thunderous yes. At the end of Gladstone's first ministry she had drawn a comparison between the two charismatic figures, the German and the British:

> She [Queen Victoria] has felt that Mr. Gladstone w[oul]d have liked to *govern* HER as Bismarck governs the Emperor. Of course not to the same extent or in the *same* manner; but she always felt in his manner an overbearing obstinacy and imperiousness (without being actually wanting in respect as to form) w[hic]h she never experienced from *anyone* else and w[hic]h she found most disagreeable.[32]

In 1892, after the Liberals had triumphed at the polls, she groaned at the prospect of "that dangerous old fanatic" being "thrust down her throat":

> Independent of the real misfortune for the country and Europe, the idea of a deluded excited man of 82 trying to govern England and her vast Empire with the miserable democrats under him is quite ludicrous. It is like a bad joke![33]

32. Arthur Ponsonby, *Henry Ponsonby, Queen Victoria's Private Secretary: His Life from his Letters* (London: Macmillan and Co., 1943), Queen Victoria to Ponsonby, November 18, 1874, p. 251 (emphasis in the original).
33. Ibid., Queen Victoria to Ponsonby, July 13, 1892, p. 216, and June 4, 1892, p. 216.

It is not necessary here to sketch again the personalities of the two men—more particularly the fundamental differences in their affective ties—in order to refute the words of a monarch who herself could be a model of imperiousness. What is remarkable about Gladstone—in contrast to Bismarck—is the relatively minor role anger played in his prolonged leave-taking. To be sure, Gladstone experienced angry feelings—separation without such feelings is impossible—but he never manufactured rage of Bismarckian proportions. It was equanimity, rather than occasional outbursts of vehemence and ill-temper, that set the tone of his last decade.

In 1886, with his decision to champion the cause of Irish Home Rule, Gladstone had found a renewed sense of purpose. Thereafter he remained in public life, as he frequently remarked, "for the Irish question only."[34] That issue had steadied his position in politics, and from the political world he could not withdraw. On his seventy-seventh birthday he reiterated the commitment which bound him fast:

> I think a year of some progress; but of greater absorption in interests which, though profoundly human, are quite off the line of an old man's direct preparation for the passing the River of Death. I have not had a chance given me of creeping from this whirlpool, for I cannot abandon a cause which is so evidently that of my fellow-men, and in which a particular part seems to be assigned to me.[35]

While he continued to hold to his course, Gladstone did not give up hope. Even in 1890, when one of the main supports for his policy—a united Irish party in the House of Commons—shattered in the wake of the Parnell divorce case, he refused to despair. Instead he expressed his conviction that "at no distant time, not only will Home Rule in Ireland have been carried, but people will have a difficulty in understanding the state of mind which postponed the carrying of it so long."[36]

In the realm of practical politics, Gladstone was to experience disappointment and failure.[37] The hopes he had nourished at the begin-

34. Gladstone to Lord Acton, January 13, 1887, quoted in John Morley, *The Life of William Ewart Gladstone* (London: Macmillan and Co., 1903), III: 355.

35. Gladstone's Diary, December 29, 1886, quoted in ibid., III: 355.

36. Lionel A. Tollemache, *Talks with Mr. Gladstone* (London: Edward Arnold, 1903), January 2, 1892, p. 67; see also F. E. Hamer, ed., *The Personal Papers of Lord Rendel* (London: Ernest Benn, 1931), February 7, 1892, p. 94.

37. For policy development within the Liberal party during these years, see D. A. Hamer, *Liberal Politics in the Age of Gladstone and Rosebery: A Study in Leadership and Policy* (Oxford: Clarendon Press, 1972), and Michael Barker, *Gladstone and*

ning of the electoral campaign in 1892 vanished as the votes were counted. Instead of the three-figure majority in the Commons of which he had dreamed—a majority large enough both to pass Home Rule and to induce the Lords to concur—he awoke to find that the Liberals and Irish Nationalists together outnumbered their opponents by a mere forty seats. Strive as Gladstone might to assure the passage of a Home Rule bill in the House of Commons—and his performance in the long drawn-out session of 1893 ranked as a prodigy of courage and endurance[38]—the majority in favor proved too paltry to wring acquiescence from the Lords. That the measure would be thrown out by the upper House had been predicted from the outset. His mission thwarted, his hearing and eyesight seriously impaired, Gladstone still shrank from entering that much postponed "interval between parliament and the grave."[39]

Throughout the year and a half of his last ministry, he was isolated in his own cabinet. The diary of his private secretary Sir Algernon West provides ample testimony to the lack of personal contact between the prime minister and his colleagues. Clearly Gladstone remained engrossed with Ireland and sought to reserve his strength for that question. For their part, his associates acknowledged his commitment as justified by the electoral results: if forty was too small a majority to overawe the House of Lords, it was too large a figure to permit abandoning the Irish cause. They concurred in the priority Gladstone assigned the Home Rule measure; more than that, they watched with respect and admiration the heroism of "a man at his age struggling for a thing he could not see consummated."[40] But it was on that matter alone that they felt compelled to defer to their aged leader. Though they might differ among themselves about the most appropriate moment for Gladstone to withdraw, they were no longer prepared to accept his political guidance. When in February 1894 the Grand Old Man sounded a last-ditch battle cry against the House of Lords, they remained stone deaf.

Radicalism: The Reconstruction of Liberal Policy in Britain 1885-94 (Hassocks, Sussex: Harvester Press, 1975). See also Peter Stansky, *Ambitions and Strategies: The Struggle for Leadership of the Liberal Party in the 1890s* (Oxford: Clarendon Press, 1964).

38. For an account of Gladstone's performance in the House of Commons, see Henry W. Lucy, *A Diary of the Home Rule Parliament 1892-1895* (London: Cassell and Co., 1896), pp. 25-236.

39. W. E. Gladstone, "1879-1894," July 11, 1894, in John Brooke and Mary Sorensen, eds., *The Prime Minister's Papers: W. E. Gladstone*, I: *Autobiographica* (London: H.M.S.O., 1971), p. 112.

40. H. G. Hutchinson, ed., *Private Diaries of the Rt. Hon. Sir Algernon West* (London: John Murray, 1922), February 7, 1893, p. 138.

The following month the weak links which bound Gladstone to his colleagues were severed, and he resigned as prime minister. He had found himself alone in his opposition to a large increase in the naval budget.[41] Despite repeated appeals from his associates, he had refused to be moved. At other times when he had been outnumbered, West noted, he had been "angry and argumentative," and when he had "cooled down," he had become "more amenable to persuasion, but in this crisis he was quiet and pathetic." Gladstone could not, as he put it, "stultify the work of his life by adopting what he looked upon as militarism." He would not break the "continuous action of his political life, nor trample on tradition received from every colleague who had ever been his teacher."[42]

These last remarks suggest how the vividness of Gladstone's recollection of his own past offered comfort and helped alleviate the sting of the solitary future that now loomed ahead. Anger did not linger; it did not feed on itself; it did not need to be aired. Although Gladstone listed as a "Recorded Error" his appointment in 1892 of Lord Rosebery as foreign secretary—an appointment which paved the way for Rosebery to succeed him as prime minister—unlike Bismarck, he refrained from publicizing judgments of this sort.[43] In the words of James Bryce: "He gave vent to no disparaging criticisms on those who from time to time filled the place that had been his in the government of the country or the leadership of his party."[44]

Gratitude, not bitterness, colored his final assessment, penned shortly before his death, of the effort he had made:

> Upon the whole, when I look back upon 1886, and consider the inveterate sentiment of hostility flavored with contempt towards Ireland which has from time immemorial formed the basis of English tradition, I am much more disposed to be thankful for what we then and afterwards accomplished than to murmur or to wonder at what we did not.[45]

41. For Gladstone's own account of his resignation, see "Crisis of 1894 as to the Lords and Dissolution," February 13, 1897, "1894 The Final Imbroglio," November 10, 1896, and "Way Opened for Retirement," March 19, 1894, in *Autobiographica*, pp. 115-122.

42. *Diary of Sir Algernon West*, January 8, 1894, p. 235; January 4, 1894, p. 233; January 24, 1894, p. 257. For accounts of Gladstone's last cabinet meeting, see Earl of Rosebery, "Mr. Gladstone's Last Cabinet," Part I, *History Today* (December 1951): 31-41, Part II (January 1952): 17-22; Lucy Masterman, ed., *Mary Gladstone: Her Diaries and Letters* (London: Methuen and Co., 1930), March 2, 1894, p. 424.

43. W. E. Gladstone, "Recorded Errors," November 7, 1896, in *Autobiographica*, p. 135.

44. James Bryce, *William Ewart Gladstone* (New York: The Century Co., 1898), p. 73.

45. W. E. Gladstone, "Third Cabinet 1885-8," July 11, 1894, in *Autobiographica*, p. 112.

Indeed what struck his visitors most was the equanimity with which Gladstone had accepted his separation from politics. As a close friend noted:

> The change of life has been an unalloyed gain in spirits and vigour. It is surely a good illustration of the great power, flexibility, and elasticity of his mind, that he can quit, at his age and with ease, the absorbing occupation of sixty years, and only the more enjoy the opportunity and leisure of giving his thought and time to possibly more congenial occupation.[46]

Scholarship and religious concerns both enlarged and reflected inner resources which left little room for regret.

One deep regret lingered: the queen's ingratitude. When Gladstone left Windsor for the last time, he did so without having received a word of appreciation from his sovereign. If political differences had, as he confessed, made him harden his "heart into a flint," his loyalty and devotion to the monarchy through more than six decades had never wavered.[47] Though he attempted to "keep down that regret . . . and to attain . . . to indifference in the matter," a dream forced him to confront his hurt. Four years before Freud published *The Interpretation of Dreams*, Gladstone glimpsed the significance of the visions which appeared in sleep:

> We may sometimes, even if it be rarely, obtain a morsel of self knowledge through the medium of a dream. . . . Last night I dreamed that I was at Windsor. There had been a sort of breakfast, fugitive and early, at which several attended, and the Queen appeared, but without incident. However it was conveyed to me through one of the "pages" (servants out of livery?) that *I* of all people in the world was to breakfast alone with the Queen at ten o'clock: a circumstance which was not accordant with what is known as to H.M.'s (very judicious) habits with reference to the early part of the day. Well, the time slid on, and the hour approached, and I was getting duly into what I may call a small perturbation as to the how and where of access. But the dream had lost its tail. The hour never came. And the sole force and effect of the incident is to show that the subject of my personal relations to the Queen, and all the unsatisfactory ending of my over half a century of service, had more hold upon me, down at the root, than I was aware.

What Gladstone put down immediately after recounting the dream can stand as further associations to it:

46. *The Personal Papers of Lord Rendel*, September 23, 1895, p. 122.

47. Ponsonby, *Henry Ponsonby*, Gladstone to Ponsonby, March 5, 1894, p. 264. On the relations between Victoria and her prime minister, see Philip Guedalla, *The Queen and Mr. Gladstone*, 2 vols. (London: Hodder and Stoughton, 1933), and Herbert, Viscount Gladstone, *After Thirty Years* (London: Macmillan and Co., 1928), pp. 317–383.

I take the opportunity of recording another point. Granted that the absence of every act and word of regard, regret, and interest is absolutely
deserved. But then I have a wife. Of her, H.M. in her concluding letter,
wrote in terms (which conveyed some implication of reproach to me) of
the warm[est] interest and praise. What a fine opportunity of conveying by
language and by token to this wife herself some voluntary offering, which
would have been so well merited and appropriate, and would have furnished a conclusive answer to any criticism which might have been suggested by the cold negations of her conduct to me. But there was nothing
of the kind.[48]

Clearly on one level the dream represented a wish that did not get
fulfilled. So much Gladstone himself understood. Certain details,
however, require further explication. The phrase "*I* of all people in
the world" recalls Gladstone's autobiographical fragment, penned
four years earlier: he had been "singled" out by his parents to accom-
pany them on their journeys. Their solicitude, more particularly his
mother's, had conveyed that there was something in him which made
such a choice fully appropriate.[49] The "small perturbation as to the
how and where of access" refers, then, not only to the queen, but to
his mother as well. The sexual note is apparent and is underlined by
the mention of a lost tail. Freud might have seen here a deeper wish
that the dream actually fulfilled: a wish to comply with the incest
taboo. Or to shift from a genital to an oral interpretation: though
Gladstone's mother, unlike the queen, had fed him (breakfast), he
experienced a lingering anxiety about his own hunger.

What is striking is the way in which the dream's inhibitions are
extended in Gladstone's additional associations to it. He cannot
bring himself to voice his personal claims to attention and gratitude;
he advances his wife's instead. In so doing he seems to confront a
further check; Victoria has been ungenerous to his surrogate. It is,
however, not only with his wife that Gladstone is identifying. A sup-
pressed statement along the lines of "if I were Queen Victoria" binds
the discussion of his wife to the dream itself. The second identification alone offers Gladstone a way to overcome the checks he has
encountered, whether of his own or the queen's devising. To put it
simply: if Victoria has not known how to take care of him, he, at
least, knows how to take care of his wife. In sum, Gladstone's dream
prompted recognition of hurt at the hands of his sovereign—with
anxiety about his own responsibility thrown in—which he mitigated

48. W. E. Gladstone, "Incidental to Resignation," January 2, 1896, in *Autobiographica*, pp. 168–169 (emphasis in the original).
49. W. E. Gladstone, "Infancy-Family-Childhood," July 8, 1892, in ibid., p. 19.

by imagining himself behaving as solicitously as he remembered his mother had behaved toward him.

■

How well did Gladstone take care of his colleagues? The answer to this question has often been couched in negative terms. Gladstone has frequently been faulted for having failed to prepare his associates for his retirement, for having made no plans for an orderly transfer of authority. The facts are not in dispute: Gladstone ignored the baffling question of who should succeed him; he offered no guidance to those responsible for picking the next prime minister; and he considered the eventual choice of Rosebery a poor one. Once he had accepted the reality of his own departure, however, he did not try to cling to power by installing personal agents who he might imagine would act on lines he had laid down. Just as during his lifetime he eagerly rid himself of a large portion of his wealth—posthumous benevolence he considered no benevolence at all[50]—so too he freely surrendered what remained of his political ascendancy. If Gladstone be judged to have committed a sin of omission, that very sin may have been nothing more grievous than an act of self-effacement.

His associates had, as it were, taken leave of him by slow stages over the previous years. Whatever mix of grief and anger they may earlier have suffered, when he actually withdrew, they had largely accomplished their work of mourning, and they were already prepared to entertain a generous view of his memory. This generosity was apparent in the eulogies delivered in Parliament on his death in 1898. Yet no apotheosis occurred. Rather the speakers sought to set the record straight, to define the role Gladstone had played in the lives of those who had stood both with and against him in politics. From the Liberal front bench in the Commons, Sir William Harcourt felt obliged to stress Gladstone's graciousness as a leader:

> I have heard men who knew him not at all, who have asserted that the supremacy of his genius and the weight of his authority oppressed and overbore those who lived with him and those who worked under him. Nothing could be more untrue. Of all chiefs he was the least exacting. He was the most kind, the most tolerant, he was the most placable. How seldom in this House was the voice of personal anger heard from his lips.

50. *The Personal Papers of Lord Rendel,* February 9, 1897, p. 145; see also Balfour to Mary Lady Elcho, September 1–2, 1896, Balfour Papers, Add. MS. 49834. Note the contrast with Bismarck's zeal for acquiring wealth: Fritz Stern, *Gold and Iron: Bismarck, Bleichröder, and the Building of the German Empire* (New York: Alfred A. Knopf, 1977), ch. 12.

In the Lords, the Marquess of Salisbury—once again prime minister—who more than thirty years earlier had fixed his stand in opposition to Gladstone, acknowledged the moral impulses of his opponent: he would be "long remembered not so much for the causes in which he was engaged or the political projects which he favoured, but as a great example ... of a great Christian man." Salisbury's nephew Arthur Balfour, in his capacity as Conservative leader in the Commons, summed up Gladstone's enduring significance by sounding the note of "civic virtue":

> He added a dignity, as he added a weight, to the deliberations of this House ... which I think it is impossible adequately to replace.... He brought to our debates a genius which compelled attention, he raised in the public estimation the whole level of our proceedings, and they will be most ready to admit the infinite value of his service who realise how much of public prosperity is involved in the maintenance of the worth of public life.[51]

The reassurance Gladstone had offered his co-workers had been generalized and indirect. He had not served as a controlling presence giving order and purpose to their lives. Rather he had confirmed a meaning they had already found. That someone of his moral stature and multifarious interests had devoted more than sixty years to public service had simply corroborated the worthwhileness of such an endeavor. By the same token, Gladstone's departure was insufficient in itself to shatter the confidence his associates had achieved. It did not trigger a set of devastating anxieties. He left behind him no emotional wasteland.

III. The Omnipresent Heir: Chamberlain

Of the younger generation one figure alone could lay claim to the charismatic power which had been Gladstone's. Indeed textbook writers in search of a chapter title often refer to the last decade of the nineteenth century as the age of Joseph Chamberlain. His usefulness in this regard is doubtless enhanced by the fact that he represented the accession to the political heights of the long heralded "rising middle classes." The trumpets had sounded at the time of the first Reform Bill in 1832, yet the landed aristocrats, as readers of textbooks surely know, retained their preeminence until the 1880s. Though Gladstone himself had been born the son of a prosperous merchant, through education and marriage he had moved upward

---

51. Quoted in Morley, *Gladstone*, III: 530–531; see also A. G. Gardiner, *The Life of Sir William Harcourt* (London: Constable and Co., 1923), II: 458–460.

socially and had developed a keen attachment to, if not reverence for, the aristocracy. Only Chamberlain, among the protagonists of this study, remained without ties to the landed classes.

He too had moved up in the world, but his starting point had been humbler than Gladstone's.[52] His father, a master cordwainer and staunch Unitarian, had, like his forebears, belonged to the radical and nonconformist London artisan class. Born into this milieu in 1836, Chamberlain had suffered no material deprivation. Yet his educational opportunities had been limited; the most advanced training he had received consisted of two years at the University College School, which he had left at the age of sixteen to take his place beside his father. At eighteen he had moved to Birmingham—a city with its own strong nonconformist and radical traditions. Sent there by his father to oversee the latter's investment in a relative's screw manufacturing establishment, the young Chamberlain spent the next twenty years amassing a moderate fortune. When he withdrew from the enterprise to devote himself entirely to politics, he had capital sufficient to provide the leisure and accoutrements for a parliamentary career. Clearly his class position had improved. Through business success and marriage he had entered the circle of prosperous Birmingham industrial families who were the natural beneficiaries of Britain's widening suffrage. If Chamberlain could thus lay claim to represent the new democratic constituency, by the mid-1880s he also stood well placed to become Gladstone's heir.

Before entering the House of Commons in 1876, Chamberlain had spent the better part of a decade building what was to be an impregnable political base in Birmingham. One need not recount his accomplishments as mayor of his adopted city and as political organizer, more particularly as founder of the caucus system, which grew into the National Liberal Federation. Suffice it to say that though Chamberlain entered Parliament at the comparatively late age of forty, he came equipped with a national reputation as a radical politician. From the start he was not just another backbencher, but rather a contender for a prominent place in the Liberal party leadership. Gladstone himself judged that "after Cobden and Bright, Cham-

52. The standard account of Chamberlain's early career is J. L. Garvin, *The Life of Joseph Chamberlain*, I: *Chamberlain and Democracy, 1836–1885* (London: Macmillan and Co., 1932), pp. 3–214; see also N. Murrell Marris, *The Right Honourable Joseph Chamberlain: The Man and the Statesman* (London: Hutchinson and Co., 1900), pp. 3–133, and Denis Judd, *Radical Joe: A Life of Joseph Chamberlain* (London: Hamish Hamilton, 1977); pp. 1–76. For the most recent assessment of his career, see Richard Jay, *Joseph Chamberlain: A Political Study* (Oxford: Clarendon Press, 1981).

berlain was the finest specimen of the Reformed Parliament."[53] And following the Liberals' victory in 1880, to which the National Liberal Federation made no mean contribution, Chamberlain's species could not be excluded from the cabinet. During Gladstone's tenure in office, Chamberlain's influence and activity extended far beyond his bailiwick at the Board of Trade. As the next general election approached, he harbored the image of himself as heir apparent. With "history" on his side—for surely the tide must flow in the radical direction—Chamberlain "meant to be the next Prime Minister in succession to Gladstone."[54]

Ten years later he appeared likely to become Salisbury's heir instead. He had resigned from Gladstone's Home Rule ministry and together with Hartington had taken charge of the "Unionist" secession. Throughout Salisbury's second ministry, the secessionists remained on the opposition benches alongside their erstwhile colleagues, and they continued to sit with the Liberals after Gladstone returned to power in 1892. Yet through the intervening period the alliance with the Conservatives they had forged in antagonism to Home Rule had solidified, and by 1895, after the Conservatives had triumphed at the polls, Chamberlain was ready both to sit and to return to office with them. When he took over as colonial secretary, a position he was to occupy for the next eight years, he seemed to have undergone a political metamorphosis. His radical past, though not entirely silenced, was muted in favor of the imperial present. From the herald of social reform he was transformed into the impresario of imperial expansion. In both guises he exhibited an autocratic manner which appeared to set him apart from Liberal and Conservative alike.

Does Chamberlain stand as an exception, differing psychologically as well as socially from the political leaders whose ranks he had joined? The answer is no. Chamberlain, it will be argued, represents a variant of what, up to now, has figured as dominant among British statesmen. Still more, if he of all people turns out to resemble his colleagues, then not only does the style of British political cohesion remain intact, but the disparity between this mode and the German correspondingly subsists. One may conclude that until the end of the century—possibly down to the First World War—political behavior in the two countries continued to gravitate toward contrasting poles.

53. *Diary of Sir Algernon West*, July 25, 1894, p. 296.

54. J. S. Sandars, "Memorandum on a Conversation with Mr. Chamberlain," February 25, 1902, Balfour Papers, Add. MS. 49835; also quoted in Julian Amery, *Life of Joseph Chamberlain*, IV: *At the Height of his Power, 1901–1903* (London: Macmillan and Co., 1951), p. 461.

■

Whereas Gladstone's concern over Ireland harked back four decades, Chamberlain's was of recent origin. In the case of the younger man this new found interest soon became intense. Indeed throughout Gladstone's second ministry Chamberlain had taken the lead in urging his colleagues to deal generously with Irish complaints. From the very outset he had found himself in opposition—along with his chief—to the coercive measures recommended by the Irish secretary. When two years later the secretary handed in his resignation, Chamberlain had already emerged as a likely successor. In the intervening period he had established contact with Parnell, acting as a conduit and mediator between the Irish leader and his own colleagues. For the post in question Chamberlain was passed over twice, in the first instance by the ill-fated Lord Frederick Cavendish whose assassination upon his arrival in Dublin had so shocked both Parliament and public. Yet on Irish matters Chamberlain remained out in front. In the spring of 1885, just before the ministry fell, he was again setting the pace—proposing an extensive scheme of local government for the troubled island. This scheme marked the farthest he was ever to go in meeting the Irish demand for Home Rule.[55]

When Chamberlain resigned from Gladstone's third ministry in March 1886, after the prime minister had revealed the main outlines of his Home Rule bill, the point at issue was Chamberlain's strong distaste for "anything like a really coordinate authority in Ireland."[56] He would be satisfied with nothing less than recasting the whole bill and bringing it back to his own earlier proposals. Nevertheless for the better part of a year there were those among Chamberlain's former colleagues who sought to induce him to return to the Liberal fold.[57] It seemed incomprehensible that he should secede just at the time that the Whig defection, led by Hartington, was opening bright vistas of reorienting the party in a radical direction. How bright those prospects actually were is open to question. It may well be that the poor Liberal showing in urban constituencies in the election of 1885 had convinced Chamberlain that he would have to

55. The fullest account of Chamberlain's Irish involvements is in Garvin, *Chamberlain*, I: 312–375, 575–624.
56. Chamberlain to Dilke, May 6, 1886, quoted in Stephen Gwynn and Gertrude M. Tuckwell, *The Life of the Rt. Hon. Sir Charles W. Dilke, Bart., M.P.* (London: John Murray, 1917), II: 222.
57. For an account of the efforts to put the party back together, see Michael Hurst, *Joseph Chamberlain and Liberal Reunion: The Round Table Conference of 1887* (London: Routledge and Kegan Paul, 1967).

"look for new sources of support outside traditional radicalism," and hence would have "little to gain by giving further thought to radicalism."[58] Be that as it may, it is unclear whether Chamberlain had anything to gain by separating himself from Gladstone.

It was this period which furnished the climax of what has come to be called Chamberlain's *Political Memoir*. The bulk of his account covering the years 1880–1892 was dictated in 1891, with a final chapter being added the following year. Though it was not meant for immediate publication, it had the character of a public record. Indeed it largely consisted of a compilation of documents, correspondence and memoranda, held together by Chamberlain's guiding purpose of defending himself against the oft-repeated charge of disloyalty to Gladstone.[59]

By his own admission, Chamberlain had been an insubordinate, if not quite a rebellious, lieutenant. In 1880 he had recognized Gladstone's dominant position within the party, but at the same time had emitted a groan at the prospect of serving with him. The prospective prime minister, Chamberlain commented to his friend John Morley, "would be King Stork, and ... some of us frogs would have a hard time of it under him."[60] As far as Chamberlain himself was concerned, his prediction proved accurate. He continually chafed at the constraints which Gladstone believed should guide his conduct. He himself manifested no overriding moral obligation to self-suppression:

> I will only say that it must be to the interest of every Government that its several members should not entirely lose their individuality in the corporate existence, but that they should retain their representative character and thus continue to bring to the Government of which they form part whatever influence they may have possessed in this capacity.[61]

Gladstone's subsequent response gave Chamberlain scant satisfaction:

> It is I know difficult and disagreeable to maintain these reserves, and rein in a strong conviction, a masculine understanding, and a great power of clear expression: but pray be as cruel as you can to your own gifts.[62]

58. A. B. Cooke and John Vincent, *The Governing Passion: Cabinet Government and Party Politics in Britain 1885–1886* (Brighton: Harvester Press, 1974), pp. 14, 15.

59. Editor's "Introduction" and "Note on the Text," in Joseph Chamberlain, *A Political Memoir 1880–1892*, edited from the original manuscript by C. H. D. Howard (London: Batchwork Press, 1953), pp. ix–xix.

60. Chamberlain to Morley, January 25, 1880, quoted in John, Viscount Morley, *Recollections* (London: Macmillan and Co., 1917), I: 166.

61. Chamberlain to Gladstone, July 2, 1883, quoted in Chamberlain, *Political Memoir*, p. 89.

62. Gladstone to Chamberlain, December 3, 1883, quoted in ibid., p. 90.

Clearly, Chamberlain's separation from Gladstone betokened his wish to unbridle his "masculine understanding."[63]

The crux of Chamberlain's apologia lay in his claim that behind Gladstone's conversion to Home Rule lurked a reluctance to recognize Chamberlain's own preeminence. To avoid "giving up the initiative and following where he had been accustomed to lead the way," the prime minister had introduced Home Rule, thereby throwing "every other object into the background." "In these circumstances," Chamberlain added, it was "not easy to fix the exact date when Mr. Gladstone 'found salvation.' "[64] The indictment lodged in Chamberlain's aggressive self-defense has been echoed more than once by subsequent historians.[65] There is no doubt that the older man can be faulted for his failure to communicate more fully and openly with Chamberlain. Yet that is about all one can hold against him.

Preoccupied with devising his own policy, he failed to recognize not only Chamberlain's preeminence, but more importantly his colleague's mood. He did not appreciate—something which would have been hard to do in any case—the paradoxical nature of Chamberlain's heightened aggressiveness. What looked like an Oedipal challenge derived from a reopening of earlier psychic wounds.

■

In March 1886, just at the point Chamberlain was resigning from Gladstone's Home Rule ministry, Arthur Balfour met him at a dinner party. For his uncle Lord Salisbury, Balfour provided an account of the political conversation as well as an assessment of his interlocutor's frame of mind:

I have a strong suspicion that Dilke's position and W. E. G.'s [Gladstone's] refusal to have anything to do with him count for something in

63. Sir Charles Dilke had earlier recorded in his diary: "Chamberlain came into my room much worried and excited and broke out against Mr. G. 'I *don't* like him really. I *hate* him.'" Dilke's dismay at his friend's anger is suggested by the fact that the following day he "warned Mr. G. as to Chamberlain's state of mind." Diary entries, October 28, 1884, and October 29, 1884, Dilke Papers, Add. MS. 43926 (emphasis in the original; I have written out Dilke's abbreviations).

64. Chamberlain, *Political Memoir*, pp. 179, 180. Chamberlain repeated these charges orally to Balfour: Balfour to Salisbury, July 24, 1892, Balfour Papers, Add. MS. 49690; see also Morley's notes on a conversation with Chamberlain in 1894: *Recollections*, I: 297.

65. See, for example, Garvin, *Chamberlain*, I: 535–536, and Cooke and Vincent, *The Governing Passion*, p. 15.

the decision at which Ch[amberlain] has apparently arrived . . . to break up the Liberal party.[66]

The previous July, Sir Charles Dilke, Chamberlain's closest political ally, had been named corespondent in a divorce case. It would be tedious to rehearse the complexities of the two trials which ensued.[67] What really mattered was that the moment Dilke stood accused, his political career was effectively ruined. Hence when Gladstone set about forming his ministry in January 1886, he felt obliged to ex- clude Dilke from the cabinet. Dilke himself had readily understood the prime minister's action; from the outset he had not deceived him- self about the magnitude of the blow inflicted on him. Chamberlain, however, had clung to the illusion of his friend's rehabilitation. He was evidently resisting letting go of a close relationship that had helped to assuage a long-standing depression of his own and to defuse the anger which accompanied it.

If the friendship between Chamberlain and Dilke had not been so fixed a feature of the political landscape, observers might have judged it incongruous. Though not of a landed family, Dilke fitted easily into the governing elite. Privately educated before going to Cambridge, widely traveled, with an international network of influ- ential friends and acquaintances, Dilke cut a cosmopolitan yet se- rious figure in London society. In picking Dilke as his *arbiter elegentarium,* Chamberlain chose wisely; the radical from Bir- mingham found himself introduced to the mores of the capital with no trace of condescension marring his friend's hospitality. Staunch in his radicalism, Dilke claimed to have inherited his politics from a much-loved grandfather; nonetheless, unlike Chamberlain, he felt comfortable among his more conservative colleagues. He experi- enced no personal difficulty in working with Hartington; Gladstone considered him far more congenial than Chamberlain—and even reckoned him a future leader of the House. In fact, Dilke enjoyed a stronger position within the parliamentary party than his ally. Though not a brilliant speaker, he ranked as an excellent House of Commons man and as a conspicuously hard-working administrator. In brief, he had assets which Chamberlain lacked. Still more,

66. Balfour to Salisbury, March 24, 1886, Balfour Papers, Add. MS. 49688; also quoted in Arthur James Balfour, *Chapters of Autobiography* (London: Cassell and Co., 1930), p. 220.

67. The standard biography of Chamberlain's friend is Gwynn and Tuckwell, *Dilke.* See also Roy Jenkins, *Sir Charles Dilke: A Victorian Tragedy* (London: Collins, 1958), and Hon. Betty Askwith, *Lady Dilke: A Biography* (London: Chatto and Windus, 1969).

through mutual respect, the two had transformed incongruity into complementarity.

For more than a full decade Chamberlain had worked in tandem with Dilke. Radical political interests had brought them together even before Chamberlain's election to Parliament. After he had taken his seat, he and his friend had quickly fallen into a habit of mutual confidence and concerted action. In 1880—as the prospect of office opened before them—Chamberlain had put in writing his sense of their accord: "What I should like—what I hope for with you—is a thorough offensive and defensive alliance, and in this case our position will be immensely strong."[68] Two years later, in a letter to Granville, Dilke had underlined this solidarity: "Neither he nor I would ever be likely to let the other resign alone. Our relations are so close that I should resign with him if he were to resign because he thought Forster [the Irish Secretary] did not have his hair cut sufficiently often."[69] Admiration and approval had grown so great between the two that Dilke could write of delighting in his friend's triumphs even more than Chamberlain himself: "It is absurd that this should be so between politicians, but so it is."[70]

Not until Chamberlain determined to vote against the Home Rule bill did he and his ally have a serious disagreement. Dilke expressed his dismay:

> It is a curious fact that we should without a difference have gone through the trials of the years in which we were rivals, and that the differences and the break should have come now that I have—at least in my own belief, and that of most people—ceased for ever to count at all in politics.[71]

Chamberlain demurred:

> We have never been rivals. Such an idea has not at any time entered my mind. . . . We have been so closely connected that I cannot contemplate any severance. I hope, as I have said, that this infernal cloud on your public life will be dispersed; and if it is not I feel that half my usefulness and more—much more—than half my interest in politics are gone.[72]

In short, if this partnership between equals—and latent rivalry implied equality—had not been so drastically unsettled, Chamberlain

68. Chamberlain to Dilke, April 1880, quoted in Gwynn and Tuckwell, *Dilke*, I: 304.
69. Dilke to Granville, April 1882, quoted in ibid., I: 424.
70. Dilke to Granville, December 1882, quoted in ibid., I: 502.
71. Dilke to Chamberlain, May 5, 1886, quoted in ibid., II: 218.
72. Chamberlain to Dilke, May 6, 1886, quoted in ibid., II: 221.

might well have muted his own opposition to Gladstone's Home Rule proposal.[73] In so doing he would have been acting in accordance with a promise he had given Dilke a year earlier:

> The malice and ingenuity of men is so great that I should be afraid they would some day break our friendship if it had not victoriously stood the strain of public life for so many years. I will swear that I will never do anything knowingly to imperil it, and I hope that we are both agreed that if by any chance either of us should think that he has the slightest cause of complaint he will not keep it to himself for a day, but will have a frank explanation. In this case I shall feel safe, for I am certain that any mistake would be immediately repaired by whoever might be at fault.[74]

Why did the relationship with Dilke give Chamberlain a feeling of safety? The nub of the matter is that each had gone through an identical ordeal: the death of a wife in childbirth. Indeed, Chamberlain had lost two wives in this fashion. His first had died in 1863 when his elder son, Austen, was born, while Dilke's spouse had failed to survive the birth of their boy, Wentie, in 1874. A year later Chamberlain's second wife—a cousin to the first—and her infant had expired together. Still more, as his biographer noted, "his own sorrow helped to shorten his mother's life. She had tried to comfort him, but knew he was beyond all comfort." Seven months after he buried his second wife, his mother died. The burden of these deaths extinguished "hope and joy in his personal life."[75] Nor did a fund of religious belief offer him solace; for the shocks he had suffered had undermined his faith.

Chamberlain faced the outer world with "mocking grimness";[76] at the same time he attempted to inter his emotional needs and hurt along with his wives and mother. The persistence of his depression—accompanied by severe headaches—suggests that he was unable to rebuild his endangered inner world. (Until the mourner begins to sense, albeit only dimly, that he can relinquish his own anger at having been "deserted," the "deserters" haunt rather than reassure.) Empathy with Dilke (and vice versa) aided Chamberlain in the task. It allowed him to admit—in a guarded fashion, to be sure—the pain of yearning, and in so doing helped soothe that very pain. It likewise offered a remedy—indeed the only possible one—for emotional loneliness: involvement in a mutually committed relationship.

73. On this point, see diary entry, March 4, 1886, Dilke Papers, Add. MS. 43927.
74. Chamberlain to Dilke, January 11, 1885, quoted in Gwynn and Tuckwell, *Dilke*, II: 107.
75. Garvin, *Chamberlain*, I: 208.
76. Ibid., I: 210.

The fact that you are by nature such a reserved fellow that all *demonstration* of affection is difficult, but you may believe me when I say that I feel it—none the less. I suppose I am reserved myself. The great trouble we have both been through has had a hardening effect in my case, and since then I have never worn my heart on my sleeve.[77]

Chamberlain's grief may well have been intensified by his own share in the death of his wives. Evidently he had been unwilling to curb his "masculinity"—not only in politics, as Gladstone advised, but sexually as well. His first had died after having given birth to two children, while his second succumbed on the termination of her fifth pregnancy. In all, Chamberlain had been married for only ten years. If it is a common childhood fantasy that when an infant bursts forth from the womb, the mother dies, then surely the father must figure in such a fantasy as an accomplice to murder.

Though Chamberlain blotted out his own part in his first wife's death, her son, Austen, came to appreciate that he at least stood condemned in his father's eyes:

It was one day in my 'teens that I spoke critically to him of a friend of his [Dilke], left early a widower with an only child. "He doesn't seem to care much for the boy," I said, "or to see much of him," and my father, quick as always in a friend's defence, blurted out before he saw the implication of what he was saying, "You must remember that his mother died when the boy was born," and in a flash I saw for the first time what he had so carefully concealed from me, that in my earliest years I had been to him the living embodiment of the first tragedy of his life.[78]

Toward the boy in question, Chamberlain behaved as a surrogate parent. For close to two years in the early 1880s, Wentie Dilke, who seemed to suffer from a combination of physical and emotional handicaps,[79] lived in Birmingham with Chamberlain's children.[80] To be sure Chamberlain did not occupy himself with the boy's daily care; but his generosity does suggest his identification with Dilke's loss and, still more, why this identification helped alleviate his own depression. In his concern for Wentie—and subsequently for the

77. Chamberlain to Dilke, December 6, 1882, quoted in Gwynn and Tuckwell, *Dilke*, I: 501 (emphasis in the original).

78. Sir Austen Chamberlain, *Politics From Inside: An Epistolary Chronicle 1906–1914* (London: Cassell and Co., 1936), pp. 16–17. For an account of Austen's political career, see Sir Charles Petrie, *The Life and Letters of the Right Hon. Sir Austen Chamberlain*, 2 vols. (London: Cassell and Co., 1939–1940).

79. Askwith, *Lady Dilke*, p. 181.

80. For evidence of Chamberlain's concern for Wentie, see his letter to Dilke, September 12, 1882, Dilke Papers, Add. MS. 43885; see also Gwynn and Tuckwell, *Dilke*, I: 358.

woman who became Dilke's second wife[81]—Chamberlain attempted
to make good the loss his friend had suffered. The solicitous regard
he found himself extending his political ally enabled him to trust
himself and, as he had earlier commented, gave him a feeling of
safety.

But Chamberlain could not repair the damage done to Dilke by
the divorce case. The very fact that his friend may also have been his
rival made Chamberlain's need to protect him all the more compelling. And his inability to do so increased his own anxiety and vulnerability. In these circumstances his heightened aggressiveness is
not to be wondered at. Nor is it surprising that Gladstone should
have been its primary target; for the Grand Old Man alone had it in
his power to rehabilitate Chamberlain's friend.

To take stock briefly and simply: to most observers Chamberlain's
aggressiveness made him appear out of step with Britain's political
leaders. It has been argued here that this aggressiveness derived from
his unfinished mourning, from the projection outward of anger at
losses he could not repair. In similar vein, it is logical to suppose that
his difficulty in making amends—and his wish to do so—sprang from
the same source: his relationship with his mother.

Though information on Chamberlain's mother is scanty, the closeness of the tie between the two is not in doubt. Chamberlain's comment about her after her death, though an idealization, surely rested
on a reality he had experienced: "No one ever lived of a more loving,
kindly and sympathising disposition."[82] "Sunny-natured," with "a
particularly soft gentle voice," Chamberlain's mother had been devoted to her firstborn.[83] His talent may well have contributed to her
interest; she had urged that he be allowed to go on from school to
University College. But when his father had refused to give his eldest son an education he could not afford to provide the younger
children and had insisted that this son join him in his business, she
had acquiesced in the realities of the situation.[84] Evidently she understood what was required of her: to facilitate her son's passage to
the world of adult responsibility.

She did not do so without anxiety. Hers was not the anxiety of an

81. *Dilke*, II: 91–92, 167–168.
82. Quoted in Garvin, *Chamberlain*, I: 84.
83. See the description of Chamberlain's mother by one of his sisters quoted in
ibid., I: 31.
84. Ibid., I: 37.

intrusive mother who fears that her son will fall short of fulfilling her own grandiose fantasies. Rather it was the young child's aggressive self-assertion which prompted her worry. One might add parenthetically that this kind of uneasiness, while marking a deviation from "good-enough" mothering, is possibly the most common divergence from the type. The very empathy such a mother displays in sustaining her child's real and ideal world may turn into acute distress when he appears intent on destruction. In the case of Chamberlain's mother, her anxiety can be glimpsed in her exaggerated response—masked by a nursery variety of gallow's humor—to a minor act of vandalism committed by her three-year-old son. About the target of the boy's aggression, she wrote:

> This thimble was given to Caroline Harben [her maiden name] on her fourteenth birthday by her grandmother ... and had she continued Caroline Harben, might still have been in her service. But her little son Joey (more ruthless than Time) stamped upon its worn frame and finished what the old Destroyer might have spared much longer (January 17, 1840).[85]

Chamberlain's biographer adds that the "battered little silver thimble, carefully laid away in cotton-wool, was cherished by the statesman to the end of his days."

Chamberlain's mother may have experienced his acts of naughtiness as personal assaults and may have detected in them the ambivalence about her which the boy was unable to voice. Whatever the cause, she seems to have found it difficult to pardon the offender. In this regard a report by Chamberlain's childhood playmate is illuminating: "Once when he was put to bed for punishment he said to his mother: 'You keep telling me that we must forgive seventy times seven and you won't forgive me even once.' "[86] Without his mother's forgiveness, Chamberlain could not be sure that she accepted as reparation what he offered. Instead he sought to make amends indirectly by meticulously carrying out his tasks as a student. According to his teacher at the age of eight:

> As a child Joseph Chamberlain didn't take things easily; he went deeply into them, and was very serious for a boy. He didn't care much for games; he was not so solitary as *solid,* industrious, and intelligent, but rather too anxious about his lessons, conscientious and very solemn as a rule.[87]

85. Quoted in ibid., I: 25.
86. Report by Mrs. Russell Martineau, quoted in ibid., I: 26.
87. Recollections of Miss Pace, quoted in Marris, *Chamberlain,* p. 12 (emphasis in the original).

Even this scrupulousness may not have been enough; or at least it proved insufficient to alleviate the depression his mother—and perhaps Joe himself—suffered when he was around the age of ten. Her youngest child, Frank, had died. Between the birth of her eldest and that of his brother, seven other children had arrived. But the survivors could not console the mother for the loss of her littlest. Her despondent mood is suggested by the fact that she could no longer bear the house in which the tragedy had occurred.[88] To escape that spot the family moved, in 1846, to Highbury Place; Chamberlain was later to name his home in Birmingham after this London residence. His brother's death—and the fratricidal wish it fulfilled—as well as his mother's depression, reinforced Chamberlain's doubt of his ability to make whole again what in fantasy he had destroyed. In these circumstances the task of trusting himself to understand and comfort another human being loomed up as daunting indeed.

Yet evidently he did not despair of finding a loving partner. By all accounts the two marriages that ended so tragically had been happy. In his comments about his second wife, written for her children after their mother's death, Chamberlain spelled out what he considered the essential ingredients for a successful marital relationship:

> I have had in my wife a friend and counsellor, intensely interested in the objects for which I have striven, heartily rejoicing in my success and full of loving sympathy in occasional failure and disappointment. And looking back I see how the path has been smoothed for me by her unselfish affection and how much strength I have gained from the just confidence I have reposed in the judgment and devotion she has displayed in the part reserved for her.... And the result of this complete similarity and identity of interests has naturally been to knit us together so that I can now say that there is no thought or action of my later years which my wife has not shared with me.[89]

No difference of view had arisen to mar the mutual comprehension between Chamberlain and his second wife. This fortunate identity of interests had enabled him to circumvent the latent depression under which he had suffered since childhood.

The absence of such common ground frustrated Chamberlain's initial endeavor to find a third wife. In the mid-1880s his courtship of Beatrice Potter—the future Mrs. Sidney Webb—foundered on her unwillingness to *"think and feel like* him." Rather than trying to please her, he wooed the budding young social investigator by at-

---

88. Garvin, *Chamberlain*, I: 30.
89. Quoted in ibid., I: 207.

tempting to "drag" her "into his interests."[90] Her account of a conversation between them highlights the strenuousness of his effort.

"It pains me to hear any of my views contradicted," and with this preface he begins with stern exactitude to lay down the articles of his political creed. I remain modestly silent; but noticing my silence, he remarks that he requires "intelligent sympathy" from women. "Servility," Mr. Chamberlain, think I; not sympathy, intelligent servility: what many women give men, but the difficulty lies in changing one's master, in jumping from one *tone* of thought to the exact opposite—*with intelligence*. And then I advance as boldly as I dare my feeble objections to his general proposition, feeling that in this case I owe it to the man to show myself and be absolutely sincere. He refutes my objections by reasserting his convictions passionately, his expression becoming every minute more gloomy and determined.[91]

But Chamberlain's arrogance—if such it was—masked a profound sorrow which eventually revealed itself. Toward the end of their relationship he wrote to Beatrice Potter:

Why cannot we be friends— "camarades"—to use your own expression? I like you very much, I respect and esteem you, I enjoy your conversation and society, and I have often wished that fate had thrown us more together. If you share this feeling to any extent, why should we surrender a friendship which ought to be good for both of us? . . .

The circumstances of my past life have made me solitary and reserved, but it is hard that I should lose one of the few friends whose just opinions I value, and the sense of whose regard and sympathy would be a strength and support to me.[92]

In 1888 Chamberlain married for a third time and at last found the sympathy he had craved. The previous year Prime Minister Salisbury had sent him to the United States to negotiate a fisheries agree-

90. "The Diary of Beatrice Webb 1873-1943," VI, March 18, 1884 (emphasis in the original). For published extracts from her diary in which she recorded her impressions of Chamberlain, see her autobiography entitled *My Apprenticeship* (London: Longmans, Green, and Co., 1926), pp. 123-128; see also "Appendix: Beatrice Webb and Joseph Chamberlain," in Margaret Cole, ed., *Beatrice Webb's Diaries*, II: 1924-1932 (London: Longmans, Green, and Co., 1956), pp. 311-316. For balanced accounts of the relationship between Chamberlain and Miss Potter, see Peter Fraser, *Joseph Chamberlain: Radicalism and Empire, 1868-1914* (New York: A. S. Barnes and Co., 1966), pp. 112-129, and Jeanne MacKenzie, *A Victorian Courtship: The Story of Beatrice Potter and Sidney Webb* (London: Weidenfeld and Nicolson, 1979), pp. 20-33, 36-40, 46-49.

91. "The Diary of Beatrice Webb 1873-1943," VI, January 12, 1884 (emphasis in the original); also quoted (not entirely accurately) in *Beatrice Webb's Diaries*, II: 315.

92. Chamberlain to Beatrice Potter, August 3, 1887, quoted in Fraser, *Chamberlain*, p. 127, and MacKenzie, *A Victorian Courtship*, pp. 48-49.

ment, and there he had met and fallen in love with Mary Endicott, the twenty-four year old daughter of the American secretary of war. Miss Endicott seemed to meet his requirements perfectly, combining devotion to his interests with an attractive manner. One observer described her as:

> a woman in a thousand, and one who is, above all, thoroughly feminine, not clouding one's appreciation of a cultured and clever intellect by advocacy of any fad or theory likely to cause a sensation—a true woman. . . .
> While assisting her husband in every possible manner, and constantly attending political meetings with him, Mrs. Chamberlain is the very opposite of the so-called advanced woman who dabbles in politics; indeed I feel sure that her husband would never have countenanced anything of that kind.[93]

Once again Chamberlain had found a mate whose readiness to shoulder the burdens of his career eased his corresponding task of comprehending another human being. Still more, though they had no children of their own—and one may only speculate on the reasons— the third Mrs. Chamberlain recreated for her husband a cohesive family life. He recognized that she brought his children nearer to him, while his eldest daughter commented that her new stepmother, who was younger than herself, "unlocked his heart," enabling her and her siblings "to enter in as never before."[94] Clearly Chamberlain's domestic happiness proved a tonic to his spirits. Paradoxically, however, while his good fortune relieved his depression, this stroke of luck deprived him of the necessity of ever fully mastering it.

■

In early 1886, as Dilke watched Gladstone form his Home Rule ministry, he wrote to John Morley, the newly appointed chief secretary for Ireland, urging him to stand with the Birmingham leader, who was an intimate friend of them both: "My *one* hope is that you will work—my hope, not for your own sake, but for the sake of Radical principles—as completely with Chamberlain as I did."[95] He might have added for Chamberlain's sake as well. Early the follow-

93. Ralph Nevill, ed., *The Reminiscences of Lady Dorothy Nevill* (London: Edward Arnold, 1906), p. 195; see also Balfour to Mary Lady Elcho, quoted in Kenneth Young, *Arthur James Balfour* (London: G. Bell and Sons, 1963), p. 139, and Cecil Headlam, ed., *The Milner Papers: South Africa 1897–1905* (London: Cassell and Co., 1931–1933), II, Milner to Lady Edward Cecil, January 3, 1903, p. 434.

94. Quoted in J. L. Garvin, *The Life of Joseph Chamberlain*, II: *Disruption and Combat, 1885–1895* (London: Macmillan and Co., 1933), p. 373.

95. Dilke to Morley, February 2, 1886, quoted in Gwynn and Tuckwell, *Dilke*, II: 210 (emphasis in the original).

ing year, with his hopes dashed and Chamberlain isolated from his former Liberal colleagues, Dilke wrote in his diary: "All this split has spoilt Chamberlain and . . . he will be very difficult for all men to work with in the future."[96]

At first glance what is striking about the rupture between Chamberlain and Morley that eventually occurred is the vulnerability of the hard-hitting politician to criticism aimed in his direction. Their relationship dated from the 1870s, and during Chamberlain's years of bereavement Morley had been his trusted friend.[97] Despite the severance of their political ties through their disagreement on Home Rule, Chamberlain had hoped to preserve their personal intimacy. One need not recount here the vicissitudes of that bond, the abortive efforts at restraint, the sharp words and the apologies which followed. Suffice it to say that in 1891 the tie finally snapped—to be reknit in a looser form toward the end of Chamberlain's career. A biting political assault on Gladstone by the Birmingham leader provoked a personal rejoinder by Morley. In hurt tones Chamberlain wrote his adversary:

> What is the excuse for this virulence of language in speaking of one to whom you admit some obligation and who has never made a similar attack upon you throughout the controversy in spite of gross and reiterated provocation?
>
> It appears that you are animated by a chivalrous sentiment which makes it necessary for you to accuse an old friend of dishonourable conduct in order to defend a new one who is at least able to take care of himself without the protecting *aegis* of your shield.[98]

Morley's censure could not accomplish his former friend's moral regeneration. Chamberlain did not withdraw his attack on Gladstone. Instead, he felt that it was himself rather than the Liberal chief who was threatened. Behind his vulnerability lay an implicit appeal for reassurance about his own aggressiveness. Only by answering that appeal could his political associates encourage his self-restraint.

96. Diary entry, February 4, 1887, Dilke Papers, Add. MS. 43927. (I have written out Dilke's abbreviations.)

97. Sir Austen Chamberlain, *Down the Years* (London: Cassell and Co., 1935), pp. 193–205, and Morley, *Recollections*, I: 147–148. For a perceptive account of the relationship between Morley and Chamberlain, see D. A. Hamer, *John Morley: Liberal Intellectual in Politics* (Oxford: Clarendon Press, 1968), pp. 112–118, 162–182, 221–223; see also Garvin, *Chamberlain*, I: 156, and II: 488–490.

98. Chamberlain to Morley, October 30, 1891, quoted in Chamberlain, *Political Memoir*, p. 305.

IV. The Resourcefulness of Balfour

In late 1888 Balfour penned for his uncle Salisbury an assessment
of the coalition between the Conservatives and the Liberal Unionists. His concern to keep Chamberlain as a strong ally led him to
conclude that the time was not yet ripe for a fusion of the two parties. While Hartington might find it possible to join the Conservatives, Chamberlain would not:

> If he [Chamberlain] is deserted by Hartington and his followers he would
> probably rapidly drift back into the bosom of the True Liberal Church,
> and we should lose the value of his support. I rate this more highly than
> perhaps you do. . . . It is true that he will hardly leave us while Gladstone
> lives, and that after Gladstone dies he would probably leave us anyhow.
> Nevertheless I am convinced that Joe as leader ... of eighty Liberal
> Unionists—and Joe as leader of half a dozen Radical Unionists, would be
> very different people indeed.[99]

Subsequently Balfour elucidated his last remark when he commented
that it was "within a strong and united party that the disintegrating
effects of Joe's personality and propaganda" would do the least
damage.[100] In short, Balfour considered the capture of Chamberlain
as crucial to his own party and the strength of that party as crucial to
the capture of Chamberlain. To put it another way, taking Chamberlain into camp ranked as the ultimate test of political cohesion.

If the containment of Chamberlain was the most difficult test, it
would not appear to have been the only one confronting Britain's
political leaders. After all, the Conservative party, though it dominated the political scene, with a brief interruption, for twenty years,
did confront a Liberal opposition. The fact that the Liberal summit
was in disarray from the time of Gladstone's retirement until Sir
Henry Campbell-Bannerman took over at the end of the century
would suggest that even for the British the reestablishment of cohesion was no easy matter. How can one justify passing over so obvious
a failure in order to concentrate on the comparative success of Balfour and the Conservatives?

The answer is simply that the failure can be accounted for with
relative ease. The character of Lord Rosebery—the personal touchi-
ness and hysterical moods of the man who bore the chief responsibility for Liberal leadership in those troubled years—in itself provides

99. Balfour to Salisbury, November 23, 1888, Balfour Papers, Add. MS. 49689;
also quoted in Blanche E. C. Dugdale, *Arthur James Balfour, First Earl of Balfour*
(London: Hutchinson and Co., 1936), I: 202.
100. Balfour to Lord Hugh Cecil, July 19, 1905, Balfour Papers, Add. MS. 49835.

an adequate explanation. It is Rosebery, not Chamberlain, who stands out as an exception among British political leaders. And because Chamberlain's behavior may well be viewed as merely a variant, it—and not Rosebery's—must be included in the style of British political cohesion delineated earlier. Hence for this study, as had been true for Balfour, the accommodation of Chamberlain's deviance constitutes the ultimate test.

Skeptics might be tempted to judge Balfour a failure also. Not even his devoted niece-biographer considered his prime ministry from 1902 to 1905 his finest hour.[101] Though his accomplishments in that office should not be underestimated—throughout he demonstrated a tenacity and stoicism which Rosebery altogether lacked—cabinet solidarity would not be listed among them. In Balfour's case, as earlier in that of Gladstone, Chamberlain severely taxed the leader's power of personal management. Here the similarity ends. For Chamberlain's decision to resign from Balfour's cabinet in 1903 in order to pursue his vision of tariff reform bore little resemblance to his break with Gladstone in 1886.[102] There was no rupture in the friendship of the departing minister and his chief; Austen Chamberlain's continued presence in the cabinet bore witness to the bond between the two and helped to preserve it. More to the point, the three years of Balfour's prime ministry should not be allowed to overshadow his two decades as conservative leader in the House of Commons. The nub of the matter would seem to be that it was when Balfour was not in the foremost position that his particular talents as mediator were most in evidence.

Throughout those twenty years Balfour set a premium on party unity. Consistently and self-consciously he defined his own role in terms of harnessing men of diverse views to work together. Self-restraint and decorous behavior ought, he wrote his sister-in-law, to keep dissent within bounds and minimize friction:

> Can a single case be produced in which I have shown the smallest irritation in the House of Commons on the subject of a difference of opinion expressed with good manners and supported only by argument? I think not. . . . What I do resent, and what I think myself perfectly justified in resenting, is being treated by one's friends as if they were one's enemies.

101. Dugdale, *Balfour*, I: 363–364; see also Lady Frances Balfour, *Ne Obliviscaris* (London: Hodder and Stoughton, 1930), II: 179.

102. On the split over tariff reform, see Alfred Gollin, *Balfour's Burden: Arthur Balfour and Imperial Preference* (London: Anthony Blond, 1965), and Julian Amery, *The Life of Joseph Chamberlain*, V and VI: *Joseph Chamberlain and The Tariff Reform League* (London: Macmillan and Co., 1969). See also Alan Sykes, *Tariff Reform in British Politics 1903–1913* (Oxford: Clarendon Press, 1979).

Differences of opinion there must be in any Party. Sometimes, though by no means always, when they exist they ought to be expressed, but they should never be expressed with the accompaniment of imputations either on character or motive. Such a course does infinite mischief to a party, and, in my opinion, is inconsistent with party loyalty.[103]

An examination of Balfour's comparative success in enforcing these principles should define the limits within which Chamberlain was "tamed," and in so doing shed light on the psychological resourcefulness of a ruling elite whose power was gradually being eroded.

■

And what of Salisbury? After all, it was he who formed the government in 1895 and held the post of prime minister for the next seven years. Indeed until 1900 he served as foreign secretary as well—the office that gave him the greatest satisfaction and where he won his greatest repute. Yet Salisbury's leadership had always been characterized by emotional distance, and advancing years merely accentuated his practice of minimum personal interaction with his colleagues. Even in cabinet meetings his voice was often muted. Lord Lansdowne, the then secretary for war, provided a glimpse of the blurred fashion in which the prime minister exercised his influence. In defending himself against the charge of having "set at nought a 'clear decision' of the Cabinet," Lansdowne wrote:

I was quite unaware of any such decision but our decisions are very often impalpable, and perhaps I ought to have been able to construct one from the materials afforded by Devonshire's [Hartington's] yawns, and casual interjections round the table.[104]

After regretfully turning over the Foreign Office to Lansdowne, recognizing that the work had become too heavy for him, Salisbury had little zest for the tasks which remained. As one observer noted:

Lord Salisbury is no more now than when Foreign Secretary an effective Prime Minister; the ingrained habit of leaving the Premiership to look after itself keeps him as reluctant as ever to undertake its burdens.[105]

By the time Salisbury left the Foreign Office, his wife was dead. She died in late 1899; her robust health had begun to fail two years

---

103. Balfour to Lady Frances Balfour, May 23, 1899, Balfour Papers, Add. MS. 49831.

104. Lansdowne to Balfour, April 22, 1900, Balfour Papers, Add. MS. 49835.

105. Sir Almeric Fitzroy, *Memoirs* (London: Hutchinson and Co., n.d.), I, April 9, 1901, p. 50.

earlier, and the summer before her death she had suffered a stroke. The family was naturally anxious about the spouse who survived. Salisbury's had been a very close marriage; he had long ago come to rely on his wife's exuberance and energy both to lift the depression that frequently clung to him and to calm the violent passions that in his youth had been the psychic counterpart of his gloom. Under Lady Salisbury's ministrations, the heated language of his younger days had largely given way to controlled irony. But the undercurrent of dejection had never entirely disappeared, and with his wife's death and the approach of his seventieth birthday, it began to sap a vitality which had never been abundant.

Unlike Gladstone, Salisbury had no sense of mission either to steady him or to spur him on. No consuming vision gave purpose to his political life. If the young Salisbury had resembled Chamberlain in transforming an excess of melancholy into bursts of outward aggression, the old man had forsworn that defensive technique. With "a certain pathos in the voice" he told a niece the year his wife died: " 'I have been beaten all my life, and do not mind now.' "[106]

■

"Within was that refuge from inharmonious conditions, whether in public or personal life, that never failed him, and which may have been the secret of the unruffled grace and ease with which he walked through the world." Thus Balfour's niece attested to his inner resources. "His power of becoming aloof at will was perhaps the most important thing for an understanding of his character and the only way of explaining a paradox that lurked in the depths. He basked all his days in affection, and repaid it to the full. Yet no misfortune, no bereavement, could have broken him, for he was a solitary at heart."[107]

A paradox? Not really: the memory of his cherished dead remained so vivid that Balfour could not bring himself to believe that his severance from them was final. In writing to a woman friend who had lost two sons in the First World War, he gave voice to his faith that separation from loved ones was no more than temporary:

> I am . . . sure that those I love and have lost are living. . . . The bitterness lies not in the thought that they are really dead, still less in the thought that I have parted with them for ever; for I think neither of these things.

106. Lady Frances Balfour to George Saintsbury, 1899, quoted in Lady Frances Balfour, *Ne Obliviscaris*, II: 155.
107. Dugdale, *Balfour*, II: 19.

The bitterness lies in the thought that *until I also die* I shall never again see them smile or hear their voices.[108]

So too had it been with Balfour's attachment to Salisbury. He had entered politics at his uncle's urging, and loyalty to Salisbury had been the guiding force of his political activity. In later years, his biographer reported, "often when speaking of the past, he would date not in terms of his own career, but say 'that was before (or after) uncle Robert went.' "[109] Salisbury's treatment of him had given Balfour little reason to feel his dependence as personally threatening; the older man had always acknowledged the younger as a free agent. In turn, Balfour never tried to cast off his reliance on his uncle; rather he transformed it into a grateful remembrance of things past.

During Salisbury's last ministry, Balfour increasingly sought to ease his uncle's burden. When Salisbury's health required stays in southern France, Balfour deputized for him at the Foreign Office. Salisbury had no qualms about delegating whatever matters might require immediate decision, though he apologized for the extra load imposed on his nephew. Balfour's response is indicative of his concern to protect his uncle in an unobtrusive fashion:

As regards F[oreign] O[ffice] work do you think that in future it might be found possible for me or some other colleague to take over for (say) a month each year when nothing in particular is going on? It is not the severity of the work which I at all fear for you; it is its unrelieved continuity.[110]

More than a year and a half later, when British troops suffered unexpected and stunning reverses at the outset of the Boer War at the very time Salisbury was burying his wife, Balfour stepped in once again. A contemporary's description of him imparting dread tidings suggests how he doubtless related the same facts to his grieving uncle: "the extreme gentleness and slow choice of words . . . in no way detracted from the clearness and courage of one who softens the blow of bad news without concealing truth."[111]

Nowhere were such qualities more in evidence than in Balfour's

108. Balfour to Lady Desborough, August 5, 1915, quoted in ibid., II: 297 (emphasis in the original).

109. Ibid., I: 318.

110. Salisbury to Balfour, April 9, 1898, and Balfour to Salisbury, April 14, 1898, Balfour Papers, Add. MS. 49691; both letters are also quoted in Dugdale, *Balfour*, II: 257–261.

111. Sir James Percy Fitzpatrick, *South African Memories* (London: Cassell and Co., 1932), p. 144, quoted in Dugdale, *Balfour*, I: 295.

long-standing relationship with Mary Lady Elcho. Sixteen years his junior, she had married a man eminently suitable from a worldly point of view, but whose changeable temper made him emotionally unreliable. Their daughter penned a vivid description of her father:

> He was as unpredictable as the weather; I never knew what kind of experience a visit to him might prove. One day, perhaps, something I said or did would provoke loud chortles of explosive laughter—delightfully contagious laughter. Then I would feel happy and pleased with myself. Next day, though I had acted in precisely the same way, he might be completely unnoticing. His receiver would be off.[112]

The daughter also provided a lively portrait of her mother as chatelaine of a great country house, organizing games and amusements for her myriad guests:

> Before long . . . I realised that my mother's nature, far more than her circumstances, was answerable for her overcrowded life. Kindness of heart, combined with total lack of system, made her utterly defenceless. She could no more refuse demands on her time than others can refuse demands on their purse.[113]

Into Mary Elcho's world Balfour came as a most agreeable guest,[114] and from the late 1880s on, his hostess was the only woman he loved. Whether that love ever extended to physical intimacy is unclear. Probably not: self-restraint as a means of protecting those dear to him had long since become ingrained and may have served to deplete Balfour's stock of sexual energy. Unlike Bülow, who persistently and successfully pressed divorce—with the foreseeable consequence that his wife-to-be was obliged to abandon her children—Balfour made no such proposal. If his conscience did not permit him to ask Mary to forsake all, she too suffered from scruples which weighed heavily against drastic action. Her love for Balfour, she wrote him, threatened to be "death to the soul."[115] The actual death

112. Cynthia Asquith, *Haply I May Remember* (London: James Barrie, 1950), p. 129.

113. Cynthia Asquith, *Remember and Be Glad* (London: James Barrie, 1952), p. 7.

114. For a highly colored description of that world, see Nicholas Mosley, *Julian Grenfell: His Life and the Times of His Death 1888–1915* (London: Weidenfeld and Nicolson, 1976).

115. Mary Lady Elcho to Balfour, c. 1890, quoted in Young, *Balfour*, p. 135; for contrasting accounts of the relationship, see ibid., pp. 47, 81–84, 102, 134–139, and Max Egremont, *Balfour: A Life of Arthur James Balfour* (London: Collins, 1980), pp. 117–121. Lord Egremont would seem to have the better of the argument in denying that the relationship was ever consummated.

of one of her little boys at Christmastime 1892 may have served as a grim reminder of the risks she was running.[116] Though she appears to have been the more exigent of the two, by the late 1890s she was ready to find safety in a platonic friendship.

What was remarkable about their attachment was not the story of passion unsatisfied, but rather the transformation of that passion into lifelong mutual concern. From the diaries of Mary's daughter, dating from the war years, one can glimpse the relationship which had taken shape. The secret of Balfour's success lay in his ability to free Mary from the illusion of the omnipotence of her own passionate need. By what he once referred to as a series of "gentle rearguard actions,"[117] he continued to indulge her, while discouraging possessiveness on either side. Though he gradually deprived her of emotional symbiosis, he remained constant to her—a totally reliable and sympathetic friend. He thus empowered her to loosen the tie between them without allowing it to break.

In so doing Balfour gave Mary emotional support in her role as "good-enough" mother. Her daughter testified to her success in this regard:

> Perhaps her greatest merit was combining with the maximum of fondness the minimum of possessiveness. Her unintrusive love for her sons and daughters never put fetters on them. She was indeed so unexacting that though her ceaseless concern for her children was touchingly evident, she did not expect—far less demand—their confidences. She longed to know, but she never asked.

Balfour's resources buttressed those of a mother who had it in her to foster feelings her daughter described in glowing terms:

> To be cherished—made to feel valuable—quickens in all but the utterly graceless a sense of obligation: above all I believe that early happiness, natural, taken-for-granted happiness, instils . . . a predisposition which creates a kind of loyalty to life, a loyalty that not all the slings and arrows of outrageous fortune—not even two World Wars—can utterly abolish or destroy.[118]

■

116. On the death of the boy in question, see Asquith, *Haply I May Remember*, p. 135.

117. Lady Cynthia Asquith, *Diaries 1915-1918* (London: Hutchinson and Co., 1968), July 10, 1916, p. 190.

118. Asquith, *Remember and Be Glad*, pp. 20, 23. On the grandmother, Mary Elcho's own mother, see Edith Olivier, *Four Victorian Ladies of Wiltshire* (London: Faber and Faber, 1945), pp. 85-101.

How did Balfour woo Chamberlain? Scarcely a year after Balfour had written Salisbury that he expected Chamberlain to return to the Liberal fold when Gladstone died, Dilke noted in his diary the attractive force on his erstwhile ally which Salisbury's nephew exerted.[119] Less than six years later, in 1895, as Chamberlain received news of his and Balfour's success at the polls, he wrote his new colleague: "I am anxious to be exactly on the same lines as yourself, and I believe there will be no difficulty, but it would be of great advantage to have a quiet talk with you."[120] If Chamberlain did not go as far as he had with Dilke in proposing a "thorough offensive and defensive alliance," he seemed ready to find in Balfour a replacement for his disgraced friend. To be sure, the personal intimacy of the old relationship was never duplicated; no point of contact comparable to the shared experience of losing a wife in childbirth existed between the two. And by the time Chamberlain was becoming closely associated with Balfour, he was happily remarried and had less need of such intimacy. Dilke and Balfour had in common, however, an ability to "contain" Chamberlain's domineering personality by helping him regain trust in himself. Just as Balfour's reliability aided Mary Lady Elcho in relinquishing her passion, so too this same quality helped free Chamberlain from the illusion of the omnipotence of his anger—from the unconscious conviction that he endangered those close to him.

The terrain on which Chamberlain made contact with Balfour was the Irish bog. When in 1887 Salisbury had sent his nephew to Dublin as Irish secretary, he had appointed him to the very post Chamberlain five years earlier had unsuccessfully claimed as his own. In so doing, Salisbury had not only forged a link between the two men, but raised Balfour to the status of potential rival. At once, his fate became personally as well as politically significant for Chamberlain. Still more, the memory of Lord Frederick Cavendish's murder haunted those who watched Balfour depart for Ireland. In that case the vengeance wreaked on the innocent man who had unwittingly usurped Chamberlain's place had been terrible and swift. In contrast, Balfour emerged unscathed. The reassurance he provided his conservative colleagues by his performance in Dublin and Westminster has already been discussed. In Chamberlain's eyes, Bal-

119. Diary entry, December 1889, quoted in Gwynn and Tuckwell, *Dilke*, II: 274. On the political importance of the relationship between Balfour and Chamberlain, see Garvin, *Chamberlain*, II: 617, and J. L. Garvin, *The Life of Joseph Chamberlain*, III: *Empire and World Policy, 1895–1900* (London: Macmillan and Co., 1934), p. 7.

120. Chamberlain to Balfour, July 23, 1895, quoted in Dugdale, *Balfour*, I: 224; see also Chamberlain to Balfour, December 8, 1894, Balfour Papers, Add. MS. 49773.

four demonstrated a capacity for withstanding aggression and at the same time drawing the sting from such assaults. Balfour's fortitude could be admired; it might be copied; above all, it remained unchanging.

More than that, Balfour's record in Ireland—to which Chamberlain made a contribution by vocal support in the House and on the public platform—served to vindicate the stance the renegade Liberal had adopted toward Gladstonian Home Rule.[121] It justified Chamberlain's refusal to give way to obstruction in Westminster and disorder in Ireland; it confirmed his view that pacification did not require dismantling the Union—on the contrary, the preservation of the Union afforded an opportunity for constructive reform. What had earlier been for Chamberlain a disintegrating outburst of aggression had acquired solidity as imperial sentiment. With that sentiment validated by Balfour's steadfastness and success, Chamberlain went on to construct a usable and sustaining system of belief.

Before long, observers noted the change. In the late 1890s one commentator remarked that Chamberlain "talked of China and West Africa, and of France and Russia, with an amplitude of view and phrase that would have astonished Birmingham ten years ago."[122] By that time he was not alone in his growing enthusiasm for empire; but the widespread nature of such enthusiasm does not explain its psychological significance for him. Though imperial affairs had figured only fleetingly in his past—in contrast, for example, to Gladstone's lifelong concern for Ireland—not even Chamberlain's detractors suggested that the marked shift in his political priorities was nothing more than opportunism. Lord Milner was surely close to the mark when he wrote of him:

> In the long run he is swayed by big permanent ideas, and they are not external to him, but, wherever he gets them from, *they have roots inside him,* which alone can ensure any vitality to a policy or any greatness to its possessor.[123]

Only a few remarks need to be made about those "big permanent

---

121. While Chamberlain remained adamant in his opposition to Home Rule, over the years his animus against Gladstone dissipated: by the time he paid Gladstone a visit shortly after the Grand Old Man's retirement, his anger had been transformed into esteem. For Chamberlain's own account of the visit (July 28, 1894), see his memorandum quoted in Garvin, *Chamberlain,* II: 594–595.

122. Maurice V. Brett, ed., *Journals and Letters of Reginald Viscount Esher 1870–1910* (London: Ivor Nicholson and Watson, 1934), I, January 29, 1898, p. 210.

123. *The Milner Papers,* II, Milner to Lady Edward Cecil, May 16, 1903, p. 448 (emphasis in the original).

ideas." One can find in them echoes of Chamberlain's past, testifying to the abiding influence of his experience as a successful businessman and municipal administrator. The qualities he praised derived from his Birmingham days, just as the persona he projected in his speeches was that of a practical man with a vision which was correspondingly practical.[124] Spliced into this fabric were marks of respect for Britain's landed elite:

> It is not enough to occupy certain great spaces of the earth's surface unless you can make the best of them, unless you are willing to develop them. We are landlords of a great estate; it is the duty of the landlord to develop his estate.[125]

In whatever images Chamberlain clothed his favored attributes, one emotion tied them together. The bright thread of loyalty ran through his imperial pronouncements, providing the ideal that colored his vision of empire. In the altered perspective afforded by his ideological shift, his self-esteem rose: once again—as when he had worked in tandem with Dilke—he had succeeded in binding his aggressiveness to higher ends.

Yet binding aggression to higher ends does not necessarily guarantee self-restraint; on the contrary these ends may simply serve as rationalizations for ruthless self-aggrandizement. When Chamberlain's aggression had earlier been turned to lofty purposes in working with Dilke, the safety he derived from the friendship had kept that assertiveness in check. In comparable fashion, while Chamberlain's subsequent imperial vision buttressed his self-esteem and alleviated his depression, it was his relationship with Balfour which induced him to dampen his explosive charge. For Balfour's role in confirming Chamberlain's vision did not cease with his own performance in Ireland. The very fact that he never entered fully into Chamberlain's dreams meant that that confirmation remained selective.[126] And the hope for such confirmation acted on Chamberlain as a restraining

124. David Daiches, "Joseph Chamberlain: Splendid Isolation," in Helmut Viebrock, ed., *Rhetorik und Weltpolitik: Eine interdisziplinäre Untersuchung politischer Reden von W. E. Gladstone, J. Chamberlain und B. v. Bülow* (Wiesbaden: Franz Steiner Verlag, 1974), p. 130. For his successive utterances on the subject, see Charles W. Boyd, ed., *Mr. Chamberlain's Speeches*, 2 vols. (London: Constable and Co., 1914).

125. Quoted in William L. Strauss, *Joseph Chamberlain and the Theory of Imperialism* (Washington, D.C.: American Council on Public Affairs, 1942); see also Bernard Semmel, *Imperialism and Social Reform: English Social-Imperial Thought 1895–1914* (London: George Allen and Unwin, 1960), pp. 74–88.

126. For Balfour's views on empire, see Denis Judd, *Balfour and the British Empire: A Study in Imperial Evolution 1874–1932* (London: Macmillan and Co., 1968).

force. He was not prepared to jeopardize the assurance which Balfour's fortitude provided—the assurance that his own anger was not deadly. As he had formerly told Dilke, in this second case also he would "do nothing knowingly to imperil" his colleague.

A tamed Chamberlain is not the usual image conveyed by descriptions of Salisbury's cabinet. The fact of his leading position, his transformation of the previously obscure post of colonial secretary into one of preeminence, cannot—and for that matter, need not—be disputed. The point at issue is not whether Chamberlain was a powerful figure, but whether he curbed that power in deference to his colleagues. Recent scholarship suggests that the answer is yes. And ironically the charge which contemporary political opponents most often leveled against him—summed up in referring to the Boer War as "Joe's War"—is the one which has most effectively been laid to rest.[127] Without entering into the continuing debate over whose war it was if not Joe's, one should stress Chamberlain's efforts to keep from getting too far ahead of his colleagues in South African affairs. A letter to his undersecretary written three months before hostilities broke out is indicative of the line he took:

> The difficulty—which only presents itself in full force to those who are actually responsible—is not so much to make up one's own mind as to keep perfect faith with one's colleagues and friends.
>
> I have no idea that in this case they will differ with me, but the more loyal they are the more I am bound not to commit them further than they have agreed to go.[128]

By the time the reality of the war in South Africa was upon him, the theme of loyalty which was central to Chamberlain's notion of empire had become a governing ideal in his relations with his colleagues also.

127. See, for example, Ronald Robinson and John Gallagher with Alice Denny, *Africa and the Victorians: The Climax of Imperialism* (London: Macmillan and Co., 1961), pp. 410–461, and J. A. S. Grenville, *Lord Salisbury and Foreign Policy: The Close of the Nineteenth Century* (London: Athlone Press, 1964), pp. 235–264. For evaluating the newer points of view, I have found the following particularly helpful: *The Milner Papers*, I; British Cabinet Papers, Cab. 41/25/14, June 24, 1899; Cab. 41/25/16, July 11, 1899; Cab. 41/25/17, August 1, 1899; Cab. 41/25/18, September 8, 1899; Cab. 41/25/19, September 23, 1899. The most recent account of the war itself is Thomas Pakenham, *The Boer War* (New York: Random House, 1979).

128. Chamberlain to Selborne, June 23, 1899, quoted in Garvin, *Chamberlain*, III: 414. See also Andrew N. Porter, "Lord Salisbury, Mr. Chamberlain and South Africa, 1895–9," *The Journal of Imperial and Commonwealth History* 1 (October 1972): 3–26, and by the same author, *The Origins of the South African War* (Manchester: Manchester University Press, 1980).

■

The task of containing Chamberlain had not been easy. It was one which had overtaxed the ingenuity of Gladstone. While the Grand Old Man had been able to work out his own salvation, the path he had followed had offered no wide opening for Chamberlain. Not until Chamberlain had both charted a new course of his own and accepted realistic limits on that course could he enter upon his long-postponed inheritance as Gladstone's charismatic heir. For this achievement, Balfour had served as his trusted ally. In so doing, Balfour epitomized the true resourcefulness of the British landed elite— the fact that it could produce men capable of playing the role of "good-enough" mother.

Chapter 7

Conclusion

Two Dissonant Tempers

That tempers deeply rooted in childhood, more particularly in contrasting experiences of maternal care, set the parameters for interpersonal behavior among British and among German statesmen—such is the argument I have advanced. The resulting incomprehension between the leaders of the two countries—their missing of each other's mental track—need no longer be wondered at. The British were perplexed; the Germans were frankly distrustful. Where the British hoped that patient negotiation might dispel suspicion, the Germans viewed a lack of ready compliance as a sure sign of enmity. In short, diplomatic discourse between the two summits echoed the clash of two dissonant tempers.

I. The Scrupulous Temper

A text from George Eliot's *The Mill on the Floss* may serve to recall the temper earlier attributed to the British protagonists of this study. It is of no moment that in the novel the question at issue is in the private, not the public, realm. Once again—as throughout this work—a sharp demarcation between public and private seems inappropriate; a continuum, rather than separate compartments, represents emotional reality.

Will Maggie go off with Stephen and marry him? Their mutual attraction and affection has grown throughout the novel, and indeed has overwhelmed Stephen. Both, however, have previous ties. It is the conversation in which Maggie conveys her refusal that merits attention:

> 'If the past is not to bind us, where can duty lie? We should have no law but the inclination of the moment.... Faithfulness and constancy mean something else besides doing what is easiest and pleasantest to ourselves. They mean renouncing whatever is opposed to the reliance others have in us—whatever would cause misery to those whom the course of our lives has made dependent on us.'

To Stephen's assertion of his own claim, Maggie responds:

> 'There are memories, and affections, and longing after perfect goodness, that have such a strong hold on me; they would never quit me for long; they would come back and be pain to me—repentance.... We can only choose whether we will indulge ourselves in the present moment, or whether we will renounce that, for the sake of obeying the divine voice within us—for the sake of being true to all the motives that sanctify our lives. I know this belief is hard: it has slipped away from me again and again; but I have felt that if I let it go for ever, I should have no light through the darkness of this life.'[1]

For Maggie the "divine voice" is within her. Her sense of obligation does not derive from what the world believes; rather it is self-generated and deeply personal. Or to put it another way: her sense of obligation has its origin in past attachments between herself and others. The fact that she has been trusted, that others have come to rely on her, weighs heavily. Dependence is freely acknowledged; it is welcomed with gratitude. Indeed Maggie's remembrance of those who have confided in her draws the sting from what might otherwise be unbearably painful recollections. She can still vividly recall her own experience of suffering and of having "no one to pity" her. All the more reason, in her mind, for a scrupulous regard for those who have accepted her love and loved her in return. Toward them, her overriding wish is to make reparation for the damage she may have already inflicted; she cannot "take a good" for herself "that has been wrung out of their misery."[2] Scruples of this sort are not a matter of rote responses to be lightly cast aside; they are the bedrock on which one can build a life.

■

A letter that Anthony Trollope's Duke of Omnium addresses to his son Silverbridge, upon learning of the young man's election to the

1. George Eliot, *The Mill on the Floss*, Book 6, ch. 14.
2. Ibid., Book 6, ch. 14.

House of Commons, illuminates the same scrupulous temper at work in the political realm.

Though the duke prefers that his son should follow in his footsteps, at least to the extent of adhering to the same political party, he cannot regard as treasonous the young man's decision to do otherwise. Difference of party affiliation—and as a corollary, disagreement on substantive matters—is no ground for rebuke, let alone a breach. This tolerance is worth underlining, not only in terms of the relationship between father and son, but for the light it sheds on British public life in general. It suggests that those who participated in it were not so dazzled by the cut and thrust of politics that they failed to appreciate the shared values which guided their conduct. In the duke's eyes, agreement on a mode of behavior, rather than on a series of issues, defines the mental universe in which disputes are waged. What is important to him is that Silverbridge be conscious of the moral and psychological qualities required of someone who has entered the public arena.

The burden of the duke's lecture is to warn his son against the snares and delusions of self-aggrandizement. Not himself the stuff from which heroes or charismatic leaders are made, the older man has no wish to see the younger aspire to such heights. The duke's ideal-typical statesman would be a homelier figure:

> 'And I would have you remember also that the work of a member of Parliament can seldom be of that brilliant nature which is of itself charming; and that the young member should think of such brilliancy as being possible to him only at a distance. It should be your first care to sit and listen so that the forms and methods of the House may as it were soak into you gradually. And then you must bear in mind that speaking in the House is but a very small part of a member's work, perhaps that part which he may lay aside altogether with the least strain on his conscience. A good member of Parliament will be good upstairs in the Committee Rooms, good downstairs to make and to keep a House, good to vote, for his party if it may be nothing better, but for the measures also which he believes to be for the good of his country.
>
> 'Gradually, if you will give your thoughts to it, and above all your time, the theory of legislation will sink into your mind, and you will find that there will come upon you the ineffable delight of having served your country to the best of your ability.
>
> 'It is the only pleasure in life which has been enjoyed without alloy by your affectionate father.'[3]

When the duke suggests what the future holds for Silverbridge, it is his own past that he is describing. When he expresses his faith that

3. Anthony Trollope, *The Duke's Children*, ch. 15.

attending to parliamentary business will expand his son's understanding, he is outlining an inner transformation which he himself has experienced. At the same time he indicates that he has gained more than understanding; by doing what he believes to be his best, he has acquired a clear conscience and with it, trust in himself. In a world of "good-enough" mothers—male and female—doing one's best is recognized as "good-enough." Superior achievement is not necessary to buttress self-esteem; scrupulousness will suffice.

■

> The German Foreign Office hold to a traditional view of negotiation that one of the most effective methods of gaining your point is to show how intensely disagreeable you can make yourself if you do not. They are surprised that the recollection of these methods should rankle, and speaking generally the North Germans combine intense susceptibility as regards themselves with a singular inability to appreciate the susceptibilities of others.[4]

This comment was penned by Lord Sanderson in 1907, a year after he had retired from the post of permanent undersecretary in the Foreign Office. His observations merely echoed what had been remarked upon by British statesmen for more than a generation. Though the British might lament the bad diplomatic manners of the Germans, they were not so insular as to expect that all their interlocutors would share their own notions of decorum—or, for that matter, put the same favorable construction on their own deportment as they did themselves. Hence it behooved the British, Sanderson continued, to refrain from harsh judgment.

> The moral which I should draw from the events of recent years is that Germany is a helpful, though somewhat exacting, friend, that she is a tight and tenacious bargainer, and a most disagreeable antagonist. She is oversensitive about being consulted on all questions on which she can claim a voice, either as a Great Power, or on account of special interests, and it is never prudent to neglect her on such occasions. Her diplomacy is, to put it mildly, always watchful, and any suspicion of being ignored rouses an amount of wrath disproportionate to the offence. However tiresome such discussions may be, it is, as a general rule, less inconvenient to take her at once into counsel, and to state frankly within what limits you can accept her views, than to have a claim for interference suddenly launched on you at some critical moment. . . . But I do not think it can be

4. *British Documents on the Origins of the War 1898–1914,* III: *The Testing of the Entente 1904–6* (London: H.M.S.O., 1928), Observations by Lord Sanderson, February 21, 1907, p. 429.

justly said that she is ungrateful for friendly support. It is at all events unwise to meet her with an attitude of pure obstruction, such as is advocated by part of our press. A great and growing nation cannot be repressed. It is altogether contrary to reason that Germany should wish to quarrel with us though she may wish to be in a position to face a quarrel with more chances of success, than she can be said now to have. But it would be a misfortune that she should be led to believe that in whatever direction she seeks to expand, she will find the British lion in her path. There must be places in which German enterprise can find a field without injury to any important British interests, and it would seem wise that in any policy of development which takes due account of those interests she should be allowed to expect our good will.[5]

Sanderson set down these observations in response to the historic memorandum which Eyre Crowe, head of the Western Department in the Foreign Office, circulated on January 1, 1907. Though in substance the two documents were close, their tone differed. Crowe was less inclined than Sanderson to ignore the blackmailing technique they both attributed to the German Foreign Office—and less sanguine about the prospects of negotiation. More particularly he underlined the failure of "the kind of temporary expedients to which England has so frequently and so patiently resorted" to keep Anglo-German relations on an even keel.

It has been so often declared, as to have become almost a diplomatic platitude, that between England and Germany, as there has never been any real clashing of material interests, so there are no unsettled controversies over outstanding questions. Yet for the last twenty years, as the archives of our Foreign Office show, German Governments have never ceased reproaching British Cabinets with want of friendliness and with persistent opposition to German political plans. A review of British relations during the same period with France, with Russia, and with the United States reveals ancient and real sources of conflict, springing from imperfectly patched-up differences of past centuries, the inelastic stipulations of antiquated treaties, or the troubles incidental to unsettled colonial frontiers. Although with these countries England has fortunately managed to continue to live in peace, there always remained sufficient elements of divergence to make the preservation of good, not to say cordial, relations an anxious problem requiring constant alertness, care, moderation, good temper, and conciliatory disposition.

How, then, to account for the failure of diplomacy in the ostensibly less troublesome realm of relations with Germany? Grandiose designs on the part of the Reich, Crowe noted, was one answer frequently given. According to this view:

5. Ibid., Observations by Lord Sanderson, February 21, 1907, pp. 430–431.

Germany is deliberately following a policy which is essentially opposed to vital British interests, and . . . an armed conflict cannot in the long run be averted, except by England either sacrificing those interests, with the result that she would lose her position as an independent Great Power, or making herself too strong to give Germany the chance of succeeding in a war. This is the opinion of those who see in the whole trend of Germany's policy conclusive evidence that she is consciously aiming at the establishment of a German hegemony, at first in Europe, and eventually in the world. . . .

There is . . . perhaps another way of looking at the problem: It might be suggested that the great German design is in reality no more than the expression of a vague, confused, and unpractical statesmanship, not fully realizing its own drift; . . . that, in fact, Germany does not really know what she is driving at, and that all her excursions and alarums, all her underhand intrigues do not contribute to the steady working out of a well conceived and relentlessly followed system of a policy, because they do not really form part of any such system. This is an hypothesis not flattering to the German Government, and it must be admitted that much might be urged against its validity. But it remains true that on this hypothesis also most of the facts of the present situation can be explained.[6]

Crowe made it perfectly clear that he found the second interpretation the more accurate of the two. What eluded both Crowe and Sanderson, however, was the nature of German susceptibilities. They failed to appreciate the fatalist temper that led the Reich's leaders, in the words of General Helmut von Moltke, chief of the general staff, to agonize over whether Germany would have the courage "to enforce . . . an energetic line . . . with the sword."[7]

II. The Fatalist Temper

Once again a text (from Theodor Fontane's *Effi Briest*) may serve as a point of departure. A conversation between Baron von Innstetten and his friend Wüllersdorf—both bureaucrats in the service of the Prussian state—echoes a second and contrasting temper.

Innstetten has just discovered that his wife Effi had been unfaithful to him. Although her infidelity lay almost seven years in the past, he concludes, in the course of talking to his friend, that he must sub-

6. British Cabinet Papers, Cab. 37/86, No. 1, Eyre Crowe, "Memorandum on the present State of British Relations with France and Germany," January 1, 1907, published in *British Documents on the Origins of the War 1898–1914*, III: 407–408, 414–415.
7. Eliza von Moltke, ed., *Helmut von Moltke, 1848–1916: Erinnerungen, Briefe, Dokumente 1877 bis 1916: Ein Bild vom Kriegsausbruch, erster Kriegsführung und Persönlichkeit des ersten militärischen Führers des Krieges* (Stuttgart: Der Kommende Tag, 1922), Moltke to his wife, August 19, 1911, p. 362.

mit to his caste's code of honor and challenge the former lover to a duel.

> 'With people living all together, something has evolved that now exists and we've become accustomed to judge everything, ourselves and others, according to its rules. And it's no good transgressing them, society will despise us and finally we will despise ourselves and not be able to bear it and blow our brains out. Forgive me for giving you this lecture which, after all, is only saying what everyone has said to himself hundreds of times. But how can anyone really say anything new? So once again, there's no hatred or anything of that sort and I don't want to have blood on my hands merely for the sake of the happiness I've been deprived of, but that *something* which forms society—call it tyrant if you like—is not concerned with charm or love, or even with how long ago a thing took place. I've no choice, I must do it.'

One cannot doubt that Innstetten will be able to measure up to the task—and its consequences—which he recognizes as his. The alternative, after all, is to blow out his own brains. For the code he accepts as personally compelling is persecutory and destructive; it leaves him with the stark choice between homicide and suicide.

In the next paragraph, however, one discovers that Innstetten need not have succumbed to what might be called the fatalist temper, that his fatalism itself derives from an earlier action:

> 'Six hours ago, I'll grant you this in advance, the cards were still in my hand and I could have done one thing or another, there was still a way out. But not any longer, I'm in an impasse. I've only myself to blame; if you like, I should have been more guarded and shown more self-control, have kept everything to myself and fought it all out in my own mind. But it came so suddenly and so violently that I can hardly blame myself for not having been able to control my reactions more successfully. I went to your place and wrote you a note and by doing that the game passed out of my hands. From that moment onwards, there was someone else who knew something of my misfortune and, what is more important, of the stain on my honour; and as soon as we had exchanged our first words, there was someone else who knew all about it. And, because there is such a person, I can't go back.'

There was a path not taken—the path of "fighting it out in his own mind." Earlier in the conversation, Innstetten claims to love Effi still. But the spell he professes to be under is feeble indeed; it rouses no memory to be cherished; it forges no link to a past which cries out for preservation. Without an inner world of grateful remembrance, Innstetten's impulse to forgive Effi dies at birth. Without reassuring presences of his own, he cannot make the world safe for her.

Instead, Innstetten transfers to an *inter*personal relationship a drama that was *intra*psychic in origin. In so doing, he fabricates a persecutory authority figure as well: Wüllersdorf derives his power from Innstetten—not from "society." And the relationship thus established provides the key to Innstetten's own inner world.

> 'I'm still not sure,' repeated Wüllersdorf. 'I don't like using a stale cliché, but there's no better way of putting it: "I'll be as silent as the grave," Innstetten.'
> 'Yes, Wüllersdorf, that's what people always say. But there is no keeping a secret. And if you do as you say and are discretion itself towards others, even so *you* know about it and it doesn't help me where you're concerned if you've just expressed approval and even said: "I can understand all that you're saying." The fact of the matter is, that from this moment onwards I'm dependent on your sympathy and every word that you hear me exchange with my wife will be checked by you. . . .'

Innstetten does not or cannot trust Wüllersdorf. This lack of trust makes Innstetten's decision to confide in his friend appear, in retrospect, all the more self-destructive. Yet it is not what Wüllersdorf may do which makes him dangerous; rather the mere fact of his knowing is crucial. When knowing is projected into the future, it becomes transformed into remembering the past. Where Innstetten's memory of loving Effi fails to deter him, Wüllersdorf's memory of his friend's misfortune will always be present in both their minds. The past, then, is not forgotten; the good may be interred, but the evil lives ever after. Hence memory haunts rather than soothes. What is more, because Wüllersdorf may prove untrustworthy, Innstetten is at his friend's mercy; he is obsessed by Wüllersdorf as a power exacting submission from him.

If Innstetten cannot render his friend harmless, he can and does cut the ground out from under him:

> 'Or suppose it happens that, in some quite ordinary question of an affront having been given, I suggest that allowances might be made because no harm has been done, or some such thing, then a smile will cross your face or at least start to cross it and in your mind you'll be saying to yourself: "Good old Innstetten, where insults are concerned he really has a passion for analyzing the exact amount of offensive material they contain and he never finds a sufficient quantity of poison gas. . . ." Am I right, Wüllersdorf, or not?'
> Wüllersdorf had risen to his feet. 'It's terrifying to think that you're right, but you *are* right. I won't worry you any longer with my question as to whether it's necessary. The world is how it is and things don't go the way that we want but the way that others want. All that high-falutin' talk

about "God's judgement" is nonsense, of course, and we don't want any of that, yet our own cult of honour on the other hand is idolatry. But we must submit to it, as long as the idol stands.'[8]

The world, however, is not "how it is." All that is clear is that Wüllersdorf corresponds to the image Innstetten has fashioned. And the moment Wüllersdorf recognizes himself in Innstetten's description, he too succumbs to the fatalist temper.

■

On July 29, 1914, the German ambassador in London, Prince Lichnowsky, reported to Berlin on a conversation he had had with the British foreign secretary:

> Sir E[dward] Grey ... said to me that he had a friendly and private communication to make to me, namely, that he did not want our warm personal relations and the intimacy of our talks on all political matters to lead me astray, and he would like to *spare himself the reproach (of) bad faith.* The British Government desired now as before to cultivate our previous friendship, and it could *stand aside as long as the conflict remained confined to Austria and Russia. But if we and France should be involved,* then the situation would immediately be altered, and the British Government would, *under the circumstances, find itself forced to make up its mind quickly.* In that event *it would not be practicable to stand aside and wait for any length of time.* 'If war breaks out, it will be *the greatest catastrophe* that the *world has ever seen.'* It was far from his desire to express any kind of threat; he only wanted to protect me from disappointments and *himself* from the *reproach of bad faith,* and had therefore chosen the form of a private explanation.[9]

"Mean and Mephistophelian!" ran William II's marginal notation. "Thoroughly English, however." "England reveals herself in her true colors," he added, "at a moment when she thinks that we are caught in the toils and, so to speak, disposed of!"[10]

> The net has been suddenly thrown over our heads, and England sneeringly reaps the most brilliant success of her persistently prosecuted *anti-German world-policy,* against which we have proved ourselves helpless, while she twists the noose of our political and economic destruction

8. Theodor Fontane, *Effi Briest,* trans. Douglas Parmée (Harmondsworth: Penguin Books, 1967), ch. 27 (emphasis in the original).

9. Imanuel Geiss, ed., *July 1914: The Outbreak of the First World War: Selected Documents* (New York: W. W. Norton and Co., 1974), Lichnowsky to Jagow, July 29, 1914, pp. 289–290 (emphasis in the original).

10. Ibid., William II's marginal comments on Lichnowsky to Jagow, July 29, 1914, pp. 289–290.

out of our fidelity to Austria, as we squirm *isolated* in the net. A great achievement, which arouses the admiration even of him who is to be destroyed as its result![11]

Despite his bitter words, the emperor showed himself determined to take up the sword and thereby make his worst forebodings come to pass.

Sir Edward Grey had clung to the hope that "if once it became apparent" that Europe was "on the edge, all the Great Powers would call a halt and recoil from the abyss."[12] But the Germans refused to halt. They saw themselves confronted by a fate which posited no middle ground between homicide and suicide—except perhaps slow suffocation through poison gas. To haunted men, war appeared obligatory—and they forgot that they themselves had fabricated the "idols" to which they now felt enslaved.

When on August 3, 1914, Grey at length told the House of Commons of his own government's intentions, he could derive scant comfort from the warm response his speech evoked; instead, he groaned to a close co-worker: "I hate war, I hate war." Later that same evening, with his celebrated remark about "the lamps . . . going out all over Europe," he showed a growing awareness of what he and his colleagues had resolved to do.[13] Peering into the twilight, he dimly discerned the drastic reversal of mentality that the new emphasis on military valor would entail. In this respect, his countrymen had something rarer to lose than did the Germans in the ensuing carnage.

11. Ibid., William II's marginal comments on Pourtalès to Jagow, July 30, 1914, p. 295 (emphasis in the original).
12. Viscount Grey of Fallodon, *Twenty-Five Years 1892–1916* (New York: Frederick A. Stokes Co., 1925), I: 302.
13. Harold Nicolson, *Sir Arthur Nicolson, Bart., First Lord Carnock: A Study in the Old Diplomacy* (London: Constable and Co., 1930), p. 306; G. M. Trevelyan, *Grey of Fallodon: Being the Life of Sir Edward Grey afterwards Viscount Grey of Fallodon* (London: Longmans, Green, and Co., 1937), p. 266.

Bibliographical Note

This book does not require a formal bibliography: the sources on which it is based are fully indicated in the footnotes. The notes do not suggest, however, the background knowledge I derived from a close study of the microfilmed British Cabinet Papers, Cab./37 and Cab./41, the first a record of items circulated for cabinet discussion and the second a record of the prime minister's reports to the queen. Though my citations are preponderantly to published materials, I have also explored a number of collections of private papers. A research trip to the British Library in London enabled me to consult the papers of Gladstone, Balfour, Dilke, and Sir Edward Walter Hamilton, and a similar trip to the Bundesarchiv in Koblenz gave me access to the Eulenburg and Bülow Papers. While these explorations proved valuable in supplying detailed confirmation of my tentative hypotheses, they convinced me that further such research would not substantially alter the lines of argument I was working out from the abundant primary literature available in print.

Index

Age, old, 68, 154; Bismarck's response to, 70, 73; Gladstone's response to, 38–39, 42, 74–75, 179

Aggression, 53, 90, 112; among British political leaders, 91, 192, 193, 197, 205, 206, 207; capacity to withstand, 206; control of, 207; and the "good-enough" mother, 164

Albert, Prince Consort, 166, 167; bond with his eldest daughter, 124, 125, 126, 128, 173–174; childhood of, 171; death of, 174–175; relationship with Queen Victoria, 171–174

Alderson, Georgina (later 3rd Marchioness of Salisbury), 88–89

American Civil War, 89

Anger, 205; avoidance of, 43; British and German responses to, 90; control of, 208; in Gladstone's retirement from political life, 178, 181; toward the mother, 8

Anglican religion, 21–22, 25–26, 39–40

Anglo-German relations: antagonism in, 1, 71; differences in diplomatic manners, 213; failure of diplomacy in, 214–219; incomprehension between British and German leaders, x, 1–2, 14, 210; scrupulous vs. fatalist tempers in, 210–219. *See also* Leaders, British; Leaders, German; Political cohesion; Politics

Anxiety: from childhood traumatic experiences, 85–86; confrontation with, 24; in motherhood, 48–49, 127–128, 173–174, 192–193; and sexuality, 23, 24–28

Argyll, 8th Duke of, 33

Arnim, Harry von, 62

Augusta, Empress, 47–48, 70

Austro-German alliance, 73

Authority, 217; acceptance of, 13, 161–162; of Bülow, 147, 148, 155–162; by divine right, 133–134; plans for the orderly transfer of, 181; psychological incorporation of, 113

Authority, charismatic; and bureaucratic administration, 45–76; and parliamentary government, 15–44; and relations between leaders and colleagues, 77–78, 113–114, 181–182

"Baby worship," 127
Balfour, Arthur James, 2, 98, 100–110, 187–188, 198–209; approach toward political cohesion, 199–200; as chief secretary for Ireland, 100, 103, 105, 106–110, 111, 205–206; childhood and parents of, 101–103; compared with Bismarck, 104; fear of emotional involvement, 100–101; philosophy of, 101; political and personal relationships with his uncle Salisbury, 98, 104–106, 202, 205; political relations with Chamberlain, 198, 199, 205–209; psychological resources of, 199–209 *passim*; religion of, 101, 103; romantic attachment of, 203–204, 205; on the significance of Gladstone's political career, 182
Balfour, Lady Blanche, 88; and maternal nurturance, 102–103
Beach, Sir Michael Hicks, 94, 96; resignation of, 99
"Benign circle," 24, 28, 164
Bismarck Fronde, 116
Bismarck, Herbert von, 62; abandonment of his beloved, 70, 152; character and behavior of, 71–72; compared with Balfour, 104; friendship with Eulenburg, 137; identification with the potency of his father, 70–71; and journalistic attacks on Holstein, 121, 122; political career of, 61, 69–74, 114–115, 117; reliance of his father on, 70, 74, 104
Bismarck, Otto von, 2, 45–76, 84, 97, 145; association with Bülow's father, 149–150; attitudes on female influence in politics, 48, 84, 126; career choice of, 87; charismatic leadership of, 45–46, 77, 113; childhood of, 48–53; children of, 61, 62, 69–74 (*see also* Bismarck, Herbert von); compared with Bülow, 161–162; compared with Gladstone, 87, 91, 175–176, 178; compared with Salisbury, 82, 87, 90; death of, 158; engagement and marriage of,

50, 51, 54, 55, 150–151; erosion of his authority, 67–76, 161; Eulenburg's opinion of, 137–139; father of, 52–53; fear of emotional involvement, 47–48; health of, 58; intimate relationships avoided by, 47, 53, 62, 69, 74; maternal behavior recreated by, 114; mother of, 48–52, 53, 56, 63, 139; political career of, 45–46, 57–76; political heir of, 148, 157; power manipulated by, 58–67; power after his resignation, 115–117, 119; relationship with William II, 129, 134–135; reliance on his son, 70, 74, 104; religion of, 54–56, 87; resignation of, 45; sense of superiority and omnipotence, 47, 48, 56–57, 62, 75, 78, 90
———, colleagues and subordinates of, 59–67, 68, 69, 72–73, 74, 75–76, 77–78, 113–114, 138; acceptance of subordination, 62–67, 113–114; bureaucratic and psychological dependence of, 59, 113–114, 135; compared with Gladstone's co-workers, 77–78; compared with Salisbury's co-workers, 90, 91; control of, 59–62; reaction to Bismarck's old age and political dependence on his son, 72–74; response to the change of monarchs, 68, 113
Bismarck, Wilhelm von (Billy), 62, 70
Bismarck, Wilhelmine von, 48–52, 63, 83
Blanckenburg, Marie von, 54–55
Blanckenburg, Moritz von, 54–55
Boer War, 202, 208
Brauer, Arthur von, 72
Bright, John, 30
Britain: basis for interpersonal relations in, 13–14, 44; political power in, 3–4. *See also* Anglo-German relations; Leaders, British; Politics, British
Bryce, James, 178
Bulgaria, 29
Bülow, Bernhard von, 2, 144–162; as an authority figure, 147, 148, 155–162; childhood of, 149–152; compared with Bismarck, 161–162; contemptuous attitude toward women, 154; marriage and wife of, 152–154, 161, 203; memoirs of, 147–149, 161; psychological manipulation by, 149, 156, 158–161; relations with Eulenburg, 144,

147, 155–156, 157; relations with Holstein, 152; relations with William II, 158–161; self-image of, 148–149
Bureaucracy, and power of German leaders, 59–76, 145
Bureaucrat, ideal type of, 58

Campbell-Bannerman, Sir Henry, 198
Caprivi, Leo von, 116; political career of, 117; political goals of, 145–146
Carolath, Princess Elisabeth, 70, 152
Cavendish, Lord Frederick, 35; assassination of, 40, 185, 205
Cecil, Lady Gwendolen, 85n, 86n, 88n, 89n, 91, 104n, 105n, 106n
Cecil, Robert. *See* Salisbury, Robert Gascoyne-Cecil, 3rd Marquess of
Chamberlain, Austen, 191, 199
Chamberlain, Joseph, 2, 30, 182–197; aggressiveness of, 192, 193, 197, 205, 206, 207; attitude of Salisbury toward, 93; compared with other British leaders, 184, 192, 197, 199; containment of, 198, 200, 205–209; death of his wives and mother, 190–191; education of, 183, 192; friendship with Dilke, 188–192, 207; imperialist views of, 206–207, 208; loyalty to his colleagues, 208; marriages of, 190–191, 194–196; mother of, 192–194; as political heir of Gladstone, 182–183, 184, 209; political memoirs of, 186; political relations with Balfour, 198, 199, 205–209; political separation from Gladstone, 185–187; position on Irish Home rule, 184, 185, 187, 189–190, 197; relations with Churchill, 95
Charismatic authority. *See* Authority, charismatic
Checkland, S. G., 18n
Childbirth, death of the mother caused by, 190–191
Childrearing, 4, 5
Churchill, Lord Randolph, 100, 106, 109; intervention in the work of his colleagues, 96–97; relationship with Salisbury, 94–99
Collins, Elizabeth, 27
Compensation in the mother–child relationship, 14

Congress of Berlin, 73, 100
Conroy, Sir John, 167, 168
Corn Laws, 41
Cranbrook, 1st Earl of, 97–98
Crowe, Sir Eyre, 214–215

Daily Telegraph Affair, 160
Death, 39; blame for the cause of, 131–132, 191; of the father, 101–102, 131–132; and fratricidal fantasies, 151; impact of, 125; and marriage of Bismarck, 55; of the mother, 36, 37, 86, 165–166; and separation from loved ones, 201–202; of wives during childbirth, 190–191
Defence of Philosophic Doubt (A. J. Balfour), 101
Dependence: acceptance of the need for, 170; and acceptance of subordination, 66–67; British attitudes toward, 202, 211; bureaucratic, 59; efforts to avoid, 135; and lack of emotional support, 113–114
Derby, 14th Earl of, 81, 93
Devonshire, 7th Duke of, 36, 86
Dilke, Sir Charles, friendship with Chamberlain, 187–192, 207
Dilke, Wentie, 191–192, 196–197, 205
Diplomatic manners, differences in, 213
Disraeli, Benjamin, 81, 89, 93; relationship with Salisbury, 91–92
Distrust: based on political betrayal, 120–122; and fear of emotional involvement, 47–48, 65; in German politics, 13, 47–48, 57, 65, 78, 122, 124; and interplay of environment and personality, 124, 125
Divine right, and maternal rejection, 133–134
Dönhoff, Marie von, 152–154
Dreams: context of the retelling of, 57; interpretation of, 51, 56–57; and psychological impact of retirement from politics, 179–181

Education: of Bismarck, 51; of Chamberlain, 183, 192; of William II, 130; of Salisbury, 86; maternal anxieties about, 51, 127, 128
Edward VII, King, childhood of, 174

Egypt, 37–38

Elcho, Mary, 203–204

Eliot, George, 210–211

Electoral reform, in British politics, 40–41, 79–80, 81, 91, 93, 182, 183

Emotional safety: Bismarck's political reliance on his son, 70; among British political leaders, 190–192; and control of inner feelings, 52, 56; and inability to express love, 53; and reaction to old age and loss of power, 74–75

Emotional support, 110; in friendship, 136, 168–170; in military life, 133; for role of the "good-enough" mother, 204

Endicott, Mary, 196

Eulenburg, Botho zu, 145, 146

Eulenburg-Hertefeld, Philipp zu, 2, 70n, 136–144; artistic temperament of, 136, 137–138, 140–141; on attitude of William II toward Bismarck, 135; attitude toward Bülow, 144, 147, 155–156, 157; emotional collapse and political betrayal of, 156; on fear after Bismarck's resignation, 115–116; feminine aspect of, 138, 140; friendship with William II, 136, 140–144, 155, 156; homoerotic proclivities of, 136, 156; mother of, 139–140; opinion of Bismarck, 137–139; opinion of Holstein, 120; psychological manipulation of William II, 160–161; relations between Holstein and William II linked by, 119; relations with Holstein, 119, 142, 143–144

Evangelical religious beliefs, 18, 21, 150

Fairbairn, W. R. D., 6–7; on the Oedipus situation, 9

Family life: centrality of the mother in, 9–10; compared with public life, 13–14, 19–20; historical study of, 4–6. *See also* Father–child relationship; Mother–child relationship; Parents

Fantasy: of merger between parent and child, 166; and psychological equilibrium, 133, 141; and self-aggrandizement, 57, 144

Fatalist temper, 215–219

Father: of Bismarck, 52–53; of Bülow, 150; of Gladstone, 20, 23, 25; of Holstein, 64–65; of Hartington, 36–37; of Salisbury, 86–87, 89, 91; patriarchal role of, 9–10

Father–child relationship, 7, 8–9; bonds between Prince Albert and his eldest daughter, 124, 125, 126, 128, 173–184; and death of the father, 101–102, 131–132; and death of the mother during childbirth, 191; identification with the potency of the father, 70–71

Fear: of Bismarck after his resignation, 115–116, 119, 122, 143, 158; and dependence, 66; of emotional involvement, 100–101; in German interpersonal relations, 13

Fisher, M. H., 58n, 60n, 63n, 122n

Fontane, Theodor, 215–218

Frederick, Crown Prince and Emperor (Fritz), 67–68; death of, 129, 131–132; relations with Bismarck, 69; wife of, 57, 125–126, 127 (*see also* Frederick Crown Princess and Empress)

Frederick, Crown Princess and Empress (Vicky), 123–136; bonds with her father, 124, 125, 126, 128, 173–174; friendship with Bülow's wife, 161; and marriage of Bülow, 152n, 153; mother of, 124, 127, 165, 173–174; relationship with her son William II, 123–124, 126–134, 136, 161, 166

Friendship: among British political colleagues, 31, 106, 188–192, 197, 199, 207; among German leaders, 136, 140–144, 155, 156; platonic, 204

Freud, Sigmund: and dream interpretation, 56–57, 179, 180; legacy of, 6–9, 43; opinion of the mother of William II, 123, 124, 127

Fulford, Roger, 124n, 125n, 126n, 127n, 128n, 129n, 133n, 165n

Germany: basis of interpersonal relations in, 13; political power in, 3–4; unification of, 45. *See also* Anglo-German relations; Leaders, German; Politics, German

Gladstone, Anne, 17–18, 19, 25

Gladstone, Helen, 25–26, 27

Gladstone, John, 20

Gladstone, William Ewart, 2, 15–44; Chamberlain's political separation from, 185, 186–187; charismatic leadership of, 15, 30, 77; childhood of, 16–20, 180; compared with Bismarck, 87, 91, 175–176, 178; concern for prostitutes, 26–28; diaries of, 18–19, 22, 25, 26, 27; eulogies after the death of, 181–182; father of, 20, 23, 25; friendship with Granville, 30–32, 33, 34, 106; Irish Home Rule ministry of, 38–44, 77, 92–93, 111, 176–177, 178, 184, 185, 187, 196; marriage and wife of, 20–21, 24, 180; ministry of compared to Salisbury's government, 78, 110–112; mother of, 17–18, 20, 21, 25; political career of, 20, 21, 22, 28–44, 175–182; political heir of, 181, 182–183, 184, 209; psychic crisis of, 22–28; psychological impact of retirement of, 163, 175–182, 198; religion of, 16, 18, 19, 20, 21–23, 25–26, 27, 28, 40, 87, 179; response to old age, 38–39, 42, 74–75, 179; Salisbury's opinion of, 80–82, 112; sense of sinfulness, 18, 19, 28; sisters of, 17–18, 19, 25, 27; Queen Victoria's attitude toward, 175–176, 179–180

———, colleagues of, 15–16, 30–38, 42, 75, 77–78, 91, 177–178, 181–182; attitudes before Gladstone's resignation, 177–178, 181–182; avoidance of anger by, 43–44; compared to Bismarck's subordinates, 77–78; psychological relations with Gladstone, 182; and need for personal recognition, 30–34

Glückskind motif, 148, 149

Glynne, Catherine (later Gladstone), 20

"Good-enough" mother. *See* Mother, "good-enough"

Goschen, George, 99

Granville, 2nd Earl, 33, 42; friendship with Gladstone, 30–32, 33, 34, 106

Gray Eminence. *See* Holstein, Friedrich von

Grey, Sir Edward, 218, 219

Haller, Johannes, 136, 137n, 139, 141n

Hamilton, Lord George, 96, 97, 108, 110

Harcourt, Sir William, 30, 41–42, 181

Hartington, Spencer Compton Cavendish, Marquess of (later 8th Duke of Devonshire), 2, 30, 31, 93, 99, 184,

185, 188, 200; childhood of, 36–37; death of his mother, 86; opinion of Churchill, 94–95; relationship with Gladstone, 35–36, 37–38, 43–44; scrupulousness of, 36, 43

Hatzfeldt, Paul von, 69, 71; career of, 60–61

Hawarden kite, 41

Henckel von Donnersmark, Guido, 121, 122

Hinzpeter, George, 128, 130, 131

History: assumptions about psychology in, 3; family life in, 4–6; interpretation and research in, ix–x; psychoanalytic theory used in, 6–13; standards of adequacy for psychoanalytic explanations in, 11–12

Hohenlohe-Schillingsfürst, Chlodwig zu, 146

Hohenzollern kings, divine right of, 133

Holstein, Friedrich von, 2, 58, 114–122; Bismarck criticized by, 72–73, 122; as Bismarck's political heir, 157, 158; on character of Herbert von Bismarck, 71–72; childhood of, 63–65, 158; defeat of his political goals, 136; emotional safety of, 158–159; opinion of Hatzfeldt, 60, 61; political career after Bismarck's resignation, 115–122; political cohesion and political relations guided by, 116–122; power of, 158, 160; psychic defenses of, 63, 115, 158; regarded as a gray eminence, 115; relationship with Bismarck, 62–63, 66–67, 74, 115–116, 119, 122, 158; relations with Bülow, 152, 153, 156–159; relations with William II, 118–119, 121–122, 143, 160; relations with Eulenburg, 119, 142, 143–144; relations with Hohenlohe, 146; response to political attacks on, 119–122, 157n

Home Rule for Ireland. *See* Ireland, Home Rule of

Hope, James, 23, 26, 27

Hostile environment: effect on personality, 124, 125; protection from, 48

Incest, 25, 180

Inferiority complex, 122–123

Institutional differences, 3–4

Intimate relationships: Bismarck's struggles with and rejection of, 47, 53, 54–56, 62, 69, 74; and psychic threat of children, 173–174; reasons for rejection of, 65, 66–67, 173; strains of, 142, 144, 155

Ireland, Home Rule of, 38–44, 77, 196; attitude of Chamberlain toward, 184, 185, 187, 189–190, 197, 206; debate on, 43, 111, 112; Gladstone's commitment to, 38–42, 176–177, 178; and Gladstone's psychological needs, 42; role of Balfour in, 100, 103, 105, 106–110, 205–206; role in the political career of Salisbury, 41, 92–93

Kehr, Eckart, 146n–147n
Kent, Duchess of, 165–167, 174
Kiderlen-Wächter, Alfred von, 120, 121
Kimberley, 1st Earl of, 30
Kladderadatsch, 119–122, 157n
Klein, Melanie, 10
Körner, Theodor, 150

Lansdowne, 5th Marquess of, 200
Leaders, British: characteristics of Salisbury's leadership, 200–201; good maternal behavior recreated by, 163, 164, 209; incomprehension of German statesmen, x, 1–2, 13–14, 210; psychological impact of change of, 163, 175–182; psychological resourcefulness of, 199–209; reassurance and reliability in relations among, 91, 205–206, 208; scrupulous temper of, 210–213 (*see also* Scrupulousness of British leaders); and significance of Chamberlain's leadership, 184, 192, 197, 199, 208–209; trust of, 13–14, 44, 111, 205, 213; variant behavior among, 184, 192, 197, 199
Leaders, German: distrust among, 13, 47–48, 57, 65, 78, 122, 124, 210; diplomatic manners of, 213; fatalist temper of, 215–219; incomprehension of British statesmen, x, 1–2, 14, 210; psychological impact of change of, 163; psychological instability of, 147
Lehzen, Baroness, 167–168
Leopold I, King, 170, 172

Liberal Unionists, 93, 99, 184, 198
Lichnowsky, Prince, 218
Lucius von Ballhausen, Robert, 61
Lucy, Henry W., 108n, 109, 110n
Ludwig, Emil, 123
Lyttelton, May, 103, 104n

Manchester, Duchess of, 37
Manning, Henry (later Cardinal), 23, 26, 27
Marcks, Erich, 48n, 54n, 55, 56n
Marriage: vs. bonds between father and son, 70–71; impact on Chamberlain's life, 190–191, 194–196; of Gladstone, 20–21, 24, 180; influenced by religion and death, 20, 54–55; parental objection to, 70–71, 88, 152–153; reasons for refraining from, 103; self-confidence augmented by, 87, 88–89; sexual infidelity in, 171; transformation and salvation caused by, 152–154
Marschall von Bieberstein, Adolf, 117
Martineau, Mrs. Russell, 193n
Marx, Karl, 79
Masochism, 141
Maternal behavior: recreated by Bismarck, 114; recreated by British leaders, 163, 164. *See also* Mother–child relationship
Maynooth College, 22
Melbourne, 2nd Viscount, relationship with Queen Victoria, 168–171, 172, 173
Milner, 1st Viscount, 206
Minghetti, Donna Laura, 153–154
"Ministry of Caretakers," 77, 95, 107
Moltke, Helmut von, 215
Monkswell, Lady, 39
Morley, John, 18n, 21n, 42, 43, 186, 196; friendship with Chamberlain, 197
Mother: "bad," 114; death during childbirth, 190–191; death of children of, 194; fixation on, 140; response to the death of, 36, 37, 86; surrogates for, 18, 167–175
Mother–child relationship, 7–10, 12, 36, 210; of Balfour, 102–103; Bismarck's unsatisfactory relations with his mother, 48–53, 139; of Chamberlain, 192–194; escape from maternal con-

trol, 49, 150–153; vs. father–son bonds, 53, 71; and feminine identification by the son, 139–140; Gladstone's close bonds with his mother, 17–18, 20, 21, 25; of Holstein, 63–64; in German politics, 114, 127; intrusiveness of and compensation for the mother, 49–52, 53, 126–134, 136, 166, 193; male children as surrogates for unrealized ambitions of the mother, 48–52, 114, 127; of Salisbury, 83–86; maternal affection limited by religious views, 151, 152; psychological manipulation for political purposes, 158, 161; recreated by British leaders, 163, 164; repression of longing for the mother, 51–52, 131, 133; rejection in, 130, 131, 134; and social status of servants, 167–168; symbiotic, 140; symbolized in Bismarck's relations with his subordinates, 114; between Queen Victoria and her mother, 165–168, 174; between Queen Victoria and her children, 173–174; of William II, 123–124, 126–134, 161, 166

Mother, "good enough": concept of, 164, 168, 193, 204; emotional support for realization of, 204; and resourcefulness of British leaders, 209; and scrupulousness, 213

Motherhood: anxiety and conflicts caused by, 48–49, 114; British attitudes toward, 165; health endangered by, 102; and psychic threat posed by children, 173–174; successfully combined with political interests, 84

Mourning, 56, 190–192

National Liberal Federation, 183, 184
Nepotism, 70, 74, 104–105, 202
Northbrook, 1st Earl of, 30
Northcote, Sir Stafford, 92, 94, 96

Object-relations theory, 6–10
Oedipus complex, 7, 9
Oman, Carola, 84n, 85n, 86n
O'Shea, Kitty, 107

Palmerston, 3rd Viscount, 31
Parents: rejection of, 149–152; surrogates for, 132–133, 167–175, 191–192. *See also* Father–child relationship; Mother–child relationship

Parliamentary government, 16, 187–188; and charismatic authority, 15–44; and debate on Irish Home Rule, 107–110; possibility in Germany, 145

Parnell, Charles Stewart, and Irish Home Rule, 40–41, 106n, 107, 185

Peel, Sir Robert, 22, 23, 41, 42

Personal relations: dissimilarities in, 2, 13–14, 77–78; escape from, 47; managed by Bülow, 148, 153, 156, 158–162; managed by Holstein, 116–122

Pflanze, Otto, 50n, 57n, 58n

Plamann's Institute, 51

Political betrayal, by friends, 156, 158

Political cohesion, British: after the loss of powerful leaders, 163, 181; compared with the German approach to politics, 91, 184; guided by Balfour, 107–110; impact of Chamberlain on, 198, 199, 200; Salisbury's approach to, 79–83, 90–112; shaped by Gladstone, 28–38, 44, 112

Political cohesion, German: Bismarck's motivations for destruction of, 75–76; comparison of Bismarck's and Bülow's strategies for, 161–162; and personal relations guided by Holstein, 116–122; psychological tactics used by Bülow, 155–162; shaped by Bismarck, 57–62, 68–76; during succession of monarchs, 67–68

Politics: institutional framework of, 3–4; psychological basis of, 79; role of women in, 47–48, 83–84, 124–126, 153

Politics, British: avoidance of strife among colleagues in, 106, 110–112; control of self-seeking in, 28, 38, 81–83, 98, 110–111, 112, 181, 186; friendship in, 31, 106, 188–192, 197, 207; imperialist views in, 206–207, 208; radicalism in, 185–186, 188, 189, 196; reassurance in, 91; recognition of personal value in, 30–34; retirement of leaders of, 163, 175–182; reliance on family alliances in, 104–106, 202, 205; self-restraint and courteous behavior in, 34, 37, 38, 43, 100–103, 110–112,

199–200; trust in, 13–14, 17, 28, 42, 44, 111, 205, 213

Politics, German: attempts to depersonalize, 145–146; Bismarck's view of, 47–48; distrust in, 47–48, 57, 59, 65, 78, 122, 124, 210; impact of change of monarchs on, 67–68; introduction of "feminine" sensitivities in, 138, 144; lack of personal recognition in. 59–60; psychological tactics and manipulation in, 149, 155–162; reliance on family members in, 70–74, 104; ambition in, 46–47

Ponsonby, Sir Frederick, 124n, 128n, 129n

Potter, Beatrice, 194–195

Power: Bismarck's manipulation of, 58–67; Bismarck's response to the impending loss of, 68–76; and career choices, 87; charismatic, 15; compared between Britain and Germany, 3–4; in the father–child relationship, 70–71; and loyalty to colleagues, 208; relinquishment of, 181; during succession of monarchs, 67–68

Prince, Morton, 134

Prostitutes, 26–28

Prussia: Bismarck's atttude toward, 46, 47; English crown princess of, 123, 127 (*see also* Frederick, Crown Princess and Empress)

Psychoanalytic explanations: context of, 10, 11; standards for adequacy, 10–13

Psychoanalytic theory: applied in historical studies, 6–13; concept of the good mother in, 163–164 (*see also* Mother, "good-enough"); and religion, 16

Psychohistory, data in, 12, 78. *See also* History

Psychological manipulation in German politics, 149, 156, 158–162

Public life, compared with private life, 13–14, 42, 57, 162, 210

Puttkamer, Johanna von (later Bismarck), 50, 54, 150–151

Quarterly Review, 78

Queen Victoria. *See* Victoria, Queen

Rantzau, Kuno zu, 72

Reflections and Reminiscences (Otto von Bismarck), 46, 47–48, 56

Religion: in Balfour's life, 101, 103; in Bismarck's life, 54–56; compared to science, 101; and friendship, 141; in Gladstone's life, 16, 18, 19, 20, 21–23, 25–26, 27, 28, 40; in Salisbury's life, 87–88; prevalence of, 87; and psychoanalytic theory, 16; role of the state in, 22–23

Rich, Norman, 58n, 60n, 63n, 115n, 122n

Rogge, Helmut, 59n, 64n, 66n, 115n, 118n, 120n, 146n, 156n

Röhl, John C. G., 117n, 118n, 135n, 136n, 142n

Roman Catholicism, 62; Gladstone's attitude toward, 22, 25–26

Rosebery, 5th Earl of: compared with other British leaders, 198–199; relations with Gladstone, 32–34, 178, 181

Russell, Lord John, 41

Sachs, Hanns, 56–57

Sadism, 141–142

Salisbury, Frances Mary Gascoyne-Cecil, 2nd Marchionness of, 83–86

Salisbury, Robert Gascoyne-Cecil, 3rd Marquess of, 2, 41, 42, 77–112; attitude toward political ambition and self-assertion, 81–83, 110–111; characteristics of his leadership, 200–201; childhood of, 83–87, 88, 111; class struggle viewed by, 79–81; compared with Bismarck, 82, 87, 90, 91; daughter of, 83, 85, 86, 88, 91, 104; death of his wife, 200–201; declining power of, 163; eulogy after the death of Gladstone, 181–182; father of, 86–87, 89, 91; government of compared with Gladstone's ministry, 78, 110–112, 201; marriage of, 87, 88–89, 201; mother of, 83–86; neurotic symptoms of, 83; opinion of Gladstone, 80–82, 112; political and emotional relations with his nephew, 98, 100, 104–106, 202, 205 (*see also* Balfour, Arthur James); political career of, 89–112; political heir of, 184; religion of, 87–88; self-image of, 86–89

———, colleagues of, 90–112; compared

with Bismarck's co-workers, 90, 91; Salisbury's emotional distance from, 78, 95, 107, 111, 200; as surrogates for emotional deficiencies, 91–112
Sanderson, Lord, 213–214, 215
Schweninger, Ernst, 58, 70
Science, compared with religion, 101
Scotland, 33, 34
Scrupulousness of British leaders, 36, 109; and control of self-seeking, 112; and diplomatic relations with German leaders, 210–215; and disgust for political ambition, 81–83; and domestic political differences, 43–44; genesis from childhood experiences, 17–19; in Gladstone's approach to politics, 28–30, 112; and sexuality, 23–28
Self-aggrandizement, 144, 149; of Bismarck, 57; British attitudes toward, 212; and control of aggression, 207
Self-flagellation, and sexual desires, 23, 27
Self-image: of Bismarck, 46–48; of Bülow, 148–149; depression and self-depreciation in, 86, 87; of Salisbury, 86–89; methodological approach to, 12–13; sense of worthiness in, 36; transformation of, 87–89
Self-restraint of British political leaders, 19, 37, 38, 100–103, 110–112, 203
Sempell, Charlotte, 49n, 50n, 51n, 52n
Sexuality: anxiety about, 23, 24–28; and betrayal and seduction of women, 154; and death during childbirth, 191; and the mother–daughter relationship, 167; self-restraint in, 24–28, 203
Sherwood, Michael, 10n
Smith, Paul, 79n, 81n, 82n, 88n, 93n
Smith, W. H., 96, 97, 98, 99; role in the Irish Home Rule debate, 109–110
Socioeconomic changes, role in German historiography, 146
Spencer, 5th Earl, 30
Spitzemberg, Hildegard von, 154
Stone, Lawrence, 5n
Subordination, acceptance by Bismarck's colleagues, 62–67
Surrogates: for parents, 132–133, 191–192; and political cohesion shaped by Salisbury, 90–112; for the role of

mother, 18, 167–175; for unrealized maternal fantasies, 48–49, 114, 127

Taylor, A. J. P., 146n, 147
Trollope, Anthony, 110–111, 127, 211–212
Trust: in British interpersonal relations and politics, 13–14, 44, 111, 205, 213; in Gladstone's self-perception, 17, 28, 42; and maternal nurture, 111

Vicky. *See* Frederick, Crown Princess and Empress
Victoria, Queen, 67, 123, 165–175; attitude toward Gladstone, 175–176, 179–180; attitude toward her daughter, 124, 127, 165, 173–174; childhood of, 166–168; and divine right claimed by her grandson William II, 134; experiences as a daughter, 165–168, 174; marriage and husband of, 170–175; performance as a mother, 165, 168, 173–174; psychological equilibrium of, 168, 173

Wagner, Richard, 138
Waldersee, Alfred von, 159
War guilt, 147
Weber, Max: on bureaucracy, 59; on charisma, 15, 16n
Wellington, 1st Duke of, 84
Weltpolitik, 136
West, Sir Algernon, 177, 178
Wilhelmstrasse, 59, 60, 62
William I, Emperor, 56, 57; bonds with his grandson William II, 132–133; successor of, 67–68
William II, 2; affection for his grandfather, 132–133; attitude toward Anglo-German relations, 218–219; divine right asserted by, 133–134; education of, 127, 128, 130; emotional isolation and frailty of, 135, 160; friendship with Eulenburg, 136, 140–144, 155, 156; hostile attitudes toward his parents, 68, 132–133; military career of, 129, 132–133; physical defect of, 122–123, 128; and the political downfall of Bismarck, 75–76, 114; political role after Bismarck's

resignation, 117–119, 136, 145; relationship with Bismarck, 129, 134–135; relationship with Bülow, 159–161; relationship with Holstein, 118–119, 121–122, 160; relationship with his mother, 123–124, 126–134, 136, 161, 166; self-destructiveness of, 160; wife of, 130

Winnicott, D. W., 6–7, 173n; concept of the "benign circle," 24 (*see also* "Benign circle"); and concept of the "good-enough" mother, 164n

Women: male contemptuous attitudes toward, 154; "masculine" strivings of, 114, 126; role in politics, 20, 47–48, 83–84, 124–126, 153

World War I, 218–219

Designer: Lisa Sullivan
Compositor: Computer Typesetting Services, Inc.
Printer: Braum-Brumfield, Inc.
Binder: Braum-Brumfield, Inc.
Text: 10/12 Caslon
Display: Caslon